丛书主编：常俊跃

21世纪CBI内容依托系列英语教材

Pragmatics:
A Course Book

语用学教程

刘风光　王湉　于秀成　姜晖　主编

北京大学出版社
PEKING UNIVERSITY PRESS

图书在版编目(CIP)数据

语用学教程 / 刘风光等主编. —北京：北京大学出版社，2018.6
（21世纪CBI内容依托系列英语教材）
ISBN 978-7-301-29518-2

Ⅰ. ①语… Ⅱ. ①刘… Ⅲ. ①英语–语用学–高等学校–教材 Ⅳ. ①H31

中国版本图书馆CIP数据核字(2018)第094014号

书　　　名	语用学教程 YUYONGXUE JIAOCHENG
著作责任者	刘风光　王　澍　于秀成　姜　晖　主编
责任编辑	朱丽娜
标准书号	ISBN 978-7-301-29518-2
出版发行	北京大学出版社
地　　　址	北京市海淀区成府路205号　100871
网　　　址	http://www.pup.cn　　新浪微博：@北京大学出版社
电子信箱	zln0120@163.com
电　　　话	邮购部 62752015　发行部 62750672　编辑部 62754382
印　刷　者	河北滦县鑫华书刊印刷厂
经　销　者	新华书店
	787毫米×1092毫米　16开本　14.25印张　250千字 2018年6月第1版　2018年6月第1次印刷
定　　　价	38.00元

未经许可，不得以任何方式复制或抄袭本书之部分或全部内容。
版权所有，侵权必究
举报电话：010-62752024　电子信箱：fd@pup.pku.edu.cn
图书如有印装质量问题，请与出版部联系，电话：010-62756370

编委会

丛书主编：常俊跃

本册主编：刘风光　王　澍

　　　　　　于秀成　姜　晖

前　言

随着我国英语教育的快速发展，英语专业长期贯彻的"以语言技能训练为导向"的课程建设理念及教学理念已经难以满足社会的需要。专家教师们密切关注的现行英语专业教育与中学英语教学脱节，语言与内容教学割裂，单纯语言技能训练过多，专业内容课程不足，学科内容课程系统性差，高低年级内容课程安排失衡及其导致的学生知识面偏窄、知识结构欠缺、思辨能力偏弱、综合素质发展不充分等问题日益凸显。

针对上述问题，大连外国语大学英语专业在内容与语言融合教育理念的指导下确定了如下改革思路：

（一）**遵循全新教学理念，改革英语专业教育的课程结构**。改变传统单一的语言技能课程体系，实现内容课程与语言课程的融合，扩展学生的知识面，提高学生的语言技能。

（二）**开发课程自身潜力，同步提升专业知识和语言技能**。课程同时关注内容和语言，把内容教学和语言教学有机结合。以英语为媒介，系统教授专业内容；以专业内容为依托，在使用语言过程中提高语言技能，扩展学生的知识面，提高思辨能力。

（三）**改革教学方法和手段，全面提高语言技能和综合素质**。依靠内容依托教学在方法上的灵活性，通过问题驱动、输出驱动等方法调动学生主动学习，把启发式、任务式、讨论式、结对子、小组活动、课堂展示、多媒体手段等行之有效的活动与教学内容有机结合，提高学生的语言技能，激发学生的兴趣，培养学生的自主性和创造性，提升思辨能力和综合素质。

本项改革突破了我国英语专业英语教学大纲规定的课程结构，改变了英语专业通过开设单纯地听、说、读、写、译语言技能课程提高学生语言技能的传统课程建设理念，对英语课程及教学方法进行了创新性的改革。首创了具有我国特色的英语专业内容与语言融合的课程体系；开发了适合英语专业的内容与语言融合的课程；提高学生综合运用语言的能力，扩展学生的知识面，提高学生的综合素质，以崭新的途径实现英语专业教育的总体培养目标。

经过十年的实验探索，改革取得了鼓舞人心的结果。

（一）**构建了英语专业内容与语言融合教学的课程体系**。课程包括美国历史文化、美国自然人文地理、美国社会文化、英国历史文化、英国自然人文地理、英国社会文化、澳新加社会文化、欧洲文化、中国文化、跨文化交际、《圣经》与文化、希腊罗马神话、综合英语（美国文学经典作品）、综合英语（英国文学经典作品）、综合英语（世界文学经典作品）、综合英语（西方思想经典）、英语视听说（美国社会文化经典电影）、英语视听说（英国社会文化经典电影）、英语视听说（环球资讯）、英语视听说（专题资讯）、英语短篇小说、英语长篇小说、英语散文、英语诗歌、英语戏剧、英语词汇学、英语语言学、语言与社会、语言与文化、语言与语用等。这些课程依托专业知识内容训练学生综合运用语言的能力，扩展学生的知识面，提高学生的多元文化意识，提升学生的综合素质。

（二）系统开发了相关国家的史、地、社会、文化、文学、语言学课程资源。在内容与语言融合教育理念的指导下，开发了上述课程的资源。开发的教材系统组织了教学内容，设计了新颖的栏目板块，设计的活动也丰富多样，在实际教学中受到了学生的广泛欢迎。此外还开发了开设课程所需要的教学课件等。在北京大学、华中科技大学、北京师范大学出版社、上海外语教育出版社的支持下，系列教材已经陆续出版。

（三）牵动了教学手段和教学方法的改革，取得了突出的教学效果。在内容与语言融合教育理念的指导下，教师的教学理念、教学方法、教学手段得到更新。通过问题驱动、输出驱动等活动调动学生主动学习，把启发式、任务式、讨论式、结对子、小组活动、课堂展示、多媒体手段等行之有效的活动与学科内容教学有机结合，激发学生的兴趣，培养学生自主性和创造性，提高学生的语言技能，提升思辨能力和综合素质。曾有专家教师担心取消、减少语言技能课程会对学生的语言技能发展产生消极影响。实验数据证明，内容与语言融合教学不仅没有对学生的语言技能发展和语言知识的学习产生消极影响，而且还产生了多方面的积极影响，对专业知识的学习也产生了巨大的积极影响。

（四）提高了教师的科研意识和科研水平，取得了丰硕的教研成果。开展改革以来，团队对内容与语言融合教学问题进行了系列研究，活跃了整个教学单位的科研气氛，科研意识和科研水平也得到很大提高。课题组已经撰写研究论文70多篇，撰写博士论文3篇，在国内外学术期刊发表研究论文40多篇，撰写专著2部。

教学改革开展以来，每次成果发布都引起强烈反响。在中国外语教学法国际研讨会上，与会的知名外语教育专家戴炜栋教授等对这项改革给予高度关注，博士生导师蔡基刚教授认为本项研究"具有导向性作用"。在全国英语专业院系主任高级论坛上，研究成果得到知名专家博士生导师王守仁教授和与会专家教授的高度评价。在中国英语教学研究会年会及中国外语教育改革论坛上，成果引起与会专家的强烈反响，教育部外指委领导石坚、仲伟合、蒋洪新教授等给予了高度评价。本项改革的系列成果两次获得大连外国语大学教学研究成果一等奖，两次获得辽宁省优秀教学成果奖一等奖，一次获得国家教学成果奖。目前，该项改革成果已经在全国英语专业教育领域引起广泛关注。它触及了英语专业的教学大纲，影响了课程建设的理念，引领了英语专业的教学改革，改善了教学实践，必将对未来英语专业教育的发展产生积极影响。

《语用学教程》依照内容与语言融合教学的外语教学理念编写，强调语言所传达的知识和信息，在获得信息的同时学习语言。本教材内容安排由浅至深，旨在使学生掌握语用学的基础学科知识，同时提高综合语言技能。

前 言

《语用学教程》共分 10 单元，每单元设置主要阅读文献 2 篇，补充阅读课文 3 篇。课文的选择兼顾英语语用学知识体系的同时，注重学生新词汇和语言知识的输入。教材内容涵盖语用学发展沿革、指示语、言语行为、会话含义、会话结构、礼貌和语用学界面研究等内容。教材在每单元设置一定量的基于内容与语言融合教学理念的练习，其中既包含语言知识和技能的训练练习，也包含语用学知识体系的相关练习。练习的设置有助于学生在使用教材的过程中，实现知识体系构建和语言技能训练的同步提高。

本教材在保证语用学知识体系完整的前提下，设计多样的语言输入和输出内容，以培养学生对语用学学科知识的掌握和对语言现象进行分析的能力。因此该教材在每一单元都精心设计了旨在对学生在词汇、篇章结构、语言功能等方面进行全面严格训练的基本技能练习。同时设计与语用学相关的、学生参与度较高的课堂和课外活动。这些活动的设置是本教材的亮点之一，它使得课堂教学得以延伸，亦能激发学生的学习热情，是内容与语言融合的教学理念在本教材中的最好体现。

基于内容与语言融合教学理念的《语用学教程》不仅可以作为我国高校英语专业语用学等必修或选修课程教材，同时对语用学相关话题感兴趣的英语学习者和研究者也不无裨益。

本教材是我国英语专业语言学课程改革的一项探索，凝聚了全体编写人员的艰苦努力。然而由于水平所限，还存在疏漏和不足，希望使用本教材的老师和同学能为我们提出意见和建议。您的指导和建议将是我们提高的动力。

编者

于大连外国语大学

2017 年 8 月 1 日

Contents

Unit 1 An Overview of Pragmatics ··· 1
    Text A Defining Pragmatics ·· 3
    Text B A Brief History of Pragmatics ·· 5
    Text C From Abstract Meaning to Contextual Meaning ····················· 10
    Text D Context: A Key Notion in Pragmatics ·································· 12
    Text E Appropriacy ·· 13

Unit 2 Deixis ··· 16
    Text A Deixis ·· 18
    Text B Social Deixis and Discourse Deixis ····································· 24
    Text C Deictics ·· 28
    Text D Deictic Centre and Competing Deictic Centres ····················· 30
    Text E Zonglish ··· 32

Unit 3 Speech Acts (I) ··· 34
    Text A Austin's Performatives ·· 36
    Text B Utterances as Actions ··· 38
    Text C Austin's Felicity Conditions on Performatives ······················· 44
    Text D Speech Acts: Language as Action ······································ 46
    Text E John Langshaw Austin ·· 48

Unit 4 Speech Acts (II) ·· 50
    Text A Searle's Typology of Speech Acts ····································· 52
    Text B Direct and Indirect Speech Acts ·· 55
    Text C Pragmatics and Indirectness ·· 61
    Text D Searle's Felicity Conditions ··· 63
    Text E John Rogers Searle ·· 65

Unit 5 Implicatures (I) ··· 67
    Text A Grice's Cooperative Principle ·· 69
    Text B Observing and Flouting the Maxims ·································· 72
    Text C Conventional Implicature and Conversational Implicature ········ 80
    Text D Properties of Conversational Implicature ···························· 84

	Text E	Herbert Paul Grice	87
Unit 6	Implicatures (II)		90
	Text A	Problems with Grice's Theory	92
	Text B	Developments of Grice's Theory	94
	Text C	Relevance Theory	100
	Text D	Post-Gricean Pragmatics	103
	Text E	Stephen C. Levinson	107
Unit 7	Conversational Structure		109
	Text A	What is Conversation?	111
	Text B	Turn-taking and Adjacency Pair	113
	Text C	Pre-sequences	118
	Text D	Preference and Dispreference	122
	Text E	The Place of Conversation Among the Speech-exchange Systems	124
Unit 8	Politeness		126
	Text A	Brown and Levinson's Linguistic Politeness Model	127
	Text B	Leech's Politeness Model	130
	Text C	Perspectives on Politeness	135
	Text D	Towards an Anatomy of Impoliteness	142
	Text E	Geoffrey Neil Leech	152
Unit 9	Macropragmatics		157
	Text A	Variability, Negotiability and Adaptability	158
	Text B	Pragmatic Acts and Action Theory	163
	Text C	Intercultural Pragmatics	170
	Text D	Variational Pragmatics	178
	Text E	Some Thoughts on Pragmatics, Sociolinguistic Variation, and Intercultural Communication	185
Unit 10	Pragmatics and Its Interfaces		194
	Text A	The Semantics/Pragmatics Distinction	196
	Text B	Pragmatics and Grammar	198
	Text C	Pragmatics and Prosody	206
	Text D	Literary Pragmatics: An Overview	209
	Text E	Anticipatory Pragmatics	212

Unit 1
An Overview of Pragmatics

> Language is the house of Being. In its home man dwells.
> — Martin Heidegger
>
> The meaning of a word is its use in the language.
> — Ludwig Wittgenstein

Objectives

- To understand what pragmatics is
- To get to know the development of pragmatics
- To comprehend the importance of context in pragmatics
- To learn the key notions in pragmatics
- To improve critical thinking and intercultural communicative competence and comprehensive language skills
- To improve pragmatic competence, academic ability and relevant language skills

Before You Read

1. Please think about what these children still need to learn about using language.

   1) (A little boy comes in the front door.)
   Mother: *Wipe your feet, please.*
   The boy removes his muddy shoes and socks and carefully wipes his feet clean on the doormat.

2) (A father is trying to get his 3-year-old daughter to stop lifting up her dress to display her new underwear to the assembled guests.)

Father: *We don't DO that.*

Daughter: *I KNOW, Daddy. You don't WEAR dresses.*

2. The use of natural language can often lead to unintended meanings. Often, you may see a sign like the following at a mall, *Entire store 25% off*. Do I need to buy the whole store, or can I just pick out a few items of interest? Can you think of some other examples of unintended meanings?

3. Study the following utterances and try to tell what they mean in different contexts.

1) *Cheers.*
2) *Will you marry me?*
3) *I'm going to kill you.*
4) *Shut up!*
5) *You are my true friend.*

Start to Read

Text A Defining Pragmatics

People do not always or even usually say what they mean. Speakers frequently mean much more than their words actually say. For example, people might say: *It's cold in here*! The semantic meaning of the sentence is *The temperature in this place is frigid*, but the pragmatic meaning of it can be quite different from the literal meaning. Suppose you and your mom are in the living room. Your mom asks you whether you'd like to eat dinner in the living room or in the kitchen. You reply: *It's cold in here*. What you mean is *Let's eat in the kitchen*. In another case, the Queen and her butler, Mills, are in the drawing room. The window is open. The Queen says: *It's cold in here*. The Queen means *Mills, shut the window*. The two examples show that it is not so much what the sentences literally mean that matters when we talk as how they reveal the intentions and strategies of the speakers themselves. In some cases, people can mean something quite different from what their words say, or even just the opposite. For instance, to someone who has borrowed my car for the weekend and returned it with no petrol in the tank, I might say: *It was nice of you to fill the car up! Or What a shame you couldn't find the petrol tank!* (Thomas, 2010: 1) Pragmatics is about the distinction between what a speaker's words (literally) mean and what the speaker might mean by his words. It is the study of the relationship between linguistic forms and the users of those forms.

Pragmatics is a relatively new area of linguistics. It is a rapidly growing field in contemporary linguistics. But what is pragmatics? This is a question whose answer is notoriously difficult to provide (Huang, 2007: 1). In his book *Pragmatics*, Levinson (1983: 5-35) reviewed thoroughly a number of definitions and their inherent difficulties, which serve to indicate the rough scope of linguistic pragmatics. Below are some definitions of pragmatics. Please scrutinize what elements they have in common and the differences in emphasis.

Pragmatics is the study of 'the relation of signs to interpreters'. (Morris, 1938: 6)

Pragmatics can be usefully defined as the study of how utterances have meanings in situations. (Leech, 1983: x)

Pragmatics is concerned with the study of meaning as communicated by a speaker (or writer) and interpreted by a listener (or reader). (Yule, 1996: 3)

Pragmatics studies the factors that govern our choice of language in social interaction and the effects of our choice on others. (Crystal, 1987: 120)

Pragmatics studies the use of language in human communication as determined by the conditions of society. (Mey, 2001: 6)

Pragmatics is a general cognitive, social, and cultural perspective on linguistic phenomena in relation to their usage in forms of behavior. (Verschueren, 2000: 7)

Pragmatics is the systematic study of meaning by virtue of, or dependent on, the use of language. (Huang, 2007: 2)

As can be seen from the above definitions, at the most elementary level, pragmatics can be defined as meaning in use or meaning in context (Thomas, 2010: 1-2). As pointed out in Huang (2001), two main schools of thought can be identified in contemporary pragmatics: **Anglo-American** and **European Continental.** Within the former conception of linguistics and the philosophy of language, pragmatics is treated as a core **component** of a theory of language, on a par with phonetics, phonology, morphology, syntax, and semantics. The view is known as the component view of pragmatics. Within the Continental tradition, pragmatics is defined in a far broader way. It represents the **perspective** view of pragmatics, namely the view that pragmatics should be taken as presenting a functional perspective on every aspect of linguistic behavior.

Pragmatics allows humans into the analysis. Pragmatics is appealing because it is about how people make sense of each other linguistically. The advantage of studying language via pragmatics is that one can talk about people's intended meanings, their assumptions, their purposes or goals, and the kinds of actions (for example, requests) that they are performing when they speak (Yule, 1996: 4). Pragmatics is needed if we want a fuller, deeper, and generally more reasonable account of human language behavior. Sometimes, a pragmatic account is the only one that makes sense.

Text B A Brief History of Pragmatics

Pragmatics as a modern branch of linguistic inquiry has its origin in the philosophy of language. Its philosophical roots can be traced back to the work of the philosophers Charles Morris, Rudolf Carnap, and Charles Peirce in the 1930s. Influenced by Peirce, Morris (1938: 6-7), for example, presented a threefold division into syntax, semantics, and pragmatics within **semiotics** — a general science of signs. According to this typology, **syntax** is the study of the formal relation of one sign with another, **semantics** deals with the relation of signs to what they denote, and **pragmatics** addresses the relation of signs to their users and interpreters (Levinson, 1983: 1, Horn and Ward, 2004). This trichotomy was taken up by Carnap (1942), who posited an order of degree of abstractness for the three branches of inquiry: syntax is the most and pragmatics the least abstract, with semantics lying somewhere in between. Consequently, syntax provides input to semantics, which provides input to pragmatics (Recanati, 2004).

In the 1950s, two opposing schools of thought emerged within the analytic philosophy of language: the school of **ideal language philosophy** and the school of **ordinary language philosophy**. The central ideas underlying the former were originated by the philosophers Gottlob Frege, Alfred Tarski, and Bertrand Russell. Ideal language philosophers were primarily interested in the study of logical systems of artificial languages. However, the partially successful application of its theory and methodology to natural language in the 1950s and 1960s by followers of the school such as Richard Montague, David Donaldson, and David Lewis led to the development of today's formal semantics. By contrast, within the tradition of ordinary language philosophy, emphasis was placed on natural language rather than the formal languages studied by the logicians. Under the leadership of J. L. Austin, the school of ordinary language philosophy flourished principally at Oxford in the 1950s and 1960s. Other leading thinkers of the school included the philosophers H. P. Grice, Peter Strawson, John Searle, and the later Ludwig Wittgenstein (Huang, 2003, Recanati, 2004). It was within the tradition of ordinary language philosophy that Austin developed his theory of speech acts, and Grice his theory of conversational implicature. Both theories have since become landmarks on the path towards the development of a systematic, philosophically inspired pragmatic theory of language use.

On the linguistics front, in the late 1960s and early 1970s a campaign was launched by some of Noam Chomsky's disaffected pupils in **generative semantics** (as it was then called), notably Jerry Katz, J. R. Ross and George Lakoff, to challenge their teacher's treatment of language as an abstract, mental device divorced from the uses and functions of language. In their search for the means to undermine Chomsky's position, the generative semanticists, who were attracted to the philosophical work by Austin, Grice, Strawson, and Searle, helped to empty what the philosopher Yehoshua Bar-Hillel called the 'pragmatic wastebasket' (see Harris, 1993 for a discussion of the 'linguistics wars' they waged). As a result, a great deal of important research was done in the 1970s by linguists such as Laurence Horn, Charles Fillmore, and Gerald Gazdar to 'bring some order into the content of [the pragmatic] wastebasket', as wisely advised by Bar-Hillel (1971: 405). The publication of Stephen Levinson's celebrated textbook *Pragmatics* in 1983 systematized the field and marked the coming of age of pragmatics as a linguistic discipline in its own right.

Since then, the field of inquiry has continued to expand and flourish. In the last two decades we have witnessed new developments such as Laurence Horn's and Stephen Levinson's neo-Gricean pragmatic theories, Dan Sperber's and Deirdre Wilson's relevance theory, and important work by philosophers such as Jay Atlas, Kent Bach, and Francois Recanati. 'More recently', as the editors of a newly published *Handbook of Pragmatics* declared, 'work in pragmatic theory has extended from the attempt to rescue the syntax and semantics from their own unnecessary complexities to other domains of linguistic inquiry, ranging from historical linguistics to the lexicon, from language acquisition to computational linguistics, from intonational structure to cognitive science' (Horn and Ward, 2004: xi). One thing is now certain: the future of pragmatics is bright.

(Excerpted from Yan Huang. 2007. *Pragmatics*. pp. 2-4.)

Notes

1. **Morris, C. W. (1901—1979):** an American semiotician and philosopher. Morris is most noted today for his monograph, *Foundations of the Theory of Signs* (1938), which was the first volume of the grand project *International Encyclopedia of Unified Science*. In this work he proposed his threefold divisions of semiotics as consisting of syntactics,

semantics, and pragmatics. This latter distinction became normalized in linguistics.

Pragmatics, a basic field of linguistics today, originally had its roots in Morris's idea of a division of signs concerned with 'the relations of signs to their interpreters' or users. Practically, this distinction seemed to legitimate the place of social context for language study, which was a crucial feature of both John Dewey's and Ludwig Wittgenstein's philosophies at that time.

2. **Ludwig Josef Johann Wittgenstein (1889 — 1951):** an Austrian-British philosopher who worked primarily in logic, the philosophy of mathematics, the philosophy of mind, and the philosophy of language. From 1929 — 1947, Wittgenstein taught at the University of Cambridge. During his lifetime he published just one slim book, the 75-page *Tractatus Logico-Philosophicus* (1921), one article, one book review and a children's dictionary. His voluminous manuscripts were edited and published posthumously. *Philosophical Investigations* appeared as a book in 1953 and by the end of the century it was considered an important modern classic.

His philosophy is often divided into an early period, exemplified by the *Tractatus*, and a later period, articulated in the *Philosophical Investigations*. The early Wittgenstein was concerned with the logical relationship between propositions and the world and believed that by providing an account of the logic underlying this relationship, he had solved all philosophical problems. The later Wittgenstein rejected many of the assumptions of the *Tractatus*, arguing that the meaning of words is best understood as their use within a given language-game.

After You Read

Knowledge Focus

1. Decide whether the following statements are true or false based on Text A and Text B.

1) Pragmatics is the study of how meaning and syntax are related in a language.
2) Two main schools of pragmatics are American versus European Continental.
3) The notion *pragmatics* was first proposed by Wittgenstein.
4) Pragmatics was rooted in ordinary language philosophy.
5) Grice's theory of conversational implicature is a landmark on the path towards the development of a systematic, philosophically inspired pragmatic theory of language use.

2. Discuss the following questions with your partner.

1) Would you give examples to illustrate what pragmatics is?
2) What features does pragmatics have as a branch of linguistics?
3) What are the differences between the component view and the perspective view of pragmatics?
4) How did pragmatics develop into a discipline?
5) Why was pragmatics called a 'wastebasket'?
6) Would you provide a semantic meaning and a pragmatic meaning for *I'm tired* in three different contexts?

Language Focus

1. Fill in the blanks with words or expressions in Text A and Text B.

1) Pragmatics is about the _____ between what a speaker's words (literally) mean and what the speaker might mean by his words.
2) Levinson reviewed thoroughly a number of definitions and their _____ difficulties, which serve to indicate the rough scope of linguistic pragmatics.
3) Pragmatics studies the use of language in human communication as determined by the _____ of society.
4) The Anglo-American school treated pragmatics as a core component of a theory of language, on a par with phonetics, phonology, morphology, syntax, and _____.
5) The advantage of studying language via pragmatics is that one can talk about people's _____ meanings, their assumptions, etc.
6) Influenced by Peirce, Morris, for example, presented a threefold division into syntax, semantics, and pragmatics within _____ — a general science of signs.
7) This _____ of syntax, semantics and pragmatics was taken up by Carnap, who posited an order of degree of abstractness for the three branches of inquiry.
8) When it came to the 1950s, two opposing schools of thought emerged within the _____ philosophy of language: the school of ideal language philosophy and the school of ordinary language philosophy.
9) Jerry Katz, J. R. Ross and George Lakoff challenged Norm Chomsky's treatment of language as an abstract, _____ device divorced from the uses and functions of language.
10) New developments have been witnessed in the last two decades such as Laurence Horn's and Stephen Levinson's neo-Gricean pragmatic theories. Dan Sperber's and Deirdre Wilson's _____ theory.

2. Translate the following sentences into English.

1) 语用学是对语言行为以及实施这些行为的语境的研究。（Stalnaker, 1972: 383）

2) 语用学是一种旨在描述说话人如何使用一种语言的句子以达到成功交际的理论。（Kempson, 1975: 84）

3) 语用学是对所有那些语义理论未能涵盖的意义的研究。（Levinson, 1983: 27）

3. Translate the following passage into Chinese.

During the first half of the twentieth century, philosophy of language was concerned less with language use than with meanings of linguistic expressions. Indeed, meanings were abstracted from the linguistic items that have them, and indicative sentences were often equated with statements, which in turn were equated with propositions. As Austin complained, it was assumed by philosophers that 'the business of a sentence can only be to 'describe' some state of affairs, or to 'state some fact,' which it must do either truly or falsely'. Here he also had in mind the early Wittgenstein's picture-theory of meaning. Austin observed that there are many uses of language which have the linguistic appearance of fact-stating but are really quite different. Explicit performatives like '*You're fired*' and '*I quit*' are not used to make mere statements. And Wittgenstein came to think of language not as a system of representation but as a system of devices for engaging in various sorts of social activity; hence, 'the meaning of a word is its use in the language'.

(Bach, 2006: 463)

Comprehensive Work

1. Review the development of pragmatics in China and make a summary.

2. Form groups of three or four. First, everyone writes a very short dialogue between two imaginary characters, and then dictates the dialogue to other group members. As one dictates, the other group members write down not the dialogue they hear but the contexts in which they imagine the dialogue occurs. Then all group members read out what they have written and discuss the pragmatics of the dialogue in relation to the contexts having been imagined.

Further Readings

Text C From Abstract Meaning to Contextual Meaning

Abstract meaning is concerned with what a word, phrase, sentence, etc. *could* mean (for example, the dictionary meanings of words or phrases). The underlined sentences of the following excerpt illustrate well the point I am trying to make:

'What we want is the army to take over this country. See a bit of discipline then, we would … The Forces, that's the thing. We knew what discipline was when I was in the Forces.' Pop always spoke of his time at Catterick Camp in the nineteen-forties as 'being in the forces' as if he had been in the navy and air force and marines as well. 'Flog 'em, is what I say. Give 'em something to remember across their backsides.' He paused and swigged tea. <u>'What's wrong with the cat?' he said, so that anyone coming in at that moment, Alan thought, would have supposed him to be enquiring after the health of the family pet.</u>

As Alan rightly observes, if you had not been party to the whole of the preceding discussion, you would probably have assumed that cat referred to a pet, rather than to the *cat-o'-nine-tails*. In most dictionaries cat is shown as having two abstract meanings: *a small four-legged animal with soft fur and sharp claws, often kept as a pet and a whip made from nine knotted cords, formerly used for flogging people*. But quite clearly, the first meaning is by far the more common — the second meaning is restricted to a very limited **domain of discourse** — that of military life in earlier times.

More recently, cat has acquired an additional meaning — *catalytic converter* — which belongs to yet another domain of discourse, that of cars or air pollution. In the summer of 1990, one British television commercial for Volkswagen cars showed an elderly woman, cat-basket in hand, searching her new car for the cat, which, according to the advertisement, was supplied as standard. What this somewhat sexist advertisement rather tortuously illustrated is that if a hearer is in the 'wrong' domain of discourse, if, for example he or she thinks you are talking about pets when you are actually talking about cars or life on board ships in earlier times, the possibility of wrongly assigning sense is greater. Conversely, when you are in a known domain of discourse or when you know what social roles your interactant occupies, you will probably have little difficulty in assigning the correct sense to an ambiguous lexical item. So you will have no problem in knowing that a student who comes to ask you for *a handout* probably wants lecture notes, while the tramp who asks for *a handout* equally certainly does not.

The term *abstract meaning* does not apply only to single words. It can apply equally well to phrases or even to whole sentences. Supposing at a party you heard someone saying: *The Pearsons are on coke.* Taken in the abstract (by consulting a dictionary of contemporary spoken English, for example) the word coke could (at least in theory) refer to *Coca-Cola, cocaine* or *a coal derivative*. And, accordingly, the whole expression *to be on coke* could have one of (at least) three abstract meanings: *to be drinking Coca-Cola, to use cocaine*, or *to have solid-fuel heating*. What the words actually meant on the occasion in question could only be determined in context.

In general, competent native speakers do not have to seek laboriously for the contextual meaning of a word, phrase or sentence in the way that the two previous examples may have implied. The contextual meaning is so obvious that it never even crosses our mind that there could be alternative interpretations. So, if a friend promises to send you a card from Rome, you do not agonize over whether it will be a picture postcard, a playing card or a business card. Unless your friends are particularly odd, the second two possibilities would never even enter your head. If we were not able to take such short cuts in interpretation, the process of understanding one another would be very inefficient. Nevertheless, there are occasions when we do quite genuinely experience difficulty in assigning contextual meaning and then we have to weigh up alternative interpretations.

(Excerpted from Jenny Thomas. 2010. *Meaning in Interaction: An Introduction to Pragmatics*. pp. 2-4.)

Questions for Discussion or Reflection

1. Would you illustrate what abstract meaning is?
2. What is contextual meaning? And why is it important to pragmatics?
3. What is the relationship between abstract meaning and contextual meaning?
4. Would you provide different contexts in which the same utterance *I'm hungry* would have different pragmatic meanings?

Text D Context: A Key Notion in Pragmatics

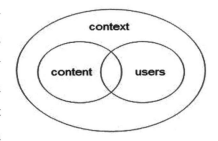

Context is one of those notions which is used very widely in the linguistic literature, but to which it is difficult to give a precise definition. From a relatively theory-neutral point of view, however, context may in a broader sense be defined as referring to any relevant features of the dynamic setting or environment in which a linguistic unit is systematically used. Furthermore, context can be seen as composed of three different sources — a view known as the 'geographic' division of context (Ariel, 1990). In the first place, there is the physical context, which refers to the physical setting of the utterance. For example, the interpretation of (1.1) depends on the knowledge computable from the physical context of the utterance, that is, the spatio-temporal location of the utterance.

(1.1) *He's* not the chief executive; *he* is. *He's* the managing director.

The second type is the linguistic context, which refers to the surrounding utterances in the same discourse. What has been mentioned in the previous discourse, for instance, plays a crucial role in understanding the elliptical construction used by Mary in (1.2).

(1.2) John: Who gave the waiter a large tip?

   Mary: Helen.

Thirdly and finally, we have the general knowledge context. The information derivable from this type of context explains why (1.3a) is pragmatically well-formed but (1.3b) is pragmatically anomalous. This is because, given our real-world knowledge, we know that whereas there is a Forbidden City in Beijing, there is no such a tourist attraction in Paris.

(1.3) a. I went to Beijing last month. The Forbidden City was magnificent.

b. I went to Paris last month. The Forbidden City was magnificent.

Clearly, what is involved here is a set of background assumptions shared by the speaker and the addressee. Stalnaker (1974) called this **common ground**. The notion of common ground has been further developed by Clark (1996), who distinguished communal from personal common ground. The former refers to the set of background assumptions shared by members of a community, and the latter to the body of background knowledge two members of a community share from their past experience of each other.

(Excerpted from Yan Huang. 2007. *Pragmatics*. pp. 13-14.)

Questions for Discussion

1. Would you illustrate the three different sources of context?
2. What does the term 'common ground' mean? Give examples to show the importance of common ground in social interactions.
3. What might be other kinds of context in addition to the ones mentioned in Text D?
4. Would you provide an example of someone who wrongly assumes that their hearers share knowledge of a context, and gives less information than is needed for them to understand?

Text E Appropriacy

Not very long ago my wife and I went out for lunch with two other couples, both a bit older than us and both slightly more important at work. We had a drink in the bar first and ordered our meal. In due course the waiter came back and announced that our lunch was ready, a communication which we all ignored. Four or five minutes later one of the more important members of the group said

(1) I think we could go in now you know

whereupon we all duly stood up and began the awkward transition from bar to dining room. The point is that in choice of words, in moment of speaking and in status of speaker this utterance was absolutely appropriate to the situation.

Similar examples are easy to find. At one stage in my career I had a senior colleague who had the bad habit of saying

(2) Are we all here

at exactly the moment a meeting was due to start and only if he could see that we were not all there. His utterance was perfectly attuned to the situation and always had the same effect, that of causing a younger member of our department to get up and go on a missing colleague hunt. And just recently when we were waiting for a colleague without whom a meeting couldn't start, another colleague said to the person sitting next to her

(3) Shall we go and get Mike

whereupon the person addressed dutifully got up and went to look for him.

Or when I begin a lecture I usually call for attention by uttering loudly

(4) Right, shall we begin

which I take to be the most appropriate utterance in the context. When I am feeling mischievous I sometimes begin a first-year pragmatics lecture by saying

(5) May I speak English

This always causes a moment of consternation when the students think their lecturer really has gone bonkers at last. But this beginning enables me to make the neat point that 'May I speak English' is not the appropriate way to begin a pragmatics lecture in Britain. And to make the still neater point that when I say 'May I speak English' in a shop in Italy, the commonest response (I know, I have done the research) is

(6) A little

This response indicates that the addressee, struggling with limited English, takes me to be saying the more appropriate or expectable 'Do you speak English?'

And then there used to be a service manager at the garage where I take my car for servicing, who could never remember my name and knew he should, so he signalled it every time I went with

(7) What's your name again

Now that they have a computer, they ask your car number first and the screen obligingly tells them who you are. But the new service manager is much more efficient than his predecessor and has begun to say

(8) What's the number again

as though he knows that he should be able to remember it.

And when I stayed for two nights in a bed-and-breakfast recently and had the same waitress each morning, she used two different ways of asking me whether I'd like tea or coffee. You can surely guess which of the following utterances she used on the first morning and which she took to be more appropriate on the second

(9) Is it tea or coffee

(10) Would you like tea or coffee?

And what is the most appropriate way of getting my fun-loving Australian friend out of the pub when I want to get home to my family before they've all gone to bed and left the milk bottles out in revenge formation on the doorstep where I'm bound to send them flying? I tried the rather feeble

(11) How are you doing

to which my friend obligingly replied

(12) Am I ready to go do you mean

Being rather a cowardly person, I of course protested that that wasn't what I meant, but I soon made it clear by bored stares at the wall and lots of posture shifts that I was getting itchy, so that it wasn't long before my friend said

(13) You're in a hurry

and since she had initiated the conversation this time, I judged it OK to reply

(14) No, well, yes I am

I cite these few examples because they are immediately recognizable as appropriate ways of using language to get business done. One of the features of language use that is of interest to pragmaticists is its appropriacy in relation to those who use it and those they address.

(Excerpted from Peter Grundy. 2000. *Doing Pragmatics*. pp. 3-5.)

Suggested Reading

Huang, Y. 2009. *Pragmatics*. Beijing: Foreign Language Teaching and Research Press. pp. 1-5; pp. 10-14.

Peccei, J. S. 2000. *Pragmatics*. Beijing: Foreign Language Teaching and Research Press. pp. 1-9.

Thomas, J. 2010. *Meaning in Interaction: An Introduction to Pragmatics*. Beijing: Foreign Language Teaching and Research Press. pp. 16-23.

Yule, G. 1996. *Pragmatics*. Oxford: Oxford University Press. pp. 3-8.

Unit 2
Deixis

> One of the most misleading representational techniques in our language is the use of the word 'I'.
> — Ludwig Wittgenstein
>
> An inner process stands in need of outward criteria.
> — Ludwig Wittgenstein

Objectives

- To understand what deixis is
- To learn the basic categories of deixis
- To comprehend the importance of context to deixis
- To learn the deictic expressions
- To improve critical thinking and intercultural communicative competence and comprehensive language skills
- To improve pragmatic competence, academic ability and relevant language skills

Before You Read

1. Please make a one-minute dialogue with your partner, without using any personal pronouns. After you have finished, discuss with your partner the functions of personal pronouns in human communication.

2. Translate the first two lines of the following poem. Pay special attention to the translation of 君 and 妾.

> 君家何处住，
> 妾住在横塘。
> 停船暂借问，
> 或恐是同乡。
> ——《长干曲》崔颢

3. Look at the picture below. Father Christmas points at the letter *G* of the word *GAP* and says, 'What's that?' Our answer might be, among other things:

1) _____   6) _____
2) _____   7) _____
3) _____   8) _____
4) _____   9) _____
5) _____   10) _____

4. How do you interpret the utterance '*You'll have to bring that back tomorrow, because they aren't here.*' without referring to the context?

5. Look at the pictures below and tell when *tomorrow* is.

6. **The use of time deictics is not always so straightforward. For example, the deictic item *today* has different references in different contexts. Please explain the following examples.**

I don't have to go to work today.

I will see to it today.

I went to the piano lesson with my son today.

Text A   Deixis

The narrowest definition of pragmatics is that it refers to the study of indexicals, expressions whose reference is a function of the context of their reference. The interpretation of indexical expressions like *now* and *I* requires an estimate of the speaker's beliefs and intentions at the time of the utterance. One of the first phenomena that scientific considerations of language use could  not ignore was the 'anchoring' of language in a real world, achieved by 'pointing' at variables along some of its dimensions. This phenomenon is called **deixis**, and the 'pointers' are **indexical expressions** and *indexicals*. There are essentially four dimensions involved: time, space, society and discourse. (Verschueren, 2000: 18) Hence, there are basically five types of deixis, namely, person deixis, spatial deixis, temporal deixis, social deixis and discourse deixis. Deixis is one of the central topics of inquiry within the Anglo-American School of thought in pragmatics.

In the second chapter of George Yule's book, he made a thorough exploration of the basic categories and the relationship between deixis and distance.

According to George Yule (2000: 9-14), deixis is a technical term (from Greek) for one of the most basic things we do with utterances. It means 'pointing' via language. Any linguistic form used to accomplish this 'pointing' is called a deictic expression. When you notice a strange object and ask, 'What's that?', you are using a deictic expression ('that') to indicate something in the immediate context. Deictic expressions are also sometimes called indexicals. They are among the first forms to be spoken by very young children and can be used to indicate people via person deixis ('me', 'you'), or location via spatial deixis ('here', 'there'), or time via temporal deixis ('now', 'then'). All these expressions depend, for their interpretation, on the speaker and hearer sharing the same context. Indeed, deictic expressions have their most basic uses in face-to-face spoken interaction where utterances such as [1] are easily understood by the people present, but may need a translation for someone not right there.

[1] I'll put this here.

(Of course, you understood that Jim was telling Anne that he was about to put an extra house key in one of the kitchen drawers.)

Deixis is clearly a form of referring that is tied to the speaker's context, with the most basic distinction between deictic expressions being 'near speaker' versus 'away from speaker'. In English, the 'near speaker', or **proximal** terms, are 'this', 'here', 'now'. The 'away from speaker', or **distal** terms, are 'that', 'there', 'then'. Proximal terms are typically interpreted in terms of the speaker's location, or the **deictic center**, so that 'now' is generally understood as referring to some point or period in time that has the time of the speaker's utterance at its center. Distal terms can simply indicate 'away from speaker', but, in some languages, can be used to distinguish between 'near addressee' and 'away from both speaker and addressee'.

Person deixis

The distinction just described involves person deixis, with the speaker ('I') and the addressee ('you') mentioned. The simplicity of these forms disguises the complexity of their use. To learn these deictic expressions, we have to discover that each person in a conversation shifts from being 'I' to being 'you' constantly. All young children go through a stage in their learning where this distinction seems problematic and they say things like 'Read you a story' (instead of 'me') when handing over a favorite book.

Person deixis clearly operates on a basic three-part division, exemplified by the pronouns for first person ('I'), second person ('you'), and third person ('he', 'she', or 'it'). In many languages these deictic categories of speaker, addressee, and other(s) are elaborated with markers of relative social status (for example, addressee with higher status versus addressee with lower status). Expressions which indicate higher status are described as **honorifics**. The discussion of the circumstances which lead to the choice of one of these forms rather than another is sometimes described as **social deixis**.

A fairly well-known example of a social contrast encoded within person deixis is the distinction between forms used for a familiar versus a non-familiar addressee in some languages. This is known as the **T/V distinction**, from the French forms '*tu*' (familiar) and '*vous*' (non-familiar), and is found in many languages including German ('*du/Sie*') and Spanish ('*tú/Usted*'). The choice of one form will certainly communicate something (not directly said) about the speaker's view of his or her relationship with the addressee. In those social contexts where individuals typically mark distinctions between the social status of the speaker and addressee, the higher, older, and more powerful speaker will tend to use the '*tu*' version to a lower, younger, and less powerful addressee, and be addressed by the '*vous*' form in return. When social change is taking place, as for example in modern Spain, where a young businesswoman (higher economic status) is talking to her older cleaning lady (lower economic status), how do they address each other? I am told that the age distinction remains more powerful than the economic distinction and the older woman uses '*tú*' and the younger uses '*Usted*'.

The Spanish non-familiar version ('*Usted*') is historically related to a form which was used to refer to neither first person (speaker) nor second person (addressee), but to third person (some other). In deictic terms, third person is not a direct participant in basic (I-you) interaction and, being an outsider, is necessarily more distant. Third person pronouns are consequently distal forms in terms of person deixis. Using a third person form, where a second person form would be possible, is one way of communicating distance (and non-familiarity). This can be done in English for an ironic or humorous purpose as when one person, who's very busy in the kitchen, addresses another, who's being very lazy, as in [2].

[2] Would his highness like some coffee?

The distance associated with third person forms is also used to make potential accusations (for example, 'you didn't clean up') less direct, as in [3a], or to make a potentially personal issue seem like an impersonal one, based on a general rule, as in [3b.].

[3] a. Somebody didn't clean up after himself.
b. Each person has to clean up after him or herself.

Of course, the speaker can state such general 'rules' as applying to the speaker plus other(s), by using the first person plural ('we'), as in [4].

[4] We clean up after ourselves around here.

There is, in English, a potential ambiguity in such uses which allows two different interpretations. There is an **exclusive** 'we' (speaker plus other(s), excluding addressee) and an **inclusive** 'we' (speaker and addressee included). Some languages grammaticize this distinction. In English, the ambiguity present in [4] provides a subtle opportunity for a hearer to decide what was communicated. Either the hearer decides that he or she is a member of the group to whom the rule applies (i.e. an addressee) or an outsider to whom the rule does not apply (i.e. not an addressee). In this case the hearer gets to decide the kind of 'more' that is being communicated.

The inclusive-exclusive distinction may also be noted in the difference between saying 'Let's go' (to some friends) and 'Let us go' (to someone who has captured the speaker and friends). The action of going is inclusive in the first, but exclusive in the second.

Spatial deixis

The concept of distance already mentioned is clearly relevant to spatial deixis, where the relative location of people and things is being indicated. Contemporary English makes use of only two adverbs, 'here' and 'there', for  the basic distinction, but in older texts and in some dialects, a much larger set of deictic expressions can be found. Although 'yonder' (more distant from speaker) is still used, words like 'hither' (to this place) and 'thence' (from that place) now sound archaic. These last two adverbs include the meaning of motion toward or away from the speaker. Some verbs of motion, such as 'come' and 'go', retain a deictic sense when they are used to mark movement toward the speaker ('Come to bed!') or away from the speaker ('Go to bed!').

One version of the concept of motion toward speaker (i.e. becoming visible), seems to be the first deictic meaning learned by children and characterizes their use of words like 'this' and 'here' (=can be seen). They are distinct from 'that' and 'there' which are associated with things that move out of the child's visual space (=can no longer be seen).

In considering spatial deixis, however, it is important to remember that location from the speaker's perspective can be fixed mentally as well as physically. Speakers temporarily away from their home location will often continue to use 'here' to mean the (physically distant) home location, as if they were still in that location. Speakers also seem to be able to project themselves into other locations prior to actually being in those locations, as when they say 'I'll come later' (=movement to addressee's location). This is sometimes described as **deictic projection** and we make more use of its possibilities as more technology allows us to manipulate location. If 'here' means the place of the speaker's utterance (and 'now' means the time of the speaker's utterance), then an utterance such as [5] should be nonsense.

[5] I am not here now.

However, I can say [5] into the recorder of a telephone answering machine, projecting that the 'now' will apply to any time someone tries to call me, and not to when I actually record the words. Indeed, recording [5] is a kind of dramatic performance for a future audience in which I project my presence to be in the required location. A similar deictic projection is accomplished via dramatic performance when I use direct speech to represent the person, location, and feelings of someone or something else. For example, I could be telling you about a visit to a pet store, as in [6].

[6] I was looking at this little puppy in a cage with such a sad look on its face. It was like, 'Oh, I'm so unhappy here, will you set me free?'

The 'here' of the cage is not the actual physical location of the person uttering the words (the speaker), but is instead the location of that person performing in the role of the puppy.

It may be that the truly pragmatic basis of spatial deixis is actually **psychological distance**. Physically close objects will tend to be treated by the speaker as psychologically close. Also, something that is physically distant will generally be treated as psychologically distant (for example, 'that man over there'). However, a speaker may also wish to mark something that is physically close (for example, a perfume being sniffed by the speaker) as psychologically distant 'I don't like that'. In this analysis, a word like 'that' does not have a fixed (i.e. semantic) meaning; instead, it is 'invested' with meaning in a context by a speaker.

Similar psychological processes seem to be at work in our distinctions between proximal and distal expressions used to mark temporal deixis.

Temporal deixis

We have already noted the use of the proximal form 'now' as indicating both the time coinciding with the speaker's utterance and the time of the speaker's voice being heard (the hearer's 'now'). In contrast to 'now', the distal expression 'then' applies to both past [7a.] and future [7b.] time relative to the speaker's present time.

[7] a. November 22nd, 1963? I was in Scotland then.
    b. Dinner at 8:30 on Saturday? Okay, I'll see you then.

It is worth noting that we also use elaborate systems of non-deictic temporal reference such as calendar time (dates, as in [7a.]) and clock time (hours, as in [7b.]). However, these forms of temporal reference are learned a lot later than the deictic expressions like 'yesterday', 'tomorrow', 'today', 'tonight', 'next week', 'last week', 'this week'. All these expressions depend for their interpretation on knowing the relevant utterance time. If we don't know the utterance (i.e. scribbling) time of a note, as in [8], on an office door, we won't know if we have a short or a long wait ahead.

[8] Back in an hour.

Similarly, if we return the next day to a bar that displays the notice in [9], then we will still be (deictically) one day early for the free drink.

[9] Free Beer Tomorrow.

The psychological basis of temporal deixis seems to be similar to that of spatial deixis. We can treat temporal events as objects that move toward us (into view) or away from us (out of view). One metaphor used in English is of events coming toward the speaker from the future (for example, 'the coming week', 'the approaching year') and going away from the speaker to the past (for example, 'in days gone by', 'the past week'). We also seem to treat the near or immediate future as being close to utterance time by using the proximal deictic 'this', as in 'this (coming) weekend' or 'this (coming) Thursday'.

One basic (but often unrecognized) type of temporal deixis in English is in the choice of verb tense. Whereas other languages have many different forms of the verb as different tenses, English has only two basic forms, the present as in [10a.], and the past as in [10b.].

[10] a. I live here now.
     b. I lived there then.

The present tense is the proximal form and the past tense is the distal form. Something having taken place in the past, as in [11a.], is typically treated as distant from the speaker's current situation. Perhaps less obviously, something that is treated as extremely unlikely (or impossible) from the speaker's current situation is also marked via the distal (past tense) form, as in [11b.].

[11] a. I could swim (when I was a child).
b. I could be in Hawaii (if I had a lot of money).

The past tense is always used in English in those if-clauses that mark events presented by the speaker as not being close to present reality as in [12].

[12] a. If I had a yacht, ...
b. If I was rich, ...

Neither of the ideas expressed in [12] are to be treated as having happened in past time. They are presented as deictically distant from the speaker's current situation. So distant, indeed, that they actually communicate the negative (we infer that the speaker has no yacht and is not rich).

In order to understand many English conditional constructions (including those of the form 'Had I known sooner ...'), we have to recognize that, in temporal deixis, the remote or distal form can be used to communicate not only distance from current time, but also distance from current reality of facts.

(Adapted from George Yule. 2000. *Pragmatics*. pp. 9-15.)

Text B Social Deixis and Discourse Deixis

In addition to the three types of deixis, namely, person, time, and space, there are two other types of deixis, namely, social and discourse deixis. Social deixis is concerned with the codification of the social status of the speaker, the addressee, or a third person or entity referred to, as well as the social relationships holding between them. The information encoded in social deixis may include social class, kin relationship, age, sex, profession, and ethnic group. Defined thus, social deixis is particularly closely associated with person deixis. (Huang, 2007: 163)

Discourse deixis is concerned with the use of a linguistic expression within some utterance to point to the current, preceding or following utterances in the same spoken or written discourse. Alternatively, discourse deixis can be said to refer to propositions (Lyons 1977, Webber 1991, Grenoble 1994, Herring 1994, Fillmore 1997: 103-6, Diessel 1999: 101). A few illustrative examples from English are given below.

> a. This is how birds evolved from predatory dinosaurs.
> b. That is tonight's evening news.
> c. Here goes the main argument.
> d. In the last section, we discussed conversational implicature; in this section, we consider conventional implicature, and in the next section, we shall compare and contrast them.
> e. As already mentioned, the three main branches of the legal profession in England are solicitors, barristers, and legal executives.

The use of the proximal demonstrative *this* in (a) anticipates information to be conveyed in an upcoming stretch of the discourse. The same is true of the use of the proximal adverb of space *here* in (c). By contrast, the use of the distal demonstrative *that* in (b) refers back to a preceding segment of the discourse. This is also the case with the use of *already* in (e). The terms *last*, *this*, and next used in (d) make reference to a preceding, current, and following portion of the discourse, respectively. The use of discourse deictics such as *those* in the examples above (a-e) can be found in most, if not all languages in the world. For example, Ambulas uses the proximal manner demonstrative *kéga* and the medial manner demonstrative *aga* to point to a forthcoming segment of the discourse, and the distal manner demonstrative waga to refer back to a preceding stretch of the discourse (Diessel 1999: 17). In Usan, one finds *ende* and *ete*, which are used only as discourse deictics. The former is the backward- and the latter the forward-referring discourse deictic (Reesink 1987: 81). Ainu is another language in which manner demonstratives function as discourse deictics (Diessel, 1999: 105). (Huang, 2007: 172)

(Excerpted from Yan Huang. 2007. *Pragmatics*. p. 163, p. 172.)

After You Read

Knowledge Focus

1. Decide whether the following statements are true or false based on Text A and Text B.

  1) Deixis expressions are among the first forms to be spoken by very young children and can be used to indicate people via person deixis, or location via spatial deixis or time via temporal deixis.

  2) Expressions which indicate lower status are described as honorifics.

  3) Third person pronouns are proximal forms in terms of person deixis.

  4) Proximal terms are 'this', 'here', 'now'.

  5) '*This is how you create a great looking Facebook page.*' The proximal demonstrative *This* in the sentence is a discourse deictic.

2. Discuss the following questions with your partner.

  1) Would you exemplify the basic categories of deixis?

  2) Would you give some examples of the use of the inclusive '*we*' and that of the exclusive '*we*'?

  3) Would you illustrate the role of context in interpreting deixis?

  4) Would you give examples which involve deictic projections?

  5) How are honorifics used in Chinese?

  6) How do you interpret '*If I hadn't been late for the train, I would be at home now.*' in terms of deixis?

  7) What are the differences between '我马上就来' and '我马上就去'?

  8) Ignoring the tense markers, identify the types of deixis in the following sentences.

   (a) I live here in Dalian and Li Hua lives there in Beijing.

   (b) Good morning, ladies and gentlemen. This train is for all stations to Cambridge.

   (c) We may get a pay rise if sales go up this year. That's what I've been told.

   (d) I came over to visit you several times last month, but you were never there.

   (e) Good morning, Madam. What can I do for you?

Language Focus

1. Fill in the blanks with words or expressions in Text A and Text B.

  1) Deictic expressions are also sometimes called _____.

2) In English, the 'near speaker', or proximal terms, are 'this', 'here', '_____'.

3) Expressions which indicate higher status are described as _____.

4) Physically close objects will tend to be treated by the speaker as _____ close.

5) We also seem to treat the near or immediate future as being close to utterance time by using the _____ deictic 'this', as in 'this (coming) weekend' or 'this (coming) Thursday'.

6) One basic (but often unrecognized) type of _____ deixis in English is in the choice of verb tense.

7) _____ deixis is concerned with the codification of the social status of the speaker, the addressee, or a third person or entity referred to, as well as the social relationships holding between them.

8) Social deixis is particularly closely associated with _____ deixis.

9) The remote or _____ forms of temporal deixis can be used to communicate not only distance from current time, but also distance from current reality of facts.

10) Speakers are sometimes able to project themselves into other locations prior to actually being in those locations. This is sometimes described as _____ _____.

2. Translate the following passage into English.

Deixis 一词源自希腊语，意思是"表示""指向"。它是一种通过词项或者语法结构指向语境信息的现象，也即表示词汇化或者语法化的语境信息，比如 they, it, here 等指示语，它们向听话人提供这样的指向：要获知话语意义，就必须参照话语的语境信息。（冉永平，2004: 14）

3. Translate the following passage into Chinese.

Indexical expressions are pragmatic determined, that is, they depend for their reference on the persons who use them. The chief linguistic means of expressing an indexical relationship are called deictic elements; we can think of such expressions as 'pointers', telling us where to look for the particular item that is referred to. But if we do not know who is pointing, using an indexical expression, our system of coordinates will be hanging in mid-air. Since all 'indexing' or 'pointing' is done by human beings, and therefore all pointing expressions have to be related to the uttering person, pointing in a particular place and at particular time involves the traditional philosophic and linguistic categories of person, place and time.

(Mey, 2001: 54)

Comprehensive Work

1. Record a conversation of your classmates and identify all the deictic expressions in it.

2. Read the following joke and find similar examples either in English or Chinese. The following is a Yiddish joke cited in Levinson (1983: 68; see also Mey, 2001: 55). What is the 'mistake' made by the Hebrew teacher?

A melamed (Hebrew teacher), discovering that he had left his comfortable slippers back in the house, sent a student after them with a note for his wife. The note read 'Send me your slippers with this boy.' When the student asked why he had written 'your' slippers, the melamed answered: "Yold (Fool)! If I wrote 'my' slippers, she would read '*my*' slippers and would send her slippers. What could I do with her slippers? So I wrote '*your slippers*', she'll read '*your*' slippers and send me mine."

3. Watch a TV programme and observe the deictic expressions used by children (preferably under 3 years old).

Further Readings

Text C Deictics

Deictics versus non-deictic expression

Deictic expressions or deictics are expressions that have a deictic usage as basic or central; non-deictic expressions are expressions that do not have such a usage as basic or central. For example, while second-person pronouns are deictic expressions, as in (1), third-person pronouns are not, as in (2).

(1) *You* and you, but not *you*, go back to *your* dorms!

(2) Mary wishes that *she* would visit the land of Lilliput.

It should be pointed out, however, that a deictic expression can be used non-deictically, as in (3), and conversely a non-deictic expression can be used deictically, as in (4).

(3) If *you* travel on a train without a valid ticket, *you* will be liable to pay a penalty fare.

(4) *She's* not the principal; *she's* the secretary.

In (3), *you* is used as impersonal, similar in function to lexical items such as *on* in French or *man* in German; in other words it is used non-deictically. On the other hand, in (4), the interpretation of each of the three instances of *she* depends crucially on a direct, moment by moment monitoring of the physical context in which the sentence is uttered. Hence the third-person pronoun here serves as a deictic expression.

Gestural versus symbolic use of a deictic expression

Within deictic use, a further distinction can be drawn between **gestural** and **symbolic** use (Fillmore, 1971: 62-3). Gestural use can be properly interpreted only by a direct, moment by moment monitoring of some physical aspects of the speech event. For example, in (1) and (4) above, the deictic expressions can be interpreted only if they are accompanied by a physical demonstration (such as a selecting gesture or eye contact) of some sort. By contrast, interpretation of the symbolic use of deictic expressions only involves knowing the basic spatio-temporal parameter of the speech event. If you hear someone uttering (5), you do not expect the utterance to be accompanied by any physical indication of the referent. Provided that you know the general location of the speaker, you can understand it without any problem.

(5) *This* town is famous for its small antiques shops.

Clearly, gestural use is the basic use, and symbolic use is the extended use. It seems that in general if a deictic expression can be used in a symbolic way, it can also be used in a gestural way; but not vice versa. Thus, there are deictic expressions in the world's languages that can only be used gesturally. The presentatives *voici/voilà* in French, *ecce* in Latin and *vot/von* in Russian, for example, belong to this category.

We can summarize the uses of deictic expressions as follows.

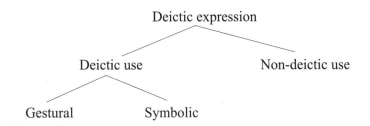

Uses of a deictic expression
(Excerpted from Yan Huang. 2007. *Pragmatics*. pp133-135.)

Questions for Discussion or Reflection

1. Discuss the following pairs of sentences. Which expressions are used deictically and which are not?

   1) a. Let's go to a *nearby* restaurant.
      b. Peter took Mary to a *nearby* restaurant.
   2) a. There was a fatal car accident in Shanghai yesterday. A *local* driver was arrested.
      b. Why not employ a *local* coach?

2. Of the following deictic expressions, which are used in a gestural way and which in a symbolic way?

   1) Hi, is Mary *there*?
   2) Press the button *now*.

3. What is the relationship between gestural use and symbolic use of deixis?

Text D Deictic Centre and Competing Deictic Centres

Generally speaking, deixis is organized in an egocentric way (Lyons, 1977: 646). The default **deictic centre** of the three major categories is the following: (i) the central anchorage point for person is the person who is speaking, (ii) that for time is the time at which the speaker produces the utterance, and (iii) that for place is the place where the speaker produces the utterance (see also Levinson, 1983: 63-4). Put informally, we may say that deixis is a 'self-centred' phenomenon, its centre being typically 'I-here-now'. (Huang, 2007: 135)

Grundy (2000: 35-36) illustrates competing deictic centres as follows. We all know how annoying it is to come across a back-in-ten-minutes notice. Our annoyance stems from not being able to calculate precisely when the writer will return because we don't know the deictic centre. I was on a train recently (there, I've done it too with *recently*); I was on a train where the announcer said that there were empty seats *at the far end of coach C*. Of course, identifying *the far end of coach C* would depend upon whether you were approaching from coach B or coach D — a case of competing deictic centres. Or another example: on 7 September 1997 I was listening to the radio when the announcer said of a panel game that was about to be broadcast

(1) This edition was recorded last summer

Was *last summer* the summer of 1996? Or was the summer of 1997 already over in England by 7 September? I wondered as I looked through the window to see what the weather was like that day. What I was trying to do, of course, was to identify a context that would help me to determine the deictic reference, just as we do, but with fewer problems, when we hear deictics like *you* or *tomorrow*. In fact, understanding pragmatic meanings is always a case of identifying a context that will make sense of an utterance.

Or to take another case of problematic context identification, when General Pinochet was arrested in London in October 1998, the BBC broadcast an interview with the British Ambassador to Chile who was speaking from Santiago. One of the answers he gave to a question the interviewer asked began

(2) What many people maybe don't realize in this country

When he said *in this country*, was he referring to Chile (where he was speaking from) or to Britain (where his audience was situated)? If you listen carefully for examples like (2), you will often be surprised as you listen to the succeeding discourse to find that the deictic centre isn't as you'd expected.

Although it may be annoying when we can't identify a deictic centre or distinguish between competing potential deictic centres, there are times when the confusion has to be avoided. A prime example is in the theatre where the left side of the stage to an actor is the right side of the stage to the director watching the rehearsal. So there is a convention that *stage-left* and *stage-right* mean left and right from the actor's perspective. Similarly, the expression local time is intended to clarify reports of news stories that occurred at, say, midnight. So at midnight is assumed to be at midnight in relation to the time in the country where the news is being broadcast, and at midnight local time refers to midnight in the country in a different time zone from which the news story originates. So as the world shrinks, it's possible to conceive of several different 'midnight'. This perhaps explains why a BBC radio reporter interviewing an official in the Japanese foreign ministry at 8:57 British Summer Time began:

(3) Good morning Mr Yakamata — good evening to you

This seems a neat way of getting both the audience's and the interviewee's deictic centres into a single greeting.

(Excerpted from Yan Huang. 2007. *Pragmatics*. p. 135 and
Peter Grundy. 2000. Doing *Pragmatics*. pp. 35-36.)

Questions for Discussion
1. Would you illustrate what deictic centre is?
2. Would you explain what competing deictic centres are?

3. Several location demonstratives include body-part terms—*ahead, behind, back, right-/left-hand side*. Think about Chinese and whether they exhibit the same phenomenon. Can you explain why body parts should be used in this way?

Text E Zonglish

Practice

Imagine a language, called Zonglish, exactly like English in all respects, except that it contains no deictic terms at all, i.e. all English deictic terms have been eliminated from Zonglish.

(1) Is *I would like a cup of tea* a well-formed Zonglish sentence?   *Yes / No*

(2) Given that a Zonglish speaker could not say *I would like a cup of tea*, would it be possible for him to inform someone that he would like a cup of tea by saying, *The speaker would like a cup of tea*?   *Yes / No*

(3) In a language like Zonglish, with no deictic terms, could one rely on one's hearers interpreting 'the speaker' when uttered as referring to the utterer?   *Yes / No*

(4) Given a speaker of Zonglish named Johan Brzown, and given that no other individual is named Johan Brzown, could he inform someone that he wanted a cup of tea by uttering *Johan Brzown wants a cup of tea*?   *Yes / No*

(5) Ignoring the problem that tense is a deictic category, could Johan Brzown inform anyone of any fact about himself if his hearer does not happen to know his name?   *Yes / No*

(6) Assuming that Johan Brzown carries a clearly visible badge announcing his name to all his hearers, how could he make it clear to his hearers that he wants a cup of tea at the time of utterance, not earlier, and not later?

(7) If Johan Brzown wants a cup of tea at 5:30 pm on November 9th, 2006, could he inform his hearer of this by uttering *Johan Brzown wants a cup of tea at 5:30 pm on November 9th 2006*?   *Yes / No*

Feedback

(1) No.

(2) No. See answers to next questions for reasons.

(3) No. If 'the speaker' were to be conventionally understood as referring to the utterer of the

utterance in which it occurred, it would in effect be a deictic expression, and therefore outlawed in Zonglish.

(4) No. Using the proper name *Johan Brzown* would get over the problem of referring to the speaker. Every speaker of Zonglish would have to use his own name instead of the personal pronoun *I*. But since tense is a deictic category, Johan Brzown still has the problem of informing his hearer that he wants the cup of tea at the time of utterance, not in the past, and not in the future.

(5) No.

(6) By using some non-deictic description of the actual time of the utterance, for example, at *5:30 pm on November 9th 2006*.

(7) Yes. With this utterance, Johan Brzown would be able to get his message across.

The point about an example like this is to show that there are good reasons for all languages to have deictic terms. A language without such terms could not serve the communicative needs of its users anything like or as well as a real human language. (Of course, all real human languages do have deictic terms.) Deictic expressions bring home very clearly that when we consider individual sentences from the point of view of their truth, we cannot in many cases consider them purely abstractly, i.e. simply as strings of words made available by the language system. The truth of a sentence containing a deictic expression can only be considered in relation to some hypothetical situation of utterance.

(Excerpted from J. R. Hurford, B. Heasley & M. B. Smith. 2007.

Semantics: A Coursebook. pp. 70-71.)

Suggested Reading

Grundy, P. 2000. *Doing Pragmatics*. London: Arnold. pp. 22-47.

Huang, Y. 2009. *Pragmatics*. Beijing: Foreign Language Teaching and Research Press. pp. 132-177.

Jaszczolt, K. M. 2004. *Semantics and Pragmatics: Meaning in Language and Discourse*. Beijing: Peking University Press. pp. 191-206.

Yule, G. 1996. *Pragmatics*. Oxford: Oxford University Press. pp. 9-16.

Unit 3
Speech Acts (I)

> The speaking of language is part of an activity, or a form of life.
> — Ludwig Wittgenstein
>
> However well equipped our language, it can never be forearmed against all possible cases that may arise and call for description: fact is richer than diction.
> — John Langshaw Austin

Objectives

- To understand what speech act theory is
- To get to know the development of speech act theory
- To comprehend the importance of speech acts to communication
- To learn the technical terms about speech acts
- To improve critical thinking and intercultural communicative competence and comprehensive language skills
- To improve pragmatic competence, academic ability and relevant language skills

 Before You Read

1. Could you perform each of the following actions by either speaking or physical gesture?

    1) Congratulate someone.
    2) Call someone's attention to the television set.
    3) Forbid someone to enter a room.
    4) Promise to go to a place on time.

2. The proverbs *Actions speak louder than words* and *Easier said than done* seem to make a clear distinction between speaking and acting. Is there often a clear distinction between the two?

3. One way of describing what the following utterances do is to say that they describe a state of affairs. But think of some contexts where each of these statements does much more than simply describe a state of affairs.

   1) There's a spider in your hair.
   2) Someone's eaten all the ice-cream.
   3) I've got a gun.
   4) You're a jerk.

4. Classify each of the following utterances as interrogative, imperative or declarative. Then decide what the speaker is using the utterance to do.

   1) You can pass the sugar.
   2) Why don't you pass the sugar?
   3) Have you got the sugar?
   4) I could use the sugar.
   5) Get me the sugar.
   6) Send the sugar down here.

5. Are the utterances below just statements?

1) I name this ship *Queen Elizabeth the Second*.

2) You are fired.

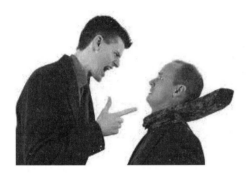 

Text A Austin's Performatives

The interest in speech acts can be traced back to the idea that we use language not only to describe phenomena in the real world but also to 'do things'. The founding father of philosophical speech act theory is the philosopher John L. Austin. In a lecture delivered at Harvard in 1955, later published as the monograph *How to do things with words* (1962), he argued against the current philosophical creed that meanings could only be assigned to sentences on the basis of their correspondence with truth, and showed that there are many different things we do with language. For example, the sentence 'I [hereby] bet you £5 it will rain' does not describe an event but constitutes a bet. Austin referred to such sentences as *performatives* and distinguished them from constative sentences such as 'It is raining', which can be true or false. Performatives have certain linguistic characteristics such as the possibility to insert *hereby* before the verb and the use of the present tense form of the verb associated with the action.

> *The 'hereby' test spotting the performative*
> *I [hereby] like apples
> I [hereby] apologize
> I [hereby] name this ship Queen Elizabeth II
> I [hereby] bet you £5 it will rain

Only in the last three sentences above can *hereby* be inserted. Pragmatically, these utterances perform the actions of apologizing, naming a ship and betting respectively. *I hereby like apples*, in contrast, does not constitute a performative utterance. Compare *I like apples* which describes or 'constates' something.

It is important that certain conditions are fulfilled for performative utterances to be successful ('felicity conditions'). Such felicity conditions are (refer to Text C for detailed discussion):

- There must be a conventional procedure having a conventional effect
- The circumstances and persons must be appropriate
- The procedure must be executed (i) correctly and (ii) completely
- Often ... the persons must have the requisite thoughts, feelings and intentions and if consequent conduct is specified, then the relevant parties must do it.

As Levinson (1983: 230) suggests, some performatives 'are ... rather special sorts of ceremony'. Ceremonial performatives are associated with specific (felicity) conventions associated with an institution such as the courtroom or the church. They must also be uttered by a person with the authority to do so, and in the manner prescribed by the institution:

- 'I sentence you to 10 years' imprisonment' (as uttered by the judge in the courtroom addressed to a person found guilty of a crime).
- 'I pronounce you husband and wife' (as uttered by a registrar or priest to a woman and man in a church or registry office in the presence of witnesses).

The above examples are 'infelicitous' if the circumstances and persons are not appropriate. This doesn't cover all types of performatives, however. Consider apologies, for example, a class of performatives which Austin described as behabitives. Here, the emphasis is on the speaker having the requisite thoughts, feelings and intentions. An example of a violation of this condition is if the speaker says 'I apologize' without feeling sorry. Such violations result in abuses with the consequence that an apology still takes place but 'unhappily'.

Explicit and implicit performatives

The examples referred to so far contain explicit pointers to the performative (I pronounce you, I sentence you …) but in some cases such pointers are missing. We therefore make a distinction between explicit performatives and implicit performatives:

- 'I promise to cook you a meal' (explicit performative)
- 'I'll cook you a meal' (implicit performative)
- 'I request you to do as I told you' (explicit performative)
- 'Do what I told you' (implicit performative)

The explicit performative is used to avoid misunderstanding or to emphasize the speaker's authority and power. It is generally present in the more ceremonial cases, but less often in casual conversation. Sometimes this leads to misunderstanding in the conversation, and a hearer might have to ask 'Is that an order?' 'Is that a promise?' or 'Is that a threat or a promise?'

(Excerpted from Archer et al. 2012. *Pragmatics: An Advanced Resource Book for Students*. pp. 35-37.)

Text B Utterances as Actions

In Chapter Eleven of his book, Austin abandons completely the original distinction between 'constatives' (statements) and all forms of performative utterance. Statements, too, are seen to have a performative aspect, and what is now needed is to distinguish between the truth-conditional aspect of what a statement is and the action it performs; between the meaning of the speaker's words and their **illocutionary force**.

Locution, illocution, perlocution

Utterances not only have sense, but also force. Austin, in fact, made a three-fold distinction:

Locution	the actual words uttered
Illocution	the force or intention behind the words
Perlocution	the effect of the illocution on the hearer

For example, I might say: *It's hot in here!* (locution), meaning: *I want some fresh air*! (illocution) and the perlocutionary effect might be that someone opens the window. Generally speaking there is a close and predictable connection between locution and perlocutionary effects as in the following example:

Example 1

The speakers are Lord Peter Wimsey, ace amateur detective, and Bunter, his butler:
'If, Bunter, you do not immediately sit down here and have your supper, I will have you drummed out of the regiment…'
Bunter [drew] up an obedient chair.

Bunter correctly interprets the illocutionary force of Lord Peter's utterance as an *invitation or request* (in the form of a mock *threat*) to join his employer for supper. All competent adult speakers of a language can predict or interpret intended illocutionary force reasonably accurately most of the time — human beings simply could not operate if they had no idea at all how their interlocutor would react, although, of course, things can go wrong, as in the following example:

Example 2

A man and a woman enter an art gallery. The man is carrying a plastic carrier bag. The woman goes to buy the admission tickets, while her husband has gone ahead into the gallery.

Official: Would the gentleman like to leave his bag here?
Woman: Oh no, thank you. It's not heavy.
Official: Only… we have had … we had a theft here yesterday, you see.

The illocutionary force of the official's first utterance is to *request* the woman's husband to leave his bag, but the woman interprets it as an *offer*. Part of the problem stems from the fact that the same **locution** could have a different **illocutionary** force in different contexts. E.g. *What time is it?* could, **depending on the context of utterance**, mean any of the following:

The speaker wants the hearer to tell her the time;
The speaker is annoyed because the hearer is late;
The speaker thinks it is time the hearer went home.

Speech acts

Austin originally (1960: 52) used the term 'speech act' to refer to an utterance and the 'total situation in which the utterance is issued'. Today the term 'speech act' is used to mean the same as 'illocutionary act'—in fact, you will find the terms **speech act, illocutionary act, illocutionary force, pragmatic force** or just **force**, all used to mean the same thing—although the use of one rather than another may imply different theoretical positions.

Just as the same words can be used to perform different speech acts, so different words can be used to perform the same speech act. The following utterances illustrate different ways of performing the speech act of *requesting someone to close the door:*

Shut the door!

Could you shut the door?

Did you forget the door?

Put the wood in the hole.

Were you born in a barn?

What do big boys do when they come into a room, Johnny?

(Excerpted from Jenny Thomas. 2010. *Meaning in Interaction: An Introduction to Pragmatics.* pp. 49-50.)

After You Read

Knowledge Focus

1. **Decide whether the following statements are true or false based on Text A and Text B.**

   1) '*I'll do you a favour*' is an explicit performative.

   2) Austin was one of the first modern scholars to recognize that 'words' are in themselves actions and that these speech acts can and should be systematically studied.

   3) Locution, illocution and perlocution are different speech acts.

   4) At the very beginning Austin isolated a number of syntactic and semantic properties of explicit performative in English, namely, I +hereby + a performative verb (simple present tense, indicative mood, and passive voice). However, as Austin himself was aware, there are some exceptions.

   5) The same words can be used to perform different speech acts, but different words cannot be used to perform the same speech act.

2. **Discuss the following questions with your partner.**

   1) Discuss and exemplify what performatives and constatives are.

   2) In each of the groups below only the (a) utterance would be explicit performative in Austin's view. Think about why the (b) and (c) utterances would not be classified as performatives.

A

(a) I admit I was wrong.

(b) I think I was wrong.

(c) I know I was wrong.

B

(a) I apologize to you.

(b) I amuse you.

(c) I flatter you.

C

(a) I promise to leave.

(b) He admits he was silly.

(c) I warned you to stop.

3) Of the following utterances, which are performatives and which are constatives according to Austin?

(a) The Smiths live in London.

(b) I object, Your Honour.

(c) John's future is bright.

(d) I declare this bridge open.

(e) I second the dash.

(f) Mary is growing long hair.

4) Illustrate what are locutionary, illocutionary, and perlocutionary acts.

5) Analyze the following utterances based on speech act theory.

(a) Mother to son: *Give me that Playboy magazine*.

(b) Dean's secretary to professor: *Coffee?*

(c) Jane: *You've interrupted me again*!

   Steve: *I was rude*.

6) Choose a particular illocutionary force (e.g. apology, threat, request) and give at least five different locutions which could express that force.

7) Give three possible perlocutions for the locution: I love tea.

8) Miscommunication can arise when the hearer has miscalculated the speaker's intention. This often forms the basis of humour as in the following rather awful joke where a **complaint** is (deliberately?) misinterpreted as **praise**.

Customer: *Waiter! There's a fly in my soup.*

Waiter: *Don't worry. There's no extra charge.*

Find similar examples.

Language Focus

1. **Fill in the blanks with words or expressions you have learned in Text A and Text B.**

   1) We use language not only to describe phenomena in the real world but also to _____ _____.

   2) 'It is raining' is a _____ sentence.

   3) It is important that certain conditions are fulfilled for perfomative utterances to be successful ('_____ conditions').

   4) _____ performatives are associated with specific (felicity) conventions associated with an institution such as the courtroom or the church.

   5) Utterances like *I pronounce you..., I sentence you...* contain _____ pointers to the performative but in some cases such pointers are missing.

   6) In Austin's three-fold distinction of a speech act, _____ is the effect of the illocution on the hearer.

   7) The _____ of a teacher's utterance *There is no chalk* may be to request a student to get some chalk.

   8) Statements also have a performative aspect, and what is now needed is to distinguish between the _____ aspect of what a statement is and the action it performs.

   9) In Chapter Eleven of his book, Austin abandons completely the original distinction between 'constatives' (statements) and all forms of _____ utterance.

   10) The same _____ could have a different illocutionary force in different contexts.

2. **Translate the following passage into English.**

   "言即行"的观点是语用学研究中广为人知的观点。在反对逻辑实证主义的背景下，牛津大学 Austin 提出关于言语行为的见解。逻辑实证主义认为，如果一个句子不可以被证实的话，从严格意义上来说它就没有意义。Austin 认为这有悖于语言使用的现实，于是他把句子划分为施为句和表述句，并进而把施为句分为带施为动词的显性施为句和不带施为动词的隐性施为句。

3. Translate the following passage into Chinese.

To utter something — either orally or in writing — is to do something. The act of speaking is, first and foremost, an act. This is the central insight behind the theory of speech acts, and although it seems relatively straightforward, it raises important questions about how the addressee is able to determine what sort of act the speaker intended to perform. The theory of speech acts, then, is inherently a pragmatic theory, since it involves an intention on the part of the speaker and an inference on the part of the hearer. We have seen in many ways how a speaker's intention can be more than is evident merely from the semantics of the sentence uttered, and we have also seen how the context must be taken into account when trying to infer a speaker's intended meaning. This is central to the study of speech acts. Without this type of inferencing, it would be impossible to tell whether a speaker uttering *I'm a little cold* intends to convey an observation about the weather, a request for the hearer to bring a blanket or close a window, a question about the thermostat setting, or an invitation to snuggle up closer — or indeed several of these things at once.

(Birner, 2013: 175)

Comprehensive Work

1. Paraphrase and exemplify the following quotes on language.
1) 'Do you think that mere words are strategy and power for war?'
2) 'Rash words are like sword thrusts, but the tongue of the wise brings healing.'

2. The same locution could have different illocutionary forces in different contexts. What are the illocutionary forces of the following utterances?
1) You have five minutes left.
2) It's been ten years since we got married.
3) I stayed up last night.

3. Find the locutions of a certain type of speech act (apology, request, promise, compliment, etc.) in movies or TV series.

4. Collect five naturally occurring examples of explicit performatives and five naturally occurring examples of implicit performatives. Explain how the addressee is able to infer that the implicit performatives are intended performatively.

Further Readings

Text C Austin's Felicity Conditions on Performatives

As already mentioned, it makes no sense to call a performative true or false. Nevertheless, Austin noticed that for a performative to be successful or 'felicitous', it must meet a set of conditions. For example, one such condition for the speech act of naming is that the speaker must be recognized by his or her community as having the authority to perform that act; for the speech act of ordering, the condition is that the speaker must be in authority over the addressee, and finally, for the speech act of promising, one condition is that what is promised by the speaker must be something the addressee wants to happen. Austin called these conditions **felicity conditions**. In other words, felicity conditions are conditions under which words can be used properly to perform actions.

Austin distinguished three different types of felicity conditions (Austin, 1975: 14—15).

Austin's felicity conditions on performatives

A. (i) There must be a conventional procedure having a conventional effect.

  (ii) The circumstances and persons must be appropriate, as specified in the procedure.

B. The procedure must be executed (i) correctly and (ii) completely.

C. Often

  (iii) the persons must have the requisite thoughts, feelings and intentions, as specified in the procedure, and

  (iv) if consequent conduct is specified, then the relevant parties must so do.

Violation of any of the conditions will render a performative 'unhappy' or infelicitous. If conditions A or B are not observed, then what Austin described as a **misfire** takes place. For instance, in England, a registrar conducting a marriage ceremony in an unauthorized place will violate condition A (i), thus committing a misfire. The same is true for a clergyman baptizing a wrong baby, because in this case, condition A (ii) is not fulfilled. Next, as an illustration of a violation of condition B (i), consider the case of a bridegroom not saying the exact words that are conventionally laid down at a marriage ceremony. As to condition B (ii), it dictates that the procedure must be complete. Thus, in making a bet, the bet is not 'on' unless *You are on* or something with the same effect is uttered by the addressee. In Austin's terminology, this counts as a satisfactory **uptake**, the absence of which will again cause a misfire. Finally, if condition C is not met, resulting in insincerities, then an **abuse** is the outcome. Examples of an abuse include congratulating someone when one knows that he or she passed his or her examination by cheating (condition C (i)), making a promise when one already intends to break it (condition C (ii)), and marrying without intending to consummate the marriage. We will return to the question of felicity conditions when we come to Searle's work.

(Excerpted from Yan Huang. 2007. *Pragmatics*. pp.98-100.)

Questions for Discussion

1. What are felicity conditions?
2. Given below are illocutionary acts, and for each act there are four suggested felicity conditions. In each case only two of the felicity conditions are correct. Please indicate the correct felicity conditions by circling your choices.

    1) promising:

    (a) The speaker must intend to carry out the thing promised.

    (b) The speaker must be inferior in status to the hearer.

    (c) The thing promised must be something that the hearer wants to happen.

    (d) The thing promised must be morally wrong.

    2) apologizing:

    (a) The speaker must be responsible for the thing apologized for.

    (b) The thing apologized for must be (or must have been) unavoidable.

    (c) The thing apologized for must be morally wrong.

    (d) The hearer must not want the thing apologized for to happen (or to have happened).

    3) greeting:

    (a) The speaker and the hearer must be of different sex.

    (b) The speaker and the hearer must not be in the middle of a conversation.

    (c) The speaker must believe the hearer to have recently suffered a loss.

    (d) The speaker feels some respect and/or sense of community (however slight) with the hearer.

    4) naming:

    (a) The thing or person named must not already have a recognized name known to the speaker.

    (b) The speaker must be recognized by his community as having the authority to name.

    (c) The thing or person named must belong to the speaker.

    (d) The thing or person named must be held in considerable respect by the community.

5) protesting:

   (a) The speaker and the hearer must have recently been in conflict with each other.

   (b) The speaker must disapprove of the state of affairs protested at.

   (c) The state of affairs protested at must be disapproved of by the community generally.

   (d) The hearer must be held to be responsible (by the speaker) for the state of affairs protested at.

Text D   Speech Acts: Language as Action

Sunday evening at home and I'm sitting at the kitchen table preparing for my pragmatics class. My then eighteen-year-old son is sitting at the top of the table turning the pages of the newspaper apparently looking for pictures. My then thirteen-year-old daughter is sitting opposite me with nothing better to do than think, and kick the underside of the table from time to time. All of a sudden, she speaks: 'Why don't we get a parrot?' My son and I ignore her. She speaks again, and looking up from my work, this time I reply:

(1) ELEANOR: They're as intelligent as three-year-olds

     ME: Some are as intelligent as eighteen-year-olds

My son continues to turn pages as though he hasn't heard.

She is not only telling me something about parrots, she is trying to persuade me that we should get one. I understand both what she says and what she does, or tries to do, by saying it.

For my part, I'm not only telling her something (doubtful) about parrots, but I'm also turning down her suggestion and insulting my son in a typical father-daughter bonding exchange. She understands both what I say and what I do by saying it.

For his part, my son, who is partly the target but not the addressee of what I say, feigns deafness. My daughter and I both understand what he means by not saying anything.

Later, I wish I'd said, 'Some eighteen-year-olds are as intelligent as three-year-olds.'

Utterances have the property of counting as actions, such as the actions of persuading, refusing, reassuring, warning and apologizing.

Language and action: understanding the phenomenon

Our butcher once asked why farmers have long ears and baldheads. When I obligingly said I didn't know, he took the lobe of one of his ears between thumb and forefinger and, pulling it downwards, said 'How much?' Next he ran his hand through his hair, saying 'Cor' as he did so. This neat joke shows how language (saying 'How much?') and action (pulling your ear lobe downwards to indicate that you can't believe what you've just heard) can be co-incident. Of course there are times when actions are preferred to words, such as when flagging down a bus or a taxi; or times when either actions, language, or both may be used, such as when greeting someone in the street; or times when both language and actions are required, as in the complicated ritual of introducing people to one another. These examples show that there is no clear-cut boundary between using actions to count as actions and using language to count as actions.

In fact, we usually realize that we are doing something with words when we talk. When my son was two years old he came into the bathroom one day when I was bent double scrubbing out the bath and said in a particularly jaunty and self-satisfied way

(2) It's me again

This struck me as a rather peculiar utterance. The sentence was an accurate description of a state of affairs in the world — indeed, it was a statement of the obvious. But when we use *It's me again* as an utterance, it is usually to apologize for troubling someone a second time. This did not seem to be my son's intention on this occasion. I wasn't able to explain his utterance to myself until I recollected that on the previous occasion when he had come into the bathroom as I was scrubbing out the bath, I had turned to him in exasperation and said

(3) It's you again

He had evidently understood the semantics but not the pragmatics of my utterance and had assumed that to get in first with it's me again was the appropriate pragmatic strategy in the bath-scrubbing context we found ourselves in.

This simple example illustrates the difference between the literal meaning of sentences like *It's me again* and *It's you again* and the use of such sentences as utterances. Knowing the literal meaning of the sentences is not enough to determine what they count as doing, what speech act is performed, when they are used.

(Adapted from Peter Grundy. 2000. *Doing Pragmatics*. pp. 48-50.)

Questions for Discussion

1. Why did the author say I wish I'd said, 'Some eighteen-year-olds are as intelligent as three-year-olds.'?
2. Explain the 'butcher' example to show why there is no clear-cut boundary between using actions to count as actions and using language to count as actions.

Text E John Langshaw Austin

According to Wikipedia, John Langshaw Austin (1911 — 1960) was a British philosopher of language, born in Lancaster and educated at Shrewsbury School and Balliol College, Oxford University. Austin is widely associated with the concept of the speech act and the idea that speech is itself a form of action. Consequently, in his understanding, language is not just a passive practice of describing a given reality, but a particular practice that can be used to invent and affect realities. His work in the 1950s provided both a theoretical outline and the terminology for the modern study of speech acts developed subsequently, for example, by John R. Searle (the Oxford-educated American philosopher), François Récanati, Kent Bach, Robert M. Harnish, and William P. Alston.

He occupies a place in philosophy of language alongside Wittgenstein and his fellow Oxonian, Ryle, in staunchly advocating the examination of the way words are ordinarily used in order to elucidate meaning, and avoid philosophical confusions. Unlike many ordinary language philosophers, however, Austin disavowed any overt indebtedness to Wittgenstein's later philosophy, calling Wittgenstein a 'charlatan'. His main influence, he said, was the exact and exacting common-sense philosophy of G. E. Moore. His training as a classicist and linguist influenced his later work.

Jenny Thomas (2010: 28-29) states that 'Austin is the person who is usually credited with generating interest in what has since come to be known as pragmatics. She says that it is not altogether clear to me why Austin's ideas on language should have been taken up so enthusiastically within linguistics, when the work of others with not dissimilar views (e.g. the ideas of the philosopher G. E. Moore and Wittgenstein's later work) has not had anything like the same impact. However, there are four factors which, taken together, may explain why the influence of Austin's work has been so great the appearance of the most influential collection of Austin's papers (*How to do things with words*, published posthumously in 1962) was very timely, coinciding as it did with a growing frustration within linguistics with the limitations of truth conditional semantics. Secondly, Austin's writing is admirably clear and accessible. Thirdly, although over the years he refined and modified his ideas considerably, his work represents a consistent line of thought. And finally, what continues to make the study of Austin's work so rewarding is that it foreshadows many of the issues which are of major importance in pragmatics today. Whatever the explanation, it is a source of mild pride that the 'father of pragmatics' should have been born here in Lancaster.

Austin was not a linguist at all (although he himself foresaw that it would be within an expanded science of linguistics that his work would be developed) but a philosopher, working at Oxford University in the 1940s and 1950s. Austin, his almost equally influential pupil H. P. Grice and a group of like-minded philosophers working at Oxford and elsewhere came to be known as ordinary language philosophers.

Austin's ideas on language were set out in a series of lectures which he gave at Oxford University between 1950 and 1954; and he delivered a version of these talks as the William James Lectures at Harvard in 1955. After Austin's sudden death in 1960, the lectures were brought together in book form by J. O. Urmson, based on Austin's own (not always complete) lecture notes and recordings of his lectures. *How to do things with words* is therefore a rather informal book, very easy to read and well worth reading. However, as Levinson (1983: 231) notes, you really need to read the book from cover to cover, because Austin developed and modified his position considerably as the series of lectures progressed. The same is true of this chapter: distinctions introduced early on will be shown to be untenable by the end, but it will help you to understand the key issues in pragmatics if you work your way through the arguments carefully.

(Excerpted from http://en.wikipedia.org/wiki/J._L. Austin, and Jenny Thomas. 2010. *Meaning in Interaction: An Introduction to Pragmatics*. pp. 28-29.)

Suggested Reading

Grundy, P. 2000. *Doing Pragmatics*. London: Arnold. pp. 48-62.

Huang, Y. 2009. *Pragmatics*. Beijing: Foreign Language Teaching and Research Press. pp. 93-104.

Jaszczolt, K. M. 2004. *Semantics and Pragmatics: Meaning in Language and Discourse*. Beijing: Peking University Press. pp. 294-297.

Yule, G. 1996. *Pragmatics*. Oxford: Oxford University Press. pp. 47-50.

Unit 4

Speech Acts (II)

> It was less a literary thing than a linguistic, philosophical preoccupation ... discovering how far you can go with language to create immediate, elementary experience.
>
> — Robert Morgan
>
> For a large class of cases — though not for all — in which we employ the word meaning it can be defined thus: the meaning of a word is its use in the language.
>
> — Ludwig Wittgenstein

Objectives

- To understand how an indirect speech act is differentiated from a direct one
- To learn the basic notions of indirect speech acts and Searle's felicity conditions
- To comprehend how speech acts are classified
- To learn the technical terms and expressions about speech acts
- To improve critical thinking and intercultural communicative competence and comprehensive language skills
- To improve pragmatic competence, academic ability and relevant language skills

Before You Read

1. How would you describe the relationship between the words and the world in the following utterances?

   1) I now pronounce you husband and wife.

2) I name this ship *Queen Elizabeth the Second*.

3) I sentence you to 20 years in prison.

4) Mary is a high school teacher.

5) I'll visit you this evening.

6) Stand up!

2. Look at the following two situations.

1) *A: Let's go to the party tonight.*

   B: I have to study for an exam.

   How do you interpret B's reply? And why do you think B responds in this way?

2) *Can you pass me the salt?*

   Does the question require a verbal response?

3. Give the direct and indirect illocutions of the following utterances. (The first one has been done for you.)

1) Why don't we go to Paris this summer?

   Direct illocution: Asking why the speaker and the hearer do not (or will not) go to Paris

   Indirect illocution: Suggesting that the speaker and the hearer go to Paris

2) I believe you may have been looking for me.

   Direct illocution:

   Indirect illocution:

3) I must ask you to leave.

   Direct illocution:

   Indirect illocution:

4) Don't you think you ought to phone your mother?

   Direct illocution:

   Indirect illocution:

4. Name three performative verbs: _____ _____ _____

5. Note down the sentence type and the main illocutionary act performed in the following utterance.

1) Boy in a toy shop: 'Is that copter expensive?'

   Sentence type: _____ Act: _____

2) Boss to employee: 'I don't want to see you in the office tomorrow.'

   Sentence type: _____ Act: _____

3) Girl helping an old lady across a road: 'Watch the step.'

   Sentence type: _____ Act: _____

4) Man in argument: 'Do you take me for an idiot?'

   Sentence type: _____ Act: _____

6. According to the conventions of everyday usage, could the utterance, in a normal situation, of *Would you like a cup of coffee*? be an act of:

1) warning?

2) thanking?

3) apologizing?

4) offering?

5) enquiring?

6) questioning?

Start to Read

Text A Searle's Typology of Speech Acts

Can speech acts be classified, and if so, how? Austin (1962) grouped them into five types: (i) **verdictives** — give a verdict, (ii) **exercitives** — exercising power, rights, or influence, (iii) **commissives** — promising or otherwise undertaking, (iv) **behabitives** — showing attitudes and social behaviour, and (v) **expositives** — fitting an utterance into the course of an argument or conversation. Since then, there have been many attempts to systematize, strengthen and develop the original Austinian taxonomy. Of all the schemes, Searle's (1975a) **neo-Austinian typology of speech acts remains the most influential.**

Under Searle's taxonomy, speech acts are universally grouped into five types along four dimensions: (i) **illocutionary point** or speech act type. (ii) **direction of fit** or relationship between words and world, (iii) **expressed psychological state**, and (iv) **propositional content**. The five types of speech act are further explained below.

(i) **Representatives** (or **assertives**; the constatives in the original Austinian performative/constative dichotomy) are those kinds of speech act that commit the speaker to the truth of the expressed proposition, and thus carry a truth-value. They express the speaker's belief. Paradigmatic cases include asserting, claiming, concluding, reporting, and stating. In performing this type of speech act, the speaker represents the world as he or she believes it is, thus making the words fit the world of belief. Representatives are illustrated in (1):

(1)
a. Chinese characters were borrowed to write other languages, notably Japanese, Korean and Vietnamese.
b. Francis Crick and Jim Watson discovered the double helix structure of DNA.
c. The soldiers are struggling on through the snow.

(ii) **Directives** are those kinds of speech act that represent attempts by the speaker to get the addressee to do something. They express the speaker's desire/wish for the addressee to do something. Paradigmatic cases include advice, commands, orders, questions, and requests. In using a directive, the speaker intends to elicit some future course of action on the part of the addressee, thus making the world match the words via the addressee. Directives are exemplified in (2):

(2)
a. Turn the TV down.
b. Don't use my electric shaver.
c. Could you please get that lid off for me?

(iii) **Commissives** are those kinds of speech act that commit the speaker to some future course of action. They express the speaker's intention to do something. Paradigmatic cases include offers, pledges, promises, refusals, and threats. In the case of a commissive, the world is adapted to the words via the speaker him- or herself. Examples of commissives are presented in (3).

(3)

a. I'll be back in five minutes.

b. We'll be launching a new policing unit to fight cyber crime on the internet soon.

c. I'll never buy you another computer game.

(iv) **Expressives** are those kinds of speech act that express a psychological attitude or state in the speaker such as joy, sorrow, and likes/dislikes. Paradigmatic cases include apologizing, blaming, congratulating, praising and thanking. There is no direction of fit for this type of speech act.

(4)

a. Well done, Elizabeth!

b. I'm so happy.

c. Wow, great!

(v) **Declarations** (or **declaratives**) are those kinds of speech act that effect immediate changes in some current state of affairs. Because they tend to rely on elaborate extralinguistic institutions for their successful performance, they may be called institutionalized performatives. In performing this type of speech act, the speaker brings about changes in the world; that is, he or she effects a correspondence between the propositional content and the world. Paradigmatic cases include bidding in bridge, declaring war, excommunicating, firing from employment, and nominating a candidate. As to the direction of fit, it is both words-to-world and world-to words.

(5)

a. President: I declare a state of national emergency.

b. Chairman: The meeting is adjourned.

c. Jury foreman: We find the defendant not guilty.

Illocutionary point, direction of fit, and expressed psychological state can be summarized as follows:

Illocutionary point	*Direction of fit*	*Expressed psychological state*
Representative	words-to-world	belief (speaker)
Directives	world-to-words	desire (addressee)
Commissives	world-to-words	intention (speaker)

| Expressives | none | variable (speaker) |
| Declarations | both | none (speaker) |

(Adapted from Yan Huang, 2007. *Pragmatics*. pp.106-108.)

Text B   Direct and Indirect Speech Acts

We have observed that performatives can be grouped into two categories, explicit performatives and implicit performatives. Implicit performatives are often subtle enough that they may at first appear to be explicit. We've already dealt with the case of saying *I'm sorry* rather than the explicitly performative *I apologize*. The promise in *I'll be sure to take out the trash* is similar, in that it describes declaratively my state of mind — in this case, my strong intent for the future, which may be taken, depending on the context, to count as a promise. The question of who is wiling to bet me in *Who'll bet me $10 that Zenyatta won't win?* makes use of Grice's maxim of Relation to count as actually offering a bet; why would I ask who'll bet me, unless I have a related intent to take them up on the bet? We have also followed Austin in expanding the category of speech acts to include not only performatives but in fact all utterances.

Notice that, in general, a speech act has a form that canonically (that is, in the default case) maps onto some general illocutionary force. For example:

a. Sam Vimes sighed when he heard the scream, but he finished shaving before he did anything about it.

b. 'Bloody stay *there*!' he yelled. 'That is an *order*! You'll go over!'

c. 'Why're you picking on me? What'm I supposed to have done?'

None of these is an explicit performative, yet each performs a **direct speech act**, in that its illocutionary force is the canonical illocutionary force for that form. For example, (a) is a **declarative** in form. Declaratives canonically have the illocutionary force of a

statement; that is, they state something. And indeed, (a), the first sentence of a novel, states something about Sam Vimes and his experience and activity. Its perlocutionary effect is a different matter; in this case, for the average reader, that effect will include not only adding this information to the discourse model, but also becoming intrigued about the source of the scream, and wondering why Sam finished shaving before he did anything about it. The perlocutionary effect does not determine whether a speech act is a direct or indirect speech act, however; that is a matter of the relationship between the form and the illocutionary force of the utterance. In the first sentence of (b), we see another direct speech act. In this case, the form is that of an **imperative**. Imperatives canonically have the illocutionary force of a **command** (or, relatedly, a request, invitation, suggestion, etc. — essentially milder forms on a scale ranging from 'suggestion' to 'command'); here we see the command *stay there*, along with the observation by the speaker that this is an order (i.e., a type of command). Finally, in (c) we have two utterances that are **interrogative** in form. Interrogatives canonically have the illocutionary force of asking a **question**, and indeed the interrogatives in (c) are asking questions of the addressee.

In addition to direct speech acts, as we have seen, we also find **indirect speech acts**, in which there is a mismatch between the linguistic form and the illocutionary force; that is, in these cases, the illocutionary force is something other than the force canonically associated with that form.

Much of the time, what we mean is actually not in the words themselves but in the meaning implied. Consider the following example:

Three students are sitting together at the 'bun lunch', the social occasion at which the university lays on filled rolls and fruit juice on the first day of the course, to welcome the students and help them to get to know each other.
MM   I think I might go and have another bun.
AM   I was going to get another one.
BM   Could you get me a tuna and sweetcorn one, please?
AM   Me as well?

In this example, we said that AM's words 'I was going to get another one' had the illocutionary force of 'expressing intentions about his own action'. It should be noted however, that he says this straight after MM's 'I think I might go and have another one.' It is possible that in fact he was implying that he would like MM to get him one while he was there and save him the bother of getting up. If this is so, he is expressing a directive, 'requesting' indirectly, with the force of the imperative 'Get me one'; this is what we call an indirect act.

Searle said that a speaker using a **direct speech act** wants to communicate the literal meaning that the words conventionally express; there is a direct relationship between the form and the function. Thus, a declarative form (not to be confused with declaration speech acts) such as 'I was going to get another one' has the function of a statement or assertion; an interrogative form such as 'Do you like the tuna and sweetcorn ones?' has the function of a question; and an imperative form such as 'Get me one' has the function of a request or order.

On the other hand, Searle explained that someone using an **indirect speech act** wants to communicate a different meaning from the apparent surface meaning; the form and function are not directly related. There is an underlying pragmatic meaning, and one speech act is performed through another speech act. Thus a declarative form such as 'I was going to get another one', or 'You could get me a tuna and sweetcorn one' might have the function of a request or order, meaning 'Get me one.' Similarly, an interrogative form such as 'Could you get me a tuna and sweetcorn one please?' or 'Would you mind getting me one?' has the function of a request or order, and 'Can I get you one while I'm there?' can be taken as an offer. Finally, an imperative form such as 'Enjoy your bun' functions as a statement meaning 'I hope you enjoy your bun'; 'Here, take this one' can have the function of an offer, and 'Come for a walk with me after the lunch' serves as an invitation.

Indirect speech acts are part of everyday life. The classification of utterances into categories of indirect and direct speech acts is not an easy task, because much of what we say operates on both levels, and utterances often have more than one of the macrofunctions ('representative', 'commissive', 'directive', 'expressive' and so on). A few examples will illustrate this.

The following excerpt from the novel *Regeneration* demonstrates that in indirect speech acts, it is the underlying meaning that the speaker intends the hearer to understand. Graves arrives after Sassoon at the convalescent home and asks:

Graves: I don't suppose you've seen anybody yet?
Sassoon: I've seen Rivers. Which reminds me, he wants to *see you*, but I imagine it'll be
        all right if you dump your bag first.'

On the surface, Sassoon's reply 'he wants to see you' is a declarative with the function of a statement and a direct representative describing Rivers' wishes. However, it appears to be intended as an order or a suggestion to Graves, meaning the same as the imperative 'Go and see him', and therefore an indirect directive, and the suggestion is reinforced by 'but I imagine it'll be all right if you dump your bag first', which is uttered as if he had actually said 'Go and see him.'

Let us take another example by Jenny Thomas (2010: 93):

This notice is displayed in the changing rooms at the swimming pool at the University of Warwick:
Would users please refrain from spitting.

What we have here (in Searle's terms) is a directive (*Don't spit*!) performed by means of an interrogative. However, all speech acts (except explicit performatives) are, as Austin and Grice demonstrated, indirect to some degree and are performed 'by means of another speech act (e.g. in making the **assertion** *It is going to charge*! I perform the speech act of warning (Austin 1962: 74)).

(Excerpted from Joan Cutting. 2002. *Discourse and Pragmatics*. p. 19; Jenny Thomas. 2010. *Meaning in Interaction: An Introduction to Pragmatics*. pp. 93-94 and Bettey J. Birner. 2013. *Introduction to Pragmatics*. pp. 191-192.)

After You Read

Knowledge Focus

1. **Decide whether the following statements are true or false based on Text A and Text B.**

   1) The five types of speech acts put forward by Searle are representatives, directives, commissives, expressives and declarations.
   2) Directives make the words match the world via the addressee.
   3) There is a mismatch between a form and an illocutionary force in an indirect speech act.
   4) All speech acts (except explicit performatives) are indirect to some degree and are performed by means of another speech act.
   5) Commissives are those kinds of speech act that commit the speaker to some future course of action. They express the speaker's intention to do something.

2. **Discuss the following questions with your partner.**

   1) What are indirect speech acts?

2) Of the following utterances, which are direct and which are indirect speech acts?

(a) If everybody could please take their seats?

(b) (At a fitness club)

   Please change your shoes before entering the room.

(c) Whatever!

(d) Have a nice day!

(e) Why don't we go to the pub nearby?

(f) Drinking is strictly prohibited in the classroom.

3) You are studying in your dorm, yet one of your roommates is listening to the music which is so loud that you feel difficult in focusing. What are the possible ways of stopping him/her? (Using direct and indirect speech acts)

4) How did Searle classify speech acts?

5) Using Searle's typology, classify the following speech acts:

(a) commanding

(b) threatening

(c) questioning

(d) reporting

(e) concluding

(f) appointing

(g) thanking

(h) praising

Language Focus

1. Fill in the blanks with words or expressions in Text A and Text B.

1) We have also followed Austin in expanding the category of speech acts to include not only performatives but in fact all _____.

2) The perlocutionary effect does not determine whether a speech act is a direct or indirect speech act, however; that is a matter of the relationship between the _____ and the illocutionary force of the utterance.

3) Searle said that a speaker using a direct speech act wants to communicate the literal meaning that the words _____ express.

4) Searle explained that someone using an indirect speech act wants to communicate a different meaning from the apparent _____ meaning.

5) The classification of utterances into categories of indirect and direct speech acts is not

an easy task, because much of what we say operates on both levels, and utterances often have more than one of the _____.

6) Since then, there have been many attempts to systematize, strengthen and develop the original Austinian _____.

7) Of all the schemes, Searle's (1975a) neo-Austinian _____ of speech acts remains the most influential.

8) Under Searle's taxonomy, speech acts are universally grouped into five types along four _____.

9) In using a _____ the speaker intends to elicit some future course of action on the part of the addressee, thus making the world match the words via the addressee.

10) _____ are those kinds of speech act that express a psychological attitude or state in the speaker such as joy, sorrow, and likes/dislikes.

2. Translate the following passage into English.

如果对塞尔及其分类进行批判，我们不能忽视这样一个事实：作为哲学家，他和奥斯丁在描写语言方面都有一些特定的目标。对于语言学研究目的来说，这些目标看起来并不总是很相关。奥斯丁和塞尔都是基于"一个句子，一个事例的准则"；也就是说，他们为了阐释理论，使用带有某一个特定言语行为特征的句子。近些年，随着语用语言学的发展，"事例方法"的缺陷日益突出了。(Mey, 2001: 125)

3. Translate the following passage into Chinese.

A different approach to distinguishing between types of speech acts is to consider whether they are direct or indirect. Indirectness captures the fact that we do not always say literally what we mean. However, hearers normally have no difficulty in interpreting what is said on the basis of inference. When there is a conventional relationship between sentence type and speech act (illocutionary force) we have a direct speech act. An example is the relation between an interrogative and a question (*Can you help me*?) or between the imperative and a command (or request).

(Archer et al., 2012: 41-42)

Comprehensive Work

1. Review the studies of a particular speech act at home and abroad.

2. Make a comment on the limitations of speech act theory based on the literature in the field.

Further Readings

Text C Pragmatics and Indirectness

As we have seen, indirectness occurs when there is a mismatch between the expressed meaning and the implied meaning. Indirectness is a universal phenomenon: as far as we know it occurs in all natural languages, a fact which in itself requires some explaining.

There are four points which should be borne in mind in this discussion of indirectness:

* We shall be concerned with intentional indirectness.
* Indirectness is costly and risky.
* We assume (unless we have evidence to the contrary) that the speakers are behaving in a rational manner and, given the universality of indirectness, that they obtain some social or communicative advantage through employing indirectness.
* For the purposes of this argument, we shall ignore the possibility that X cannot be expressed.

Intentional indirectness

Not all indirectness is intentional; some is caused by linguistic inadequacy, for example, when you do not know the correct word for some object in your own or a foreign language. This happened to me once in France, when I went into a shop to buy some coat hangers. It was only after I had attracted the attention of the shop assistant that I realized that I couldn't remember how to ask for them in French and I was forced to try to describe their use and appearance in a roundabout way. I was not trying to imply anything by my indirectness, nor was I trying to avoid an embarrassing topic, nor to spare my own or my hearer's feelings; I had simply forgotten the word. On other occasions we may have to use indirectness because of some performance error — for example, if you temporarily forget a word or, through fear, nervousness, excitement, etc., cannot get it out. The use of indirectness in these circumstances may lead the hearer to infer all sorts of things about you, but you cannot be said to have generated any implicatures. In pragmatics we are interested only in intentional indirectness.

Indirectness is costly and risky

In an excellent discussion Dascal (1983) makes the point that indirectness is costly and risky. It is 'costly' in the sense that an indirect utterance takes longer for the speaker to produce and longer for the hearer to process (a fact which has frequently been confirmed in psycholinguistic experiments). It is 'risky' in the sense that the hearer may not understand what the speaker is getting at. Consider the two interactions which follow:

Example 1

B (a non-native speaker of English) has been staying with A for several weeks. He has a passion for West Side Story and has just played the film's sound track right through for the second time in one evening:

A: Would you like to listen to something else now?
B: No.

In order to avoid making a direct complaint to his guest, which could hurt his feelings, A suggests indirectly that he has had enough of *West Side Story*. However, his strategy fails; B interprets A's utterance as a genuine question and prepares to play the record for a third time!

Example 2

The following was related to me by Elite Olshtain and I have reconstructed the dialogue from memory. An American woman was visiting Israel; one evening she went to the flat of some friends and her host asked her what she would like to drink. She replied:

'Well, I've been on whisky all day.'

The American woman intended to indicate indirectly that, having been drinking whisky previously, she would prefer to stick with whisky. Unfortunately, the host misinterpreted her indirectness and thought she was saying that, as she had been on whisky all day, she didn't want any more to drink.

(Excerpted from Jenny Thomas. 2010. *Meaning in Interaction: An Introduction to Pragmatics*. pp.119-121.)

Questions for Discussion

1. What is intentional indirectness?
2. Why is indirectness costly and risky?
3. Would you explain Example 2 based on your knowledge of indirectness?

Text D Searle's Felicity Conditions

The philosopher John Searle continued the work initiated by Austin. Searle emphasized that 'speaking a language is engaging in a rule-governed form of behaviour' (Searle, 1969: 16) and proposed a number of 'felicity conditions' (different from Austin's) for a handful of illustrative examples of speech acts.

Searle (1969) took the view that the felicity conditions put forward by Austin are not only ways in which a speech act can be appropriate or inappropriate, but they also jointly constitute the illocutionary force. Put in a different way, the felicity conditions are the **constitutive rules** — rules that create the activity itself — of speech acts. On Searle's view, to perform a speech act is to obey certain conventional rules that are constitutive of that type of act. Searle developed the original Austinian felicity conditions into a neo-Austinian classification of four basic categories, namely, (i) propositional content, (ii) preparatory condition, (iii) sincerity condition, and (iv) essential condition.

The **propositional content** condition is in essence concerned with what the speech act is about. That is, it has to do with specifying the restrictions on the content of what remains as the 'core' of the utterance (i.e. Searle's propositional act) after the illocutionary act part is removed. For a promise, the propositional content is to predicate some future act of the speaker, whereas in the case of a request, it is to predicate some future act of the addressee.

The **preparatory conditions** state the real-world prerequisites for the speech act. For a promise, these are roughly that the addressee would prefer the promised action to be accomplished, that the speaker knows this, but also that it is clear to both the speaker and the addressee that what is promised will not happen in the normal course of action. In the case a request the preparatory conditions are that the speaker has reason to believe that the addressee has the ability to carry out the action requested, and that if the addressee is not asked, he or she will not perform the action.

Next, the **sincerity condition** must be satisfied if the act is to be performed sincerely. Thus, when carrying out an act of promising, the speaker must genuinely intend to keep the promise. When making a request, the speaker must want the addressee to do the requested action. Notice that if the sincerity condition is not fulfilled, the act is still performed, but there is an abuse, to use Austin's term.

Finally, the **essential condition** defines the act being performed in the sense that the speaker has the intention that his or her utterance will count as the identifiable act, and that this intention is recognized by the addressee. Thus in the case of a promise, the speaker must have the intention to create an obligation to act, and for a request, the speaker must intend that his or her utterance counts as an attempt to get the addressee to do what is requested. Failure to meet the essential condition has the consequence that the act has not been carried out.

Searle's felicity conditions for promising can be summarized as follows (S stands for the speaker, H for the hearer, A for the action, and T for the sentence).

1) *Propositional content condition:*
   (a) S expresses the proposition that p in the utterance of T.
   (b) In expressing that p, S predicates a future act A of S.

2) *Preparatory condition:*
   (a) H would prefer S's doing A to his not doing A, and believes H would prefer his doing A to his not doing A.
   (b) It is not obvious to both S and H that S will do A in the normal course of events.

3) *Sincerity condition:*
   S intends to do A.

4) *Essential condition:*
   S intends that the utterance of T will place him under an obligation to do A.

(Adapted from Yan Huang. 2007. *Pragmatics*. pp104-106, and John Searle. 1969. pp.62-63.)

Questions for Discussion

1. How are Searle's felicity conditions different from Austin's?
2. Summarize the felicity conditions for requesting.
3. What felicity condition(s) is/are not satisfied in the following case?

   New Year's Day is soon coming, and students are going to have a big dinner party at a restaurant. S and H are both members of the class. S and some of his roommates are going out of their dorm when they see H washing something in the washing room.
   S：忙啥呢？走啊，我请你吃饭。
   H：切！

Text E John Rogers Searle

John Rogers Searle (1932 —) is an American philosopher and currently the Slusser Professor of Philosophy at the University of California, Berkeley.

John Searle, like Grice, studied under Austin at Oxford. In his philosophical writings (notably in his 1969 book *Speech Acts: An Essay in the Philosophy of Language*) Searle distinguishes between 'propositional content' and 'illocutionary force' (cf. Austin's 'locution' and 'illocution' and Grice's 'what is said' and 'what is meant') and in a later work (1975) proposes a detailed classification of the major categories of speech acts; most important of all, he points out the necessity of taking into account in the analysis of a speech act the social institution within which it was produced. (Jenny Thomas, 2010: 93)

In general, Searle's theory of speech acts is just Austin's systematized, in part rigidified, with sallies into the general theory of meaning, and connections to other philosophical issues (see Searle, 1969, 1979). If illocutionary force is somehow conventionally linked with explicit performatives and other illocutionary force indicating devices (let us call them IFIDs), then we should like to know exactly how. Searle appeals to a distinction by Rawls (1955) between **regulative rules** and **constitutive rules**. The first are the kind that control antecedently existing activities, e.g. traffic regulations, while the second are the kind that create or constitute the activity itself, e.g. the rules of a game. The latter have the conceptual form: 'doing X counts as Y', e.g. in soccer, kicking or heading the ball through the goal-posts counts as a goal. (Levison, 1983: 238)

Searle's early work, which did a great deal to establish his reputation, was on speech acts. In his 1969 book *Speech Acts*, Searle gave an account of so-called 'illocutionary acts', which Austin had introduced in *How To Do Things with Words*. Among the concepts presented in the book is the distinction between the 'illocutionary force' and the 'propositional content' of an utterance. Searle does not precisely define the former as such, but rather introduces several possible illocutionary forces by example. According to Searle, the sentences:

1. Sam smokes habitually.
2. Does Sam smoke habitually?

3. Sam, smoke habitually!

4. Would that Sam smoked habitually!

Each indicate the same propositional content (Sam smoking habitually) but differ in the illocutionary force indicated (a statement, a question, a command, and an expression of desire, respectively) (1969: 22).

According to a later account which Searle presents in *Intentionality* (1983) and which differs in important ways from the one suggested in *Speech Acts*, illocutionary acts are characterized by their having conditions of satisfaction (as idea adopted from Strawson's (1971) paper 'Meaning and Truth') and a direction of fit (an idea adopted from Elizabeth Anscombe). For example, the statement 'John bought two candy bars' is satisfied if and only if it is true, i.e. John did buy two candy bars. By contrast, the command 'John, buy two candy bars' is satisfied if and only if John carries out the action of purchasing two candy bars. Searle refers to the first as having the word-to-world direction of fit, since the words are supposed to change to accurately represent the world, and the second as having the world-to-word direction of fit, since the world is supposed to change to match the words. (There is also the double direction of fit, in which the relationship goes both ways, and the null or zero direction of fit, in which it goes neither way because the propositional content is presupposed, as in 'I'm sorry I ate John's candy bars.')

(Excerpted from Jenny Thomas. 2010. *Meaning in Interaction: An Introduction to Pragmatics*. p. 93; Levinson. 1983. *Pragmatics*. p. 238 and http://en.wikipedia.org/wiki/John_Searle)

Suggested Reading

Grundy, P. 2000. *Doing Pragmatics*. London: Arnold. pp. 63-69.

Huang, Y. 2009. *Pragmatics*. Beijing: Foreign Language Teaching and Research Press. pp. 104-115.

Jaszczolt, K. M. 2004. *Semantics and Pragmatics: Meaning in Language and Discourse*. Beijing: Peking University Press. pp. 304-309.

Levinson, S. 1983. *Pragmatics*. Cambridge: CUP.

Thomas, J. 2010. *Meaning in Interaction: An Introduction to Pragmatics*. Beijing: Foreign Language Teaching and Research Press. pp. 93-107

Yule, G. 1996. *Pragmatics*. Oxford: Oxford University Press. pp. 50-51; 53-56.

Unit 5
Implicatures (I)

> No one means all he says, and yet very few say all they mean, for words are slippery and thought is viscous.
> — Henry Brooks Adams

> Thanks to words, we have been able to rise above the brutes; and thanks to words, we have often sunk to the level of the demons.
> — Aldous Huxley

Objectives

- To understand the Cooperative Principle and its four maxims
- To learn how the Cooperative Principle and its maxims are observed and flouted.
- To comprehend the properties of conversational implicature
- To learn the technical terms and expressions about the Cooperative Principle and implicature
- To improve critical thinking and intercultural communicative competence and comprehensive language skills
- To improve pragmatic competence, academic ability and relevant language skills

Before You Read

1. What might the second speaker 'mean' in each of the following conversations?

   1) Alice: Do you like my new dress?
      Peter: It's purple.
   2) Dad: Where does the bad smell come from?
      Mom: Have you seen that room of hers?

3) Mary: Tea?

   Allan: It would keep me awake all night.

4) Mom (angrily): He hasn't finished his homework yet.

   Dad: It is a fine day today.

5) David: Are you going to Paul's garden party?

   Athena: Well, Paul's got those dogs now.

6) Parent: Was it a busy afternoon?

   Kindergarten teacher: Children are children.

2. What can be the implicature of B's utterance in each of the situations below?

1) A: Do you love me?

   B: I'm quite fond of you.

   Implicature: ……………………………………………...

2) A: Was there a pianist at the pub last night?

   B: There was a man striking the keys of a piano.

   Implicature: ……………………………………………...

3) A: Do you like my new furniture?

   B: The carpet's not bad.

   Implicature: ……………………………………………...

3. Barry Morris Goldwater was a five-term United States Senator from Arizona and the Republican Party's nominee for President in the 1964 election. He was an articulate and charismatic figure in the 1960–1964 era. Once his campaign aide said to reporters: 'Don't quote what he says. Say what he means!' What does the aide mean?

Start to Read

Text A Grice's Cooperative Principle

Grice's understanding of the inferencing process is built on the assumption that:

> Our talk exchanges do not normally consist of a succession of disconnected remarks, and would not be rational if they did. They are characteristic, to some degree at least, cooperative efforts; and each participant recognizes in them, to some extent, a common purpose or set of purposes, or at least a mutually accepted direction ... We might then formulate a rough general principle which participants will be expected (*ceteris paribus*) to observe, viz: 'Make your contribution such as is required, at the stage at which it occurs, by the accepted purpose or direction of the talk exchange in which you are engaged. One might label this the Cooperative Principle.'
>
> (Grice 1975: 47)

The four maxims

Grice famously went on to underpin his Cooperative Principle (CP) with four maxims: Quantity; Quality; Relation; and Manner. He described these maxims as follows:

> *Maxim of Quantity:* Be informative
>
>   (1) Make your contribution as informative as is required (for the current purposes of the exchange).
>
>   (2) Do not make your contribution more informative than is required.
>
> *Maxim of Quality:* Be truthful.
>
> Try to make your contribution one that is true.
>
>   (1) Do not say what you believe to be false.
>
>   (2) Do not say that for which you lack adequate evidence.
>
> *Maxim of Relation:* Be relevant.
>
> *Maxim of Manner:* Be perspicuous.
>
>   (1) Avoid absurdity of expression.
>
>   (2) Avoid ambiguity.
>
>   (3) Be brief (avoid unnecessary prolixity).
>
>   (4) Be orderly.

Grice wasn't trying to tell us how to behave as interlocutors. He was suggesting that:

1) conversation is governed by certain conventions;
2) hearers tend to assume speakers are conforming with these conventions;
3) if speakers are not conforming, they have good reason(s) not to.

Ways of breaking the maxims

If Grice didn't believe that we satisfy all the demands of the CP all of the time, why did he outline the maxims so specifically? A simplistic answer is that it provided him with the means of explaining how conversational implicatures come to be generated: hence, Grice's identification of *flouting*, in particular, whereby S deliberately fails to observe a maxim (or maxims) as a means of prompting others to look for a meaning which is different from, or in addition to, the expressed meaning. Consider the following conversation:

Peter: Do you want some coffee?
Mary: Coffee would keep me awake.

Notice that Mary opts to respond with information about what coffee does to her metabolism when a simple *yes* or *no* would have been more useful for Peter; in doing so, she flouts the Relation maxim, 'Be relevant'. Notice that we need more contextual information if we are to work out what Mary actually meant by her response. Did she mean *no* (because she will be going to bed soon, for example)? Or did she mean *yes* (because Mary has some work to finish, and needs to remain alert)? If this were a real conversation, Peter would have the context-of-utterance to help him to decipher Mary's meaning and/or be able to ask for clarification (if he needed to).

There are ways of breaking the maxims in additions to flouting, of course. For example, a *violation* constitutes a deliberate attempt by S to 'mislead' her interlocutor(s). We might note, here, that we can all-too-easily associate the intention to deceive with a malicious or selfish motive on S's part. But this needn't be the case, as the following example from Cutting (2002: 40) demonstrates: 'Mummy's gone on a little holiday because she needs a rest.' The violation of the second part of the Quality maxim, 'Do not say what you believe to be false', was motivated by a desire to safeguard H's sense of well-being, according to Cutting, for mummy had actually gone away to decide whether she should divorce her husband.

An *opt-out* involves S explicitly indicating his or her unwillingness to cooperate in the way the maxims require. We've taken the following example from a BBC (online) story relating to the cancellation of a 2011 Valentine's Day event at the Cheltenham Racecourse (in Gloucestershire, UK). As you'll see if you access the link below, a racecourse spokesman gives some brief details about a problem concerning the third-party organizers, before stating: 'We are passing the matter to our solicitors and can make no further comment at this time' (13 February 2011: http://www.bbc.co.uk/news/uk-england-gloucestershire-12442689).

An *infringement* constitutes a non-observance on S's part which is not intentional, but, rather, stems from imperfect linguistic performance. S may have an imperfect command of the language because of being an L2 speaker, for example, or because of being very young. Alternatively, his linguistic performance may be permanently impaired due to brain damage/ a degenerative disease/pre-existing condition such as autism, etc., or be temporarily impaired because of drink or drugs. Mark Haddon's (2003) *The curious incident of the dog in the night-time* provides some useful examples of infringements by the character, Christopher, who suffers from autism. Christopher has found a dead dog, but his way of communicating to the police is so different to the norm that the police initially suspect him of killing the dog. Christopher has problems with the maxim of Quantity, in particular, such that his answers to the policeman's questions are sometimes uninformative ('The dog is dead', when the dog — who's obviously dead — is in full view) and sometimes over-informative ('I am fifteen years and 3 months and 2 days'). Christopher also struggles with the Relation maxim, such that he doesn't always comprehend the communicative leaps made by his interlocutors. In one instance, for example, a woman at a subway station offers Christopher her help:

> And I was sitting on the ground and the woman knelt down on one knee and she said, 'Is there anything I can do to help you?'
>
> ... [B]ut she was a stranger, so I said, 'Stand further away' because I didn't like her being so close. And I said, 'I've got a Swiss Army Knife and it has a saw blade and it could cut someone's fingers off.'
>
> And she said, 'OK buddy. I'm going to take that as a no', and she stood up and walked away.

Although Christopher's response could be easily as a threat by the woman; that was not his intention. He merely wanted her to stand less close to him.

A second means of non-observance — that of *suspension* — was not originally identified by Grice. A suspension is said to come into play when the speech event/activity type is such that the maxims are not in operation. Consequently, there is no expectation that they will be fulfilled (see, e.g., Thomas, 2010). Imagine, if you will, an interrogation. It's very unlikely that an interrogator will start from the assumption that the interrogatee will tell them the truth from the outset. Hence, we can take it that the Quality maxim is probably suspended in such circumstance.

(Excerpted from Archer et al. 2012. *Pragmatics: An Advanced Resource Book for Students*. pp. 51-53.)

Text B Observing and Flouting the Maxims

Observing the maxims

The first maxim of the cooperative principle is the maxim of **quantity**, which says that speakers should be as informative as is required, that they should give neither too little information nor too much. Some speakers like to point to the fact that they know how much information the hearer requires or can be bothered with, and say something like, 'Well, **to cut a long story short**, she didn't get home till two.' People who give too little information risk their hearer not being able to identify what they are talking about because they are not explicit enough; those who give more information than the hearer needs risk boring them.

The second maxim is that of **quality**, which says that speakers are expected to be sincere, to be saying something that they believe corresponds to reality. They are assumed not to say anything that they believe to be false or anything for which they lack evidence. Some speakers like to draw their hearer's attention to the fact that they are only saying what they believe to be true, and that they lack adequate evidence. In

> A I'll ring you tomorrow afternoon then.
> B Erm, I shall be there **as far as I know**, and in the meantime have a word with Mum and Dad if they're free. Right, bye-bye then sweetheart.
> A Bye-bye, bye.
>
> (BNC: kc8 Gillian, 1991)

B says 'as far as I know', meaning 'I can't be totally sure if this is true', so that if A rings up and finds that B is not there, B is protected from accusations of lying by the fact that she did make it clear that she was uncertain. Most hearers assume that speakers are not lying, and most speakers know that.

The third is the maxim of **relation**, which says that speakers are assumed to be saying something that is relevant to what has been said before. Thus, if we hear 'The baby cried. The mommy picked it up' (Garfinkel 1967), we assume that the 'mommy' was the mother of the crying baby and that she picked the baby up because it was crying. Similarly, in the following exchange:

> A There's somebody at the door.
> B I'm in the bath.

B expects A to understand that his present location is relevant to her comment that there is someone at the door, and that he cannot go and see who it is because he is in the bath. Some speakers like to indicate how their comment has relevance to the conversation, as in the following from a market research meeting:

> A I mean, **just going back to your point**, I mean to me an order form is a contract. If we are going to put something in then let's keep it as general as possible.

B Yes.

(BNC: j97 British Market Research Monthly Meeting, 1994)

The last is the maxim of **manner**, which says that we should be brief and orderly, and avoid obscurity and ambiguity. In this exchange from a committee meeting, the speaker points to the fact that he is observing the maxim:

Thank you Chairman, Jus — **just to clarify one point**. There is a meeting of the Police Committee on Monday and there is an item on their budget for the provision of their camera.

(BNC: j44 West Sussex Council Highways Committee Meeting, 1994)

Grice said that hearers assume that speakers observe the cooperative principle, and that it is the knowledge of the four maxims that allows hearers to draw inferences about the speaker's intentions and implied meaning. The meaning conveyed by speakers and recovered as a result of the hearer's inferences, is known as 'conversational implicature'.

Flouting the maxims

Let us look at an example, now, of maxims *not* being observed:
When Sir Maurice Bowra was Warden of Wadham College, Oxford, he was interviewing a young man for a place at the college. He eventually came to the conclusion that the young man would not do. Helpfully, however, he let him down gently by advising the young man, 'I think you would be happier in a larger — or a smaller — college.'

(Rees, 1999: 5)

Here, Sir Maurice was not adhering to the maxim of quality, since he was not really saying what he thought. Nor was he following the maxim of manner, since he was being ambiguous and contradictory. The question is, was Sir Maurice lying to the young man in order to deceive him, or was he telling a white lie, or was he just finding a nice way of letting the young man down gently? The answer hinges on whether he thought that the young man knew the painful truth and could infer what he was trying to communicate.

It is more likely that the young man did know that Sir Maurice was trying to tell him that he had failed the interview. Obviously, if Sir Maurice had said, 'You won't do', or even 'Unfortunately you're not quite good enough for this college', he might have hurt him. If the young man knew that his 'I think you would be happier in a larger — or a smaller — college' meant 'You won't do', then it is no longer a question of lying. It is a question of face saving (We will talk about politeness in Unit 8). The young man can answer, 'OK, thanks for the advice. I'll look somewhere else', and save Sir Maurice's face in his turn.

In many cultures, it can be socially unacceptable to always say exactly what is in one's mind unless one knows the hearer very well. Thus, we might prefer not to say to a shop assistant, as we hand back a dress, 'This looks awful; I don't want it after all', but rather 'I'll go away and think about it and maybe come back later.' Similarly, in Britain, if the response to an invitation to a romantic date is 'I'm washing my hair tonight', the inviter knows that it means, 'I'm free but I don't want to go out with you.' It is quite common and acceptable in Britain to say, 'Do you find it's getting a bit chilly in here?' and mean 'I want to put the fire on.'

When speakers appear not to follow the maxims but expect hearers to appreciate the meaning implied, as in the case of the dress shop assistant, the romantic date and the chilly room, we say that they are 'flouting' the maxims. Just as with an indirect speech act, the speaker implies a function different from the literal meaning of form; when flouting a maxim, the speaker assumes that the hearer knows that their words should not be taken at face value and that they can infer the implicit meaning.

Flouting quantity

The speaker who flouts the maxim of quantity seems to give too little or too much information, in

A Well, how do I look?
B Your shoes are nice...

B does not say that the sweatshirt and jeans do not look nice, but he knows that A will understand that implication, because A asks about his whole appearance and only gets told about part of it.

Flouting quality

The speaker flouting the maxim of quality may do it in several ways. They may quite simply say something that obviously does not represent what they think. We saw an incidence of this in Sir Maurice's 'I think you would be happier in a larger — or a smaller — college', which flouts the maxim if he knew that the student would understand what he is getting at, and hear the message behind his words.

Speakers may flout the maxim by exaggerating as in the **hyperbole** 'I could eat a horse', or

Lynn   Yes **I'm starving** too.
Martin Hurry up girl.
Lynn   Oh dear, stop eating rubbish. You won't eat any dinner.

(BNC: kd6 Martin, 1992)

in which 'I'm starving' is a well-established exaggerating expression. No speaker would expect their hearer to say, 'What, you could eat a whole horse?' or 'I don't think you are dying of hunger — you don't even look thin.' Hearers would be expected to know that the speaker simply meant that they were very hungry. Hyperbole is often at the basis of humour.

Flouting relation

If speakers flout the maxim of relation, they expect that the hearers will be able to imagine what the utterance did not say, and make the connection between their utterance and the preceding one(s). Thus, in

A   So what do you think of Mark?
B   His flatmate's a wonderful cook.

B does not say that she was not very impressed with Mark, but by not mentioning him in the reply and apparently saying something irrelevant, she implies it.

Grice thought that flouting the maxim of relation was possible, but many people have disagreed since. Whether we observe or flout maxims, our utterances will always be taken as relevant to the preceding co-text.

Flouting manner

Those who flout the maxim of manner, appearing to be obscure, are often trying to exclude a third party, as in this sort of exchange between husband and wife:

A   Where are you off to?
B   I was thinking of going out to get some of that funny white stuff for somebody.
A   OK, but don't be long — dinner's nearly ready.

B speaks in an ambiguous way, saying 'that funny white stuff' and 'somebody' because he is avoiding saying 'icecream' and 'Michelle', so that his little daughter does not become excited and ask for the ice-cream before her meal.

(Excerpted from Joan Cutting. 2002. *Pragmatics and Discourse*. pp. 34-41.)

After You Read

Knowledge Focus

1. Decide whether the following statements are true or false based on Text A and Text B.

1) Grice has proposed a way of analyzing implicatures based on the Cooperative Principle and its maxims of quantity, quality, relevance and existence.
2) In some cases, the speaker may be faced with a clash of maxims. In other words, the speaker finds himself/herself unable simultaneously to observe the maxims of quality and quantity.
3) When flouting a maxim, the speaker assumes that the hearer knows that their words should not be taken at face value and that they can infer the implicit meaning.
4) A violation constitutes a deliberate attempt by S to 'mislead' her interlocutor(s).
5) An infridgement constitutes a non-observance on S's part which is intentional, and stems from imperfect linguistic performance.

2. Discuss the following questions with your partner.

1) What is the Cooperative Principle?
2) Would you illustrate the four basic maxims of the Cooperative Principle?
3) What are the ways of breaking the maxims?
4) Why do people flout the maxims?

Language Focus

1. Fill in the blanks with words or expressions in Text A and Text B.

1) Grice famously went on to _____ his Cooperative Principle (CP) with four maxims: Quantity; Quality; Relation; and Manner.
2) There are ways of breaking the _____ in addition to flouting.
3) Alternatively, his linguistic performance may be permanently _____ due to brain damage/a degenerative disease/pre-existing condition such as autism, etc., or be

temporarily impaired because of drink or drugs.

4) An opt-out involves S explicitly indicating his or her unwillingness to _____ in the way the maxims require.

5) Christopher's answer to the policeman's question *I am fifteen years and 3 months and 2 days* is _____.

6) If speakers flout the maxim of relation, they expect that the hearers will be able to imagine what the utterance did not say, and make the connection between their utterance and the _____ one(s).

7) The last is the maxim of manner, which says that we should be brief and orderly, and avoid obscurity and _____.

8) The maxim of _____ says that speakers are expected to be sincere, to be saying something that they believe corresponds to reality.

9) The third is the maxim of relation, which says that speakers are assumed to be saying something that is _____ to what has been said before.

10) Those who flout the maxim of manner, appearing to be _____, and often trying to exclude a third party.

2. Translate the following passage into English.

要了解人们的意图，就要解读他们的话语。但这确实令人头疼。误解总有可能发生，而这些误解有时似乎是规律而不是例外。正如 Leech 所言，"解读话语最终变成了一种猜测和信息假设。"

3. Translate the following passage into Chinese.

Grice makes a distinction between natural and non-natural meaning. Within the category of nonnatural meaning, Grice distinguishes between what is said and what is implicated. What is said is truth-conditional, and what is implicated is not. What is implicated, in turn, may be either conversationally or conventionally implicated, and what is conversationally implicated may be due to either a generalized or a particularized conversational implicature.

(Birner, 2013: 62)

Comprehensive Work

1. **Suppose Professor A is asked by his professional colleague Professor B to evaluate candidate X, a former student of A's, who applies for a position at an American university. A writes a letter of recommendation consisting of the following information.**
   Mr. X's command of English is excellent, and he always attended class regularly.
   Is A cooperative? What implicatures can you draw from the above example? What maxims does A seem to flout? Why do you think A phrased his/her response that way?

2. **Advertisements often flout the Maxim of Manner. Can you say in which way each of the following advertisements does this?**
   1) Ahead of current thinking (National Power)
   2) In cordless technology we have the lead (Black & Decker)
   3) BA better connected person (British Airways)
   4) Acts on the spot (advertisement for an acne preparation)
   Find at least three similar English advertisements and analyze in terms of the CP.

3. **Form groups of three or four. First each one in the group thinks of an utterance and dictates it. As each person dictates their utterance, everyone else writes down an imagined utterance spoken by the previous speaker which causes the dictated utterance to have an implicature. For example, you dictate *The shoes are nice*, and I imagine the previous speaker might have said, *How do I look today*? The implicature in this case can be that you do not quite care for what the previous speaker looks like today. When the dictation is over, share the results with other groups.**

Further Readings

Text C Conventional Implicature and Conversational Implicature

Grice distinguished two different sorts of implicature: **conventional implicature** and **conversational implicature**. They have in common the property that they both convey an additional level of meaning, beyond the semantic meaning of the words uttered. They differ in that in the case of conventional implicature the same implicature is always conveyed, regardless of context, whereas in the case of conversational implicature, what is implied varies according to the context of utterance.

Conventional implicature

There are comparatively few examples of conventional implicatures; Levinson (1983: 127) lists four: *but, even, therefore* and *yet* (to these we might add some uses of for, as in: *she plays chess well, for a girl*). Consider the following example:

… she was cursed with a stammer, unmarried but far from stupid.

Notice that although it is not actually asserted that unmarried people (or, perhaps, people who stammer) are stupid, the word *but* definitely implies that this is the case. The word *but* carries the implicature that what follows will run counter to expectations — this sense of the word *but* **always** carries this implicature, regardless of the context in which it occurs ('My friends were poor, but honest', 'He is small, but perfectly formed'). And, in everyday life, people readily respond to such conventional implicatures, as the following extract illustrates:

The American actress, Kathleen Turner, was discussing perceptions of women in the film industry.

'I get breakdowns from the studios of the scripts that they're developing... and I got one that I sent back furious to the studio that said "The main character was thirty-seven but still attractive." I circled the but in red ink and I sent it back and said, "Try again!"'

Conversational implicature

This contrasts with the implicature generated in the following example.

Late on Christmas Eve 1993 an ambulance is sent to pick up a man who has collapsed in Newcastle city centre. The man is drunk and vomits all over the ambulanceman who goes to help him. The ambulanceman says:

'Great, that's really great! That's made my Christmas!'

It would be absurd to argue that saying 'Great, that's really great! That's made my Christmas!' always generated the implicature that the speaker was furious because someone had just vomited over him! On other occasions a person producing this utterance might be genuinely expressing delight over a gift or event, or anguish because the dog has eaten the turkey. This type of implicature, which Grice termed (particularized) **conversational implicature** arises only in a particular context of utterance.

Implicature and inference

Before I go further into Grice's theory of conversational implicature, I want to interpolate a discussion of the difference between implicature and inference, implying and inferring. There are two reasons for doing this. The most important is that it is the confusion of these two levels of interpretation which is at the root of some misunderstandings of Grice's theory. The second is that in Britain, if not in other parts of the English-speaking world, there is widespread misuse of the terms themselves — people frequently say *inferring* when they really mean *implying*. To imply is to hint, suggest or convey some meaning indirectly by means of language. An implicature is generated intentionally by the speaker and may (or may not) be understood by the hearer. To infer is to deduce something from evidence (this evidence may be linguistic, paralinguistic or non-linguistic). An inference is produced by the hearer. Let us begin with a simple example:

The following extract is taken from a children's book, set in Holland under William the Silent, during the wars with Spain. Maurice was a boy caught up in the events; Theo was his manservant:

Tears filled his eyes; he cried easily in these days, not having full control of himself, and Theo's fate caused him great grief. The Duchess had told him that she had been able to discover nothing, and therefore it was assumed that he had been released as entirely innocent. Maurice was convinced that nothing of the kind had happened, and assumed that the Duchess had found out that Theo was dead and had invented the agreeable solution in order not to distress him. He could not do anything about it and had accepted the statement in silence, but he fretted a great deal over Theo's death.

This extract illustrates neatly the distinction between implicature and inference. The Duchess implied that Theo was all right. Maurice understood what she had implied, but nevertheless inferred the opposite (that Theo was dead). The next example is slightly more complicated:

Some years ago, I went to stay with my brother and his family, including his son, aged about 5. I had with me an electric toothbrush, into which I had recently put new batteries. My brother asked to see the toothbrush, but when he tried to operate it, it would not work.
Me: That's funny. I thought I put in some new batteries.
Nephew [*Going extremely red*]: The ones in my engine still work.

Let us look at these two utterances from the point of view of both the speakers and the hearers. My remark had been a genuine expression of surprised irritation, addressed to the family at large and I did not expect any response, except perhaps sympathetic murmurings about the poor quality of batteries and this is how the adults understood it. My nephew, however, misinterpreted the force of my utterance as an accusation and inferred (wrongly) that he was a suspect. We can spell out the interpretation of the boy's contribution as follows:

Step 1 The hearer's first step is to assign sense and reference to his words. In this case, this was not difficult; the boy was asserting that he had batteries in the engine of his toy train which were in working order.

Step 2 The hearer works out the speaker's intention in uttering those words; we all understood him to have implied that he was not responsible for the fact that my batteries were flat. The pragmatic force of his utterance was to deny guilt.

Step 3 Nevertheless, everyone present inferred from the evidence (from our knowledge of how little boys behave, from the fact that he blushed, from the attempt to deflect attention from his toy and, indeed, from the fact that he spoke at all) that he had in fact switched the batteries.

Grice's theory is designed to explain how hearers get from level 1 to level 2, from what is said to what is implied. Steps one and two fall within the realm of pragmatics; the third step depends on more than just linguistic factors and needs to be explained within a more general theory of social interaction. Let us take another example:

> Throughout July 1994 a minor controversy was rumbling on in the British House of Commons. For five or six years investors (known as 'Names') in the huge company of insurance underwriters, Lloyd's of London, had incurred massive losses and many had gone bankrupt. A number of Conservative M.P.s are Lloyd's Names and if M.P.s are declared bankrupt they must resign their seat. Peter Hain (a member of the opposition Labour Party) was conducting a one-man campaign to show that these M.P.s had been moved (with or without their knowledge) from the most loss-making syndicates, to avoid being declared bankrupt, having to resign their seats and (since there had been a spate of by-elections around this time and the Conservatives had lost every one) possibly precipitating a General Election. In the House of Commons Peter Hain **said**:
> 'Lord Wakeham, the leader of the House of Lords, and other leading Conservatives in 1988 were taken off selected Lloyd's syndicates which later suffered three years of catastrophic losses.'

I chose this example because Peter Hain's speech was widely reported, and so I can say with some confidence that all the political commentators were agreed that what Hain had **implied** was that knowledgeable insiders at Lloyd's had improperly tipped off Conservative sympathizers so that Conservative M.P.s could switch (or be switched) to different syndicates. But although everyone understood what Hain was implying, different listeners **inferred** a variety of different things, depending on their political persuasion, background knowledge, etc. Here is a small selection of the interpretations I came across in the days following Peter Hain's speech:

The M.P. was trying to expose dubious and possibly illegal practice.
The M.P. was trying to cause trouble for the Government.
The M.P. was trying to draw attention to himself.
Conservative M.P.s cannot be trusted in financial matters.

It was very clear what the Prime Minister, Mr Major, inferred from the speech; it was that Mr Hain could not have much evidence, or he would have gone to the police or to the newspapers instead of confining his attack to Parliament (where he could make his accusations without risking a libel action). In relation to the points put by Mr Hain, Mr Major, said:

> 'I have to say to you that inferences that are clearly underlying your question today under the privilege of Parliament is not a way that most people would regard as the right way to raise these matters.

[Note that Mr Major's use of the word *inferences* here is incorrect. He should have said *implications* or (more technically) *implicatures*. This is precisely the error I criticized in the first paragraph of this section.] There are two important things to bear in mind from the discussion of these two examples. The first is that a speaker may imply something he or she knows to be untrue and hearers may understand exactly what a speaker has implied, without in any sense believing it. The second is that Grice's theory attempts to explain how people get from the level of expressed meaning to the level of implied meaning. Many misunderstandings of Grice's work stem from the fact that people wrongly assume that he was trying to explain how inferences are formed, rather than how implicatures are generated and interpreted.

(Excerpted from Jenny Thomas. 2010. *Meaning in Interaction: An Introduction to Pragmatics*. pp. 57-61.)

Questions for Discussion

1. Would you illustrate conventional implicature and conversational implicature?
2. Would you exemplify the relationship between implicature and inference.
3. Would you interpret the example of Peter Hain's speech? What does the author want to convey in this example?

Text D Properties of Conversational Implicature

Conversational implicatures are characterized by a number of distinctive properties. In the first place, there is **defeasibility** or **cancellability**: conversational implicatures can simply disappear in certain linguistic or non-linguistic contexts. How? They are cancelled if they are inconsistent with (i) semantic entailments, (ii) background

assumptions, (iii) contexts, and/or (iv) priority conversational implicatures. Let me take them one by one.

First, conversational implicatures evaporate in the face of inconsistency with semantic entailments, as the utterances in (2) show. (I use '~+>' to signify 'does not conversationally implicate'.)

(1) His wife is often complaining.
    +> His wife is not always complaining
(2) a. His wife is often, in fact/indeed always, complaining.
    b. His wife is often, and perhaps/maybe/possibly/even always, complaining.
    c. His wife is not only often but always complaining.
    d. His wife is often, or perhaps/maybe/possibly/even always, complaining.
    e. His wife is often, if not always, complaining.
    ~+> His wife is not always complaining

All the utterances in (2) have the potential conversational implicatures indicated in (1). However, all the sentences in (2) bear the semantic entailment that his wife is always complaining due to the use of phrases such as *in fact always*. Consequently, the potential conversational implicature is defeated by the inconsistent entailment.

Next, conversational implicatures are suspended if they are not in keeping with background or ontological assumptions, often referred to as real-world knowledge. This is the case with (4).

(3) John and Mary bought an apartment near the Louvre in Paris.
    +> John and Mary bought an apartment near the Louvre in Paris together, not one each
(4) The Americans and the Russians tested an atom bomb in 1962.
    ~+> The Americans and the Russians tested an atom bomb in 1962 together, not one each

Given our knowledge about history, it was impossible for the USA and the former USSR to test an atom bomb together in 1962, because they were enemies at that time, thus the disappearance of the potential 'togetherness' conversational implicature.

Third, conversational implicatures are annulled when they run contrary to what the immediate linguistic context of utterance tells us. Imagine the following exchange in a music shop.

(5) John: This CD is eight euros, and I haven't got any money on me.

Mary: Don't worry, I've got eight euros.

~+> Mary has got only eight euros

Here, given the immediate linguistic context of utterance, Mary's response does not produce the usual conversational implicature that she has got only eight euros. This is because all the information needed here is whether or not Mary has enough money for John to buy the CD rather that the exact amount of money she might in fact have.

A second property exhibited by conversational implicatures is **non-detachability**: any linguistic expression with the same semantic content tends to carry the same conversational implicature. (A principled exception is those conversational implicatures that arise via the maxim of Manner, about which later.) This is because conversational implicatures are attached to the semantic content, rather than the linguistic form, of what is said. Therefore, they cannot be detached from an utterance simply by replacing the relevant linguistic expressions with their synonyms. This is illustrated in (6), which indicates that the use of any linguistic expression that is synonymous with *almost* will trigger the same conversational implicature.

(6) The film almost/nearly won/came close to winning an Oscar.

+> The film did not quite win an Oscar

The third property, **calculability**, means that conversational implicatures can transparently be derived via the co-operative principle and its component maxims. The fourth, **non-conventionality**, means that conversational implicatures, though dependent on the saying of what is coded, are non-coded in nature (Grice 1989: 39). In other words, they rely on the saying of what is said but they are not part of what is said. They are associated with speaker or utterance but not proposition or sentence. Fifthly, according to the principle of reinforceability, conversational implicatures can be made explicit without producing too much of a sense of **redundancy**. This is because conversational implicatures are not part of the conventional import of an utterance. For example, the conversational implicatures in (7) is made explicit in (8). But (8) is not felt to be semantically redundant.

(7) The soup is warm.

+> The soup is not hot

(8) The soup is warm, but not hot.

Finally, we have **universality**: conversational implicatures tend to be universal, being motivated rather than arbitrary. Examples from different languages all assert that some young people like pop music, and conversationally imply that not all young people like pop music. If a language has 'all' and 'some', the use of the semantically weaker 'some' will universally carry the conversational implicature 'not all'.

To sum up, conversational implicatures have the following properties, namely, defeasibility or cancellability, non-detachability, calculability, non-conventionality, reinforceablility and universality.

(Adapted from Yan Huang. 2007. Pragmatics. pp. 32-34.)

Questions for discussion

1. Would you illustrate defeasibility or cancellability?
2. Would you explain the following utterances in light of the property of non-detachability:
   1) A tried to do x.
   2) A attempted to do x.
   3) A endeavored to do x.
   4) A set himself to do x.
3. Would you exemplify how conversational implicatures can be reinforced?

Text E Herbert Paul Grice

Herbert Paul Grice (1913 — 1988), usually publishing under the name H. P. Grice, H. Paul Grice, or Paul Grice, was a British-educated philosopher of language, who spent the final two decades of his career in the United States.

Born and raised in the United Kingdom, he was educated at Clifton College and then at Corpus Christi College, Oxford. After a brief period teaching at Rossall School, he went back to Oxford where he taught until 1967. In that year, he moved to the United States to take up a professorship at the University of California, Berkeley, where he taught until his death in 1988. He returned to the UK in 1979 to give the John Locke lectures on *Aspects of Reason*. He reprinted many of his essays and papers in his valedictory book, *Studies in the Way of Words* (1989).

Grice's work is one of the foundations of the modern study of pragmatics. Grice is remembered mainly for his contributions to the study of speaker meaning, linguistic meaning, and (several of) the interrelations between these two phenomena. He provided, and developed, an analysis of the notion of linguistic meaning in terms of speaker meaning (according to his initial suggestion, 'A meant something by X' is roughly equivalent to 'A uttered X with the intention of inducing a belief by means of the recognition of this intention'). In order to explain how nonliteral utterances can be understood, he further postulated the existence of a general cooperative principle in conversation, as well as of certain special maxims of conversation derived from the cooperative principle. In order to describe certain inferences for which the word 'implication' would appear to be inappropriate, he introduced the notion of (several kinds of) implicatures.

The work of the late Paul Grice (1913 — 1988) exerts a powerful influence on the way philosophers, linguists, and cognitive scientists think about meaning and communication. With respect to a particular sentence φ and an 'utterer' U, Grice stressed the philosophical importance of separating (i) what φ means, (ii) what *U said* on a given occasion by uttering φ, and (iii) what *U meant* by uttering φ on that occasion. Second, he provided systematic attempts to say precisely what meaning is by providing a series of more refined analyses of utterer's meaning, sentence meaning, and what is said. Third, Grice produced an account of how it is possible for what *U* says and what *U* means to diverge. Fourth, by characterizing a philosophically important distinction between the 'genuinely semantic' and 'merely pragmatic' implications of a statement, Grice clarified the relationship between classical logic and the semantics of natural language. Fifth, he provided some much needed philosophical ventilation by deploying his notion of 'implicature' to devastating effect against certain overzealous strains of 'Ordinary Language Philosophy,' without himself abandoning the view that philosophy must pay attention to the nuances of ordinary talk. Sixth, Grice undercut some of the most influential arguments for a philosophically significant notion of 'presupposition.' Today, Grice's work lies at the center of research on the semantics-pragmatics distinction and shapes much discussion of the relationship between language and mind.

In a nutshell, Grice has forced philosophers and linguists to think very carefully about the sorts of facts a semantic theory is supposed to account for and to reflect upon the most central theoretical notions, notions that otherwise might be taken for granted or employed without due care and attention. To be sure, Grice's own positive proposals have their weaknesses; but in the light of his work any theory of meaning that is to be taken at all seriously must now draw a sharp line between genuinely semantic facts and facts pertaining to the nature of human interaction.

To sum up, the work of Grice's that has found its way into *Studies in the Way of Words* (1989). It constitutes a major contribution to philosophy and linguistics; as such its appearance will help to ensure that Grice is remembered as one of the most gifted and respected philosophers of the second half of the twentieth century. He set impossibly high standards for himself and others. Although he produced dozens of first-rate papers, he was always reluctant to go into print — by all accounts heroic efforts were required by editors and friends to extract from him the handful of papers that he deemed worthy of publication. The William James Lectures trickled into print in diverse places between 1968 and 1978 and consequently important connections between the Theory of Conversation and the Theory of Meaning have tended to be missed, ignored, or downplayed. No one with a serious interest in language should be without a copy of this book.

(Excerpted from http://en.wikipedia.org/wiki/Paul_Grice, Date of access: January 17, 2015, and Stephen Neale. 1989. *Review of Paul Grice, Studies in the Ways of Words*. p1; p42.)

Suggested Reading

Huang, Y. 2009. *Pragmatics*. Beijing: Foreign Language Teaching and Research Press. pp. 24-27.

Pecci, J. S. 2000. *Pragmatics*. Beijing: Foreign Language Teaching and Research Press. pp. 25-32.

Thomas, J. 2010. *Meaning in Interaction: An Introduction to Pragmatics*. Beijing: Foreign Language Teaching and Research Press. pp.78-84.

Unit 6
Implicatures (II)

> For words, like Nature, half reveal and half conceal the Soul within.
> — Alfred Lord Tennyson
>
> No matter how eloquently a dog may bark, he cannot tell you that his parents were poor but honest.
> — Bertrand Russell

Objectives

- To understand the critiques of Grice's theory
- To comprehend the developments of Gricean theory
- To learn the academic terms about implicature
- To improve critical thinking and intercultural communicative competence and comprehensive language skills
- To improve pragmatic competence, academic ability and relevant language skills

Before You Read

1. An implicature can arise through the flouting of one of the maxims by the speaker (B), in which the hearer (A) can infer something not explicitly said if the speaker (B) disregards one of the maxims (whether intentionally or not), though the hearer (A) assumes that the speaker is not doing so. Give an implicature of B's utterance in each of the following situations, and then identify the maxim(s) that has/have been flouted (thus leading the hearer to this implicature).

1) A: Professor, will you write a letter of recommendation for me?
   B: Certainly. I will say that you were always neatly dressed, punctual, and are unfailingly polite.

2) A: I'm not feeling very well today.

   B: There's a hospital across the street.

3) A: How are you today?

   B: Oh, Albany is the capital of the State of New York.

4) A: What did you think of the new movie?

   B: Well, the costumes were authentic.

5) A: Have you done your homework and taken out the garbage?

   B: I've taken out the garbage.

6) A: I may win the lottery for $83 million.

   B: There may be people on Mars, too.

7) A: How's the weather?

   B: It's 86.7 degrees Fahrenheit. The air is humid, muggy, and the pavement is so hot I can feel it through my shoes.

2. Answer the following questions:

1) Would the utterance '*Some of my friends are linguists*' normally have as an implicature that not all of the speaker's friends are linguists?

2) If a teacher said '*The students who answered questions in section A have passed the test*', can we assume that a reasonable implicature might be that students who did not answer questions in section A have not passed the test?

3) Is the sentence *Some, in fact all, of my friends are linguists* actually a contradiction, i.e. necessarily false?

4) Would the implicature in 1) be cancelled if the utterance is followed by '*In fact, all of my friends are linguists*'?

5) How can the implicature in 2) be cancelled?

6) Is the sentence *The students who answered questions in section A have passed the test, just as the students who did not answer those questions have* a contradiction?

Start to Read

Text A Problems with Grice's Theory

There are a number of problems associated with Grice's theory. However, a detailed discussion of all the issues would take us beyond the scope of an introductory book. The main problems are:

- Sometimes an utterance has a range of possible interpretations. How do we know when the speaker is deliberately failing to observe a maxim and hence that an implicature is intended?
- How can we distinguish between different types of non-observance (e.g. distinguish a violation from an infringement)?
- Grice's four maxims seem to be rather different in nature. What are the consequences of this?
- Sometimes the maxims seem to overlap or are difficult to distinguish from one another.
- Grice argued that there should be a mechanism for calculating implicature, but it is not always clear how this operates.

Let us discuss the first problem in detail. According to Grice, a flout is so blatant that the interlocutor is supposed to know for certain that an implicature has been generated (even if we are not always quite sure what that implicature is). There are times when it is really very difficult to determine whether a non-observance is intentional and hence to know whether any implicature is intended at all. I once showed a group of students an extract from a poem by Thomas Hood. The poem is devoted to boyhood reminiscences and begins as follows:

Example 1

    I remember, I remember

    The house where I was born,

    The little window where the sun

    Came creeping in at morn.

    The lilacs where the robin built

And where my brother set
The laburnum on his birthday,
The tree is living yet!
→

We could not agree whether the last line observes all the maxims and simply makes a statement of fact (that the tree is still alive) or whether it is a flout of the maxim of Quantity, implying that the brother is dead.

We have already noted that an utterance frequently has a range of possible interpretations; Grice, however, did not discuss the possibility that more than one **implicature** might be intended. If it were indeed the case that an utterance can have only one implicature, how do we know which is the intended implicature? Sometimes although the hearer perceives (and is perhaps amused by) possible alternative interpretations, the context of utterance is such that one interpretation is very much more probable than another. This is the case with my next example:

Example 2

The following was part of a speech made by the King of Matabeleland to Queen Victoria:

'I am but the louse on the edge of Your Majesty's blanket.'

The most obvious interpretation of this utterance is that the King of Matabeleland was 'generating in implicatures by means of ... a figure of speech' and that he was implying that he considered himself as nothing compared with Queen Victoria. However, there is an unfortunate presupposition contained in this utterance (namely, that the Queen's bedding was verminous) — could the King also have been implying that Queen Victoria's personal hygiene left something to be desired? Given the nature of the event (official exchange of greetings between heads of state), this was almost certainly not the case. In this instance, the context in which the utterance was made allows us to determine which of the possible implicatures was likely to have been intended, but this is not always so. There are times when it can be very difficult to decide from a range of possible implicatures which was the one intended. Consider the following example:

Example 3

This note was sent by the head of a University department to all members of her department:

To all staff:

The window cleaners will be in the building during the weekend 28th/29th November.

Please clear your windowsills and lock any valuables away.

It is now three years since I was first shown this note, and I still cannot decide whether the sender was deliberately implying that window cleaners are dishonest, or whether this is simply an unfortunate inference which some readers might draw. Within Grice's theory there is no way of explaining in cases like this which implicatures are intended.

(Adapted from Jenny Thomas. 2010. *Meaning in Interaction: An Introduction to Pragmatics.* pp87-89.)

Text B Developments of Grice's Theory

There have been extensive amendments proposed to the original Gricean theory of implicature. Grice's theory was claimed to be too weak in that it allowed for deriving all the possible implicatures rather than only the ones intended by the speaker. Moreover, some people argued that the maxims are culture-specific. It is claimed for example that in some linguistic communities the maxim of quantity does not hold. In particular, in Malagasy, on the island of Madagascar, information is normally hidden rather than revealed. However, as Brown and Levinson (1987) observe, flouting this maxim presumes the awareness of it and therefore assumes that it operates, albeit on some deeper level. So perhaps no proviso of culture-dependence is necessary. Sperber and Wilson (1986, 1987) propose to subsume all the maxims under one cognitive principle called the principle of relevance. The authors say that the human central cognitive system works by preserving the balance between the effort and the effect in conversation, that is by minimizing the expenditure on utterance processing (called processing effort) and at the same time maximizing the gain, the contextual implications (called cognitive effect). The principle says the following:

Every act of ostensive communication communicates a presumption of its own optimal relevance.

(Sperber and Wilson, 1986: 158)

Where 'ostensive communication' means communicating by manifesting an intention to make some assumptions manifest to the addressee (cf. ibid.: 49). This principle operates without exceptions; it is a general presumption about human communication. In the revised version (see Postface to the 1995 edition), this communicative principle is supplemented with the cognitive principle: 'Human cognition tends to be geared to the maximization of relevance' (p. 260). One of the benefits of such a cognitive, exceptionless principle is providing a 'cut-off point', so to speak, for deriving implicatures: once the optimal relevance is achieved, the computation of implicatures stops. The main drawback of this interesting proposal is the difficulty with 'measuring' and hence applying optimal relevance in concrete situations.

Laurence Horn (1984, 1988: 132) suggests replacing all the maxims, except for the maxim of quality, with two principles: The Q[uantity] Principle and The R[elation] Principle. The Q principle says the following:

The Q principle: 'Make your contribution sufficient;
Say as much as you can (given R).'

This principle replaces Grice's first maxim of quantity ('Be informative') and the maxims of manner: 'Avoid ambiguity', 'Avoid obscurity'. This is a principle of the *maximization of informational* content. The R principle is formulated as follows:

The R principle: 'Make your contribution necessary;
Say no more than you must (given Q).'

This principle replaces Grice's maxim of relation ('Be relevant'), the second maxim of quantity ('Do not be too informative'), and one of the maxims of manner, 'Be brief'. This is a principle of the *minimization of form*. Horn says that the use of a marked expression, such as a complex, more effortful one, when the simpler one is also available, renders an interpretation according to which the message is marked in some way. Levinson (1987a, 1987b) adds to it an important distinction of minimization of content and minimization of form: general expressions are preferred to specific ones, and shorter expressions are preferred to longer ones. Levinson amends the picture by suggesting three principles: Q I and M principles. The Q principle is as follows:

Q principle
Make your contribution as informative as is required for the current purposes of the exchange. Specifically: don't provide a statement that is informationally weaker

than your knowledge of the world allows, unless providing a stronger statement would contravene the I-principle.

(Levinson, 1987a: 67)

For example, (1a) and (2a) conversationally imply (+>) information in (1b) and (2b) respectively:

(1a) I often take sugar in my coffee.
(1b) +> I do not always take sugar in my coffee.
(2a) I believe (cf. know) that John is away.
(2b) +> He may or may not be — speaker doesn't know which.

(adapted from Levinson 1987a: 64-65). The I principle says the following:

I-principle

Say as little as necessary, i.e. produce the minimal linguistic clues sufficient to achieve your communicational ends, bearing Q in mind.

(Levinson, 1987a: 68)

For example, (3a) and (4a) conversationally implicate information in (3b)-(3d) and (4b) respectively:

(3a) John turned the key and the engine started.
(3b) +> He turned the key and then the engine started.
(3c) +> He turned the key and thereby caused the engine to start.
(3d) +> He turned the key in order to make the engine start.
(4a) Harry and Sue bought a piano.
(4b) +> They bought it together, not one each.

(Levinson, 1987a: 65)

By separating the minimization of content from the minimization of form, Levinson effectively reintroduces Grice's maxim of manner as an M principle which says do not use a prolix, obscure or marked expression without reason. Levinson (2000: 35, 37-38) generalized these three principles into the following three inferential heuristics:

Q Heuristic:
'What isn't said, isn't.'
I Heuristic:
'What is expressed simply is stereotypically exemplified.'

M Heuristic:

'What's said in an abnormal way isn't normal.'

This amendment is important as the status of these statements is that of generalizations about human communicative behaviour rather than that of rules.

Another important amendment to Grice's theory of implicature is the ordering of the application of the principles. In Levinson's revised version, Q precedes M which precedes I (Q>M>I). For example, by the I principle, (5) may seem an appropriate way of saying that John stopped the car. But the M principle triggers an implicature as in (6) because (5) is not the simplest, most 'minimal' way of conveying this message. As a result, (5) conversationally implicates (6).

(5) John caused the car to stop.
(6) John stopped the car in an unusual way.

(from Huang, 1994: 14). The procedure has been formulated as follows:

Try letting the I-principle win in the first instance, i.e. go for minimal forms; if that doesn't work escalate step by step towards a Q-principle solution.

(Levinson, 1987a: 119)

Generally, the post-Gricean developments fall into two categories: those that rearrange Grice's maxims while remaining close to the spirit of the original theory of implicature, and the one that replaces the maxims with one, general cognitive principle. Horn's and Levinson's proposals belong to the first, Sperber and Wilson's theory of relevance is the latter. The dispute is still continuing in the literature, with little interaction between the orientations.

(Adapted from K. M. Jaszczolt, 2004. *Semantics and Pragmatics.* pp.219-223.)

After You Read

Knowledge Focus

1. Decide whether the following statements are true or false based on Text A and Text B.

1) Wilson and Sperber propose to subsume all the maxims under one cognitive principle called the principle of relevance.

2) Laurence Horn developed the Gricean theory of implicature by suggesting three principles: Q, I and M principles.

3) Levinson suggests replacing all the maxims, except for the maxim of quality, with two principles: The Quantity Principle and The Relation Principle.

4) According to Horn, the use of a marked expression, such as a complex, more effortful one, when the simpler one is also available, renders an interpretation according to which the message is marked in some way.

5) Sometimes the maxims of the Cooperative Principle seem to overlap or are difficult to distinguish from one another.

2. Discuss the following questions with your partner.

1) What are the problems with Grice's theory?
2) What are the amendments of Grice's theory?
3) What are the Q, I and M principles?
4) What is Relevance Theory?

Language Focus

1. Fill in the blanks with words or expressions in Text A and Text B.

1) Grice argued that there should be a _____ for calculating implicature, but it is not always clear how this operates.

2) According to Grice, a flout is so _____ that the interlocutor is supposed to know for certain that an implicature has been generated.

3) There are times when it is really very difficult to determine whether a _____ is intentional and hence to know whether any implicature is intended at all.

4) 'I am but the louse on the edge of Your Majesty's blanket.' The implicatures of this utterance are generated by means of _____ _____ _____ _____.

5) Horn says that the use of a _____ expression, such as a complex, more effortful one, when the simpler one is also available, renders an interpretation according to which the message is marked in some way.

6) There have been extensive _____ proposed to the original Gricean theory of implicature.

7) It is claimed for example that in some linguistic communities the maxim of quantity does not _____.

8) Some people argued that the maxims are _____.

9) The authors say that the human central cognitive system works by preserving the balance between the effort and the _____ in conversation.

10) Every act of ostensive communication communicates a presumption of its own _____ relevance.

2. Translate the following passage into English.

本章简要介绍了关于话语解释过程中语用推理的三个最主要的理论。作为交际推理语用模式的先驱，Grice（1989）主张一个首要合作原则带有 9 条准则和次准则。新格赖斯学者重点关注推理的一种形式，即一般会话含义的生成。这些含义产生于所谓正常语境，但 Grice 本人很少提及。他们把格赖斯的准则归结为三条或四条以解决 Grice 三条准则之间潜在的冲突。最后，Sperber 和 Wilson 的关联理论主张用一条关联原则替代 Grice 所有的准则。该原则的运行确保说话人的话语最佳关联，也就是说，这些话语为最小处理努力提供适量的语境效果。

3. Translate the following passage into Chinese.

So what is communication? Again, there are several possible answers. The range of phenomena that could count as examples of communication is quite wide. We could say that computers are communicating with each other when software from one computer sends electrical energy in a particular form to another and causes software in the other computer to perform operations. We could say that a thermostat is communicating with a central heating system when a temperature sensor sends electricity to a pump or boiler causing it to switch off or on. While a wide range of phenomena have been described loosely as 'communication', many of these involve information transmission but not communication. Sperber and Wilson assume that there are only two possible theories of communication: a code theory and an inferential theory. What is needed, then, is a way of identifying the kinds of communication which the Communicative Principle of Relevance applies to.

(Clark, 2013: 97)

Comprehensive Work

1. **Each person in a group of three or four should think up a sentence. Write up all the sentences in random order on a piece of paper. Try to see how each sentence could be relevant in the context provided by the previous sentences. As you do this, think about the problems anyone would have in working out the connections for themselves**

and what contextual resources are required. Try inserting additional sentences to reduce the processing effort required of the reader. (Grundy, 2000: 118)

2. Work with a television or radio interview. Copy down several utterances that contain hedges. Bring them to your next class and show them to the class without the hedges. Your classmates should try to guess the original hedges.

Further Readings

Text C Relevance Theory

Sperber and Wilson go much further than the Neo-Griceans have done in revising Grice's ideas. They propose that all of the Gricean maxims be reduced to one, that of Relation, on the assumption that relevance is a natural feature of all successful communication. Indeed, they argue that:

> Communicators do not 'follow' the principle of relevance; and they could not violate it even if they wanted to. The principle of relevance applies without exceptions.
> (Sperber and Wilson, 1995: 162)

This proposal is more innovative than it might first appear, as relevance theoretic pragmatics assumes a very different view of what pragmatics is and what it entails than Grice and the Neo-Griceans. For example, whereas the latter account for the derivation of implicatures using an inductive, rationalistic perspective (and hence focus on what interlocutors *most probably* mean in context), relevance theorists seek to explain what actually goes on in hearers' minds, using deductive means. They argue, for example, that as relevance is a given, interlocutors will treat the context as the variable (ibid.: 142). Moreover, in processing the relevance of an utterance, in context X, they will identify (what they take to be) S's communicative intention by constructing (what they hope will be) an accurate representation of it in their minds. A consistent inability to construct such mental representations, moreover, may be taken to constitute some kind of pathological

condition; this helps to explain why many relevance theorists are interested in experimental tests and studies of communication pathologies.

Relevance Theory is based on a broad understanding of relevance and two Principles of Relevance. Relevance is said to encompass 'all external stimuli or internal mental representations capable of providing an input to cognitive processes', including 'sights, smells, utterances, thoughts, memories or conclusions of inferences' (Wilson, 2010: 394). The first of the two principles — the Cognitive Principle — refers to cognition on a general level: 'Human cognition tends to be geared to the maximisation of relevance' (Sperber and Wilson, 1995: 260). The second principle — the Communicative Principle — comes about because of the first, and is specific to communication (as its name implies). It captures the notion that interlocutors, by communicating something, are implicitly asserting they have something pertinent to communicate: 'Every act of ostensive communication communicates a presumption of its own optimal relevance' (ibid.). The ostensiveness of the act is important. For example, a cough can be used by the speaker to communicate intentionally as well as being simply a symptom of ill health.

The presumption of 'optimal relevance' does not mean that every utterance has the same degree of relevance for an addressee. Rather, it means that addressees will use the minimum necessary effort to obtain the most relevant interpretation, implicature or 'contextual effect'. Let's explore this by the Peter/Mary example as follows:

Peter: Would you like some coffee?
Mary: Coffee will keep me awake.

Assuming that Mary is trying to be optimally relevant, Peter focuses on finding Mary's most likely meaning (given his question). This is where the context comes into play: if Peter and Mary are shopping for groceries, for example, Peter knows that Mary knows that *want* can be pragmatically enriched to *want* to buy, and *coffee* to *a jar/packet of coffee* (not a drink); as such, Peter can assume that Mary's response means she doesn't want him to buy any coffee (because of the adverse effect it seems to have on her). If Peter and Mary are at home, he would know that Mary knows *coffee* refers to the liquid drink, on this occasion (this assumes that Peter is not writing a shopping list at the time!). At this point, however, he still needs to gauge whether *Mary does not want to stay awake and therefore does not want coffee or Mary does want to stay awake and therefore does want coffee*. This is because Mary's response, 'Coffee will keep me awake,' constitutes a weak implicature and, as such, generates a number of possible hypotheses. Indeed, much stronger implicatures are *I want to sleep tonight* (which would be heard as a no) or *I need to stay awake* (which would be heard as a yes). So why does Mary opt for an utterance that doesn't appear to be as optimally relevant as it might have been? Sperber and Wilson claim that the outcome (or cost/benefit) of Peter's extra processing effort will be an extra cognitive effect that would otherwise not have occurred to him: this might be that Peter comes to recognize what Mary plans to do that evening (i.e. sleep or not sleep).

Sperber and Wilson view communication in terms of *cognitive environment* (i.e. the set of facts that are manifest to an individual) and *mutual manifestness* (i.e. the set of potential assumptions that individuals are capable of perceiving and inferring as a result of an ostensive stimulus). Mutual manifestness, in particular, involves interlocutors' dynamically processing contextual cues 'online' as and when they occur. As the following quotation reveals, however, Sperber and Wilson believe that S has more communicative responsibility than does H:

> It is left to the communicator to make correct assumptions about the codes and contextual information that the audience will have accessible and be likely to use in the comprehension process. The responsibility for avoiding misunderstandings also lies with the speaker, so that all the hearer has to do is go ahead and use whatever code and contextual information comes most easily to hand.
>
> (Sperber and Wilson 1995: 43)

The responsibility that Sperber and Wilson give to S is understandable, in view of their stance that H always assumes S is trying to be optimally relevant (see above). However, it gives the impression that the roles of S and H are 'fixed' when, in reality, they are transient and continually interchanging — in both everyday conversation and institutional interaction. Moreover, speakers and hearers both play an active part in co-constructing the discourse. That is to say, H evaluates/provides feedback to S which, in turn, may determine S's next move. Some cognitive linguists have thus proposed an alternative cognitive pragmatics approach to RT which acknowledges 'the combined effort of an actor and a partner' who 'consciously and intentionally cooperate to construct together the shared meaning of their interaction' (Bara, 2010: 51). Arundale (2008: 243) goes further still: he proposes that we reject Gricean-influenced approaches altogether (because of their focus on H's successful recognition of S's intention and, latterly, on H's attribution of intent) and adopt, instead, a model which considers 'utterances, in sequence' and focuses, specifically, on S and H's ongoing process of 'confirming and modifying' *interconnected interpretings* and their (potential) 'proactive and retroactive effects' (cf. an approach where we focus on one utterance at a time).

(Adapted from Archer et al. 2012. *Pragmatics: An Advanced Resource Book for Students*. pp. 58-60.)

Questions for Discussion

1. What is the assumption of Sperber and Wilson's relevance theory?
2. What are the two principles of relevance?
3. What does it mean by ostensive communication?
4. What is mutual manifestness?
5. What are the main differences between relevance theory and Grice's and Neo-Gricean theories?

Text D Post-Gricean Pragmatics

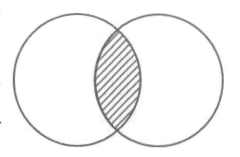

Paul Grice is generally regarded as the founding figure of the tradition in which utterance meaning is analyzed in terms of speaker's intentions. As Grice (1957: 219) put it in his seminal paper '*Meaning*', 'A meant NN something by x' is roughly equivalent to "A uttered x with the intention of inducing a belief by means of the recognition of this intention'", where meaning NN stands for non-natural meaning, or what is communicated (what is said plus implicatures), as distinguished from natural meaning where meaning that p entails that it is the fact that p. In other words, the speaker means something by uttering x when he or she intends the addressee to produce a response, recognizing that this production of a response is what the speaker intends. The view is further supported by Grice's account of rational communicative behaviour. This is spelled out in Grice's cooperative principle and maxims of conversation (Grice, 1975) which capture the predictability of speaker's meaning, some aspects of which are context-free and some context-bound.

Post-Gricean research develops these two aspects of the theory of linguistic communication. It revises Grice's set of maxims in order to reduce redundancy and overlap and aims at a more cognitively adequate generalization. These revisions adopt various degrees of reductionism. Neo-Gricean pragmatics remains close to the spirit of Grice's original maxims which were reanalyzed as (i) Horn's (1984, 1988, 2007) maximization of information content (Q principle) and minimization of form (R principle) and (ii) its less reductionist variant in Levinson's (1987, 1995, 2000) three heuristics: the Q principle (as above), aided by the minimization of content ('Say as little as necessary', I principle) and minimization of form ('Do not use a prolix, obscure or marked expression without reason', M principle). At the other end of the spectrum, relevance theory replaces the maxims with one principle defined separately for communication ('Every act of ostensive communication communicates a presumption of its optimal relevance') and for cognition ('Human cognition tends to be geared to the maximisation of relevance', Sperber and Wilson, 1995: 260). In spite of the differences in the number of principles, these post-Gricean endeavours are surprisingly similar in adhering to the overarching idea of the trade-off between informativeness and economy (expending the least effort). The principle of relevance is also spelled out in terms of a balance between two such driving forces: the processing effort and the cognitive effect in conversation, understood as minimizing the cost and at the same maximizing the information content.

Subsuming the generalizations under one principle is useful for discussing cognition and the psychology of utterance processing. On the other hand, detailed spelling out of interlocutors' rational behaviour in neo-Gricean pragmatics benefits attempts at formalization such as optimality-theory pragmatics (see Blutner and Zeevat, 2004). It also aids applications to the study of semantic change, as for example in Traugott's principles of historical pragmatics, which are founded on neo-Gricean heuristics (Traugott and Dasher, 2002; Traugott, 2004). The main difference between neo-Griceans and relevance theory lies perhaps in 'whose meaning' they model: while the neo-Griceans follow the original perspective and consider utterance meaning, including implicature, to be speaker's intended meaning, relevance theorists discuss intentional communication from the perspective of the addressee's reconstruction of speaker's assumptions.

One of the main research topics in post-Gricean pragmatics concerns the influence of pragmatic meanings, be they inferred or automatically bestowed, on truth-conditional content. Following Grice's (1978) principle of Modified Occam's Razor which says that senses are not to be multiplied beyond necessity, and since the so-called Atlas-Kempson thesis of semantic underdetermination in the 1970s, many post-Griceans have subscribed to the view that syntax renders a semantically underdetermined representation of meaning which is further enriched, embellished, modulated, etc. by the output of pragmatic processing. What is said (Recanati, 1989, 2004) and the relevance-theoretic notion of explicature (Carston, 1988, 1998, 2001, 2002) exemplify such a pragmatics-rich unit that corresponds to the development of the logical form of the uttered sentence, even though their proponents offer different principles for its delimitation (availability principle and functional independence, respectively) and uphold different hypotheses concerning the psychology of utterance processing that allows addressees to arrive at such a unit (see Recanati, 2007; Carston, 2007; Jaszczolt, 2006). The most radical form of this semantics-pragmatics mix is called Contextualism. It considers such enrichment (or, more generally, modulation of the output of syntax) to be always present. In Recanati's (2005: 179-180) words, '[c]ontextualism ascribes to modulation a form of necessity which makes it ineliminable. Without contextual modulation, no proposition could be expressed.'

In a recent strand of post-Gricean research called Default Semantics, the question of the delimitation of what is said is revised more fundamentally. What is said is assumed to be the main, primary, or most salient meaning but its relation to the logical form of the sentence is less restrictive than on the previous accounts. We know from experimental evidence that in the majority of cases speakers communicate their main message (primary meaning) through implicit content (Sysoeva and Jaszczolt, 2007). A fortiori, the unit of meaning which relies on the development of the logical form (what is said, explicature) should not be of main interest to a true post-Gricean interested in intentional communication. Instead, what is needed is a unit of primary intentional meaning in which this reliance on syntactic representation can be relaxed. Primary meanings of Default Semantics, represented formally as so-called merger representations, offer such a unit. The syntactic constraint which stipulates that what is said or is explicit must be a development of the logical form of the sentence is abandoned. The truth-conditional content pertains to the main meaning intended by the model speaker and recovered by the model addressee, irrespective of its relation to the logical form of the sentence. In other words, the logical form can not only be enriched but in some cases can be overridden when the primary meaning corresponds to what is traditionally dubbed an implicature (see Jaszczolt, 2005, 2006).

Other new aspects of post-Gricean contextualism include debates about the unit on which pragmatic processes operate, where views range from Grice's original proposition-based (thought-based), 'global' inference (Jaszczolt, 2005) to very 'local', sometimes even word- or morpheme-based inference (Levinson, 2000). In the past few years, theoretical debates have begun to be supported with evidence from experimental research. Cancellability of implicatures and aspects of what is said are also newly reopened topics in this paradigm (Weiner, 2006; Blome-Tillmann, 2008).

Not all post-Gricean pragmaticists subscribe to the contextualist semantics/pragmatics mix. Bach (2004, 2006) and Horn (2006) advocate an alternative construal in the form of radical minimalism in which the proposition, and thereby also truth conditions, are rejected. According to Bach, the semantic properties of a sentence are analogous to syntactic and phonological properties. The object of study of semantics is grammatical form rather than a proposition. Contextualists are accused of making a mistake in upholding propositionalism, the view that the grammatical form of a sentence, as in (1a), has to be completed to become fully propositional, as in (1b), evaluable by means of a truth-conditional analysis:

(1a) Tom isn't old enough.

(1b) Tom isn't old enough to stay alone in the house.

In general, questions which are currently at the forefront of post-Gricean research fall into the following categories:

(i) What principles govern utterance interpretation?

(ii) How does pragmatic content interact with semantic content?

and, for those who do not shun psychologism in pragmatics,

(iii) What are the properties of the interpretation process?

Question (i) concerns the heuristics for rational and intentional communicative behaviour. Question (ii) pertains to the boundary dispute between semantics and pragmatics in the contextualism- semantic minimalism debate. Question (iii) is spelled out as the debate over pragmatic inference vis-à-vis automatic interpretation. Cross-cutting questions (i) to (iii) is the controversy between the proponents of the grammatical basis of pragmatic enrichment ('bottom-up' process) and those advocating the theory of free, not linguistically triggered, 'top-down' enrichment. This controversy is discussed predominantly with respect to quantifier domain restriction as in (2b):

(2a) Everybody submitted an article.

(2b) Every pragmaticist invited to contribute to this Encyclopedia submitted an article.

As Stanley (2002: 152) puts it, '[m]uch syntactic structure is unpronounced, but no less real for being unpronounced.' However, according to Recanati (2002: 302), enrichment is free, 'not linguistically triggered' but 'pragmatic through and through.'

Constructions and phenomena that are most frequently studied in post-Gricean pragmatics include those expressions which were traditionally regarded as giving rise to semantic ambiguity. They include negation, sentential connectives, definite and indefinite descriptions, various quantifying expressions, and propositional attitude reports.

(Excerpted from K. M. Jaszczolt, 2010. In L. Cummings (ed.). *The Routledge Pragmatics Encyclopedia.* London: Routledge. pp806-809.)

Questions for Discussion

1. What do you know about post-Gricean pragmatics?
2. What is contextualism?
3. What are the major questions at the forefront of post-Gricean research?
4. Would you list some major figures in the development of Gricean pragmatics?
5. There is a problem known as **Grice's circle**, namely, how what is conversationally implicated can be defined in contrast to and calculated on the basis of what is said, given that what is said seems to both determine and to be determined by what is conversationally implicated. What is your proposal?

Text E Stephen C. Levinson

Stephen C. Levinson (1947 —) is director of the Language and Cognition group at the Max Planck Institute for Psycholinguistics in Nijmegen, The Netherlands. He received a BA in Archaeology and Social Anthropology from the University of Cambridge and received a PhD in Linguistic Anthropology from the University of California Berkeley. He has held posts at the University of Cambridge, Stanford University and the Australian National University.

He has written extensively on pragmatics, and in particular, furthered the work of Paul Grice on conversational implicature. He describes his theories as being 'under the Gricean umbrella'. He co-edited (with Gerald Gazdar) the first journal and wrote the first comprehensive book in this field (*Pragmatics*, CUP, 1983). Numerous research papers followed, suggesting that many patterns in both syntax and meaning may have pragmatic origins. The monograph *Presumptive Meanings* (MIT, 2000) points to very detailed, stable and universal principles of preferred interpretation or language construal. He also focuses on verbal interaction. His most influential publication is probably *Politeness: Universals in Language Usage* which he co-authored with Penelope Brown and which was a seminal work in Politeness theory. He has published 22 papers on verbal interaction in the last decade. He has done extensive field work (with P. Brown) on Tzeltal Mayan Indians and Rossel Islanders (Papua New Guinea), comparing and contrasting interactional patterns (including between infants/care-givers). He has published on e.g. gaze, repair, person-reference, and kinship contexts in interaction across these societies. He has also tried to foster interdisciplinary collaboration in this field, between anthropology, linguistics and cognitive science.

His research now focuses on language diversity and its implications for theories of human cognition. Language is the only animal communication system that differs radically in form and meaning across social groups of the same species, a fact that has been neglected in the cognitive sciences. His work attempts both to grasp what this diversity is all about, and to exploit it as a way of discovering the role that language plays in our everyday cognition. He is a recent recipient of an ERC Advanced Grant, which focuses on the interactional foundations for language.

If you want to know more about his major ideas, read the following two books: (1987) *Politeness: Universals in Language Usage* (with Penelope Brown). Pragmatics. 1983. Cambridge: CUP.

(Excerpted from http://en.wikipedia.org/wiki/Stephen_C._Levinson and http://www.mpi.nl/news/news-archive/levinson-awarded-prestigious-erc-advance-grant, Date of access: January 27, 2015.)

Suggested Reading

Jaszczolt, K. M. 2004. *Semantics and Pragmatics: Meaning in Language and Discourse*. Beijing: Peking University Press. pp. 239-245.

Huang, Y. 2007. *Pragmatics*, Oxford: Oxford University Press. Chapter 7.

Unit 7
Conversational Structure

> Conversation is an art in which a man has all mankind for competitors.
> — Ralph Waldo Emerson
>
> Conversation is an exercise of the mind; gossip is merely an exercise of the tongue.
> — Anonymous

Objectives

- To understand the structure of conversation
- To learn to describe what happens in conversation
- To comprehend the ways conversational techniques are used to convey meaning
- To learn the technical terms and expressions about conversational structure
- To improve critical thinking and intercultural communicative competence and comprehensive language skills
- To improve pragmatic competence, academic ability and relevant language skills

 Before You Read

1. Overlaps are conventionally marked by a double slash (//). Can you summarize the functions of the overlaps in the following dialogues? (The examples are taken from George Yule, 1996: 73–74.)

   1) Mr. Strait: *What's your major, Dave?*
      Dave: *English — well I haven't really decided yet.*
                  (3 seconds)
      Mr. Strait: *So — you want to be a teacher?*

Dave: No — not really — well not if I can help it.
(2.5 seconds)
Mr. Strait: Wha — // Where do you — go ahead
Dave: I mean it's a — oh sorry // I em —
2) Min: Did you see him in the video?
Wendy: Yeah — the part on the beach
Min: Oh my god // he was so sexy
Wendy: He was just being so cool
Min: And all the waves // crashing around him!
Wendy: Yeah that was really wild!
3) Joe: When they were in
// power las — wait CAN I FINISH?
Jerry: That's my point I said —

2. Discuss the differences between written and spoken language.

3. Study the following dialogue and comment on it. (The example is taken from George Yule, 1996:73.)

Caller: *If you use your long distance service a lot then you'll*
Mary: *uh-uh*
Caller: *be interested in the discount I'm talking about because*
Mary: *yeah*
Caller: *it can only save you money to switch to a cheaper service*
Mary: *mmm*

Start to Read

Text A   What is Conversation?

True conversation, of course, never is the mere exchange of formalities (even though certain conversational activities, such as greetings, come pretty close in many societies). What we want to know is how the way one talks with people functions in human communication. (Mey, 2001: 143)

Conversation is a way of using language socially, of 'doing things with words' together with other persons. (Mey, 2001: 136)

We can look at this use of language from two points of view. The first is that of *content*: then our attention will focus on what the conversation is about, on the topics discussed, and how they are brought into the conversation; whether or not these topics are overtly announced or maybe presupposed, or hidden in other ways; what kinds of topic lead to other topics and why; and so on. Here, we also focus on the topical organization of conversation and how the topics are managed, either by overt steering ('So, what's all this talk really about?', said, e.g., at a meeting), or by covert manipulation, often in the form of indirect speech acting, such as when Governor Felix told St Paul: 'Go thy way for this time; when I have a convenient season, I will call for thee' (Acts 24:25; meaning: 'I don't have to listen to this talk') [about 'righteousness, temperance, and judgement to come']. A further point to be considered is the function of conversation in creating an 'ambience', a context in which the conversationalists are able to pursue their (overt or hidden) goals; this is often the function of the kind of conversation called 'small talk' or 'chit-chat'.

Alternatively, one can focus on the *formal* aspects of conversation: how conversation works, what rules are observed, how 'sequencing' is achieved (gaining and giving up the 'floor', 'turn-taking', pausing, interrupting, and so on). (Mey, 2001: 137)

Conversation, is any interactive spoken exchange between two or more people and can be:

- face-to-face exchanges — these can be private conversations, such as talk at home between the family, or more public and ritualized conversations such as classroom talk or Question Time in the Houses of Parliament;
- non-face-to-face exchanges, such as telephone conversations;
- broadcast materials such as a live radio phone-in or a televisionchat show.

(Pridham, 2001: 2)

There are many metaphors used to describe conversation structure. For some, conversation is like a dance, with the conversational partners coordinating their movements smoothly. For others it's like traffic crossing an intersection, involving lots of alternating movement without any crashes. However, the most widely used analytic approach is based, not on dancing (there's no music) nor traffic flow (there are no traffic signals), but on an analogy with the workings of a market economy.

In this market, there is a scarce commodity called the **floor** which can be defined as the right to speak. Having control of this scarce commodity at any time is called a **turn**. In any situation where control is not fixed in advance, anyone can attempt to get control. This is called **turn-taking**. Because it is a form of social action, turn-taking operates in accordance with a local management system that is conventionally known by members of a social group. The **local management system** is essentially a set of conventions for getting turns, keeping them, or giving them away. This system is needed most at those points where there is a possible change in who has the turn. Any possible change-of-turn point is called a **Transition Relevance Place**, or TRP. Within any social group, there will be features of talk (or absence of talk) typically associated with a TRP.

This type of analytic metaphor provides us with a basic perspective in which speakers having a conversation are viewed as taking turns at holding the floor. They accomplish change of turn smoothly because they are aware of the local management system for taking those turns at an appropriate TRP. The metaphor can be applied to those conversations where speakers cooperate and share the floor equally. It can also be used to describe those conversations where speakers seem to be in competition, fighting to keep the floor and preventing others from getting it. These patterns of conversational interaction differ substantially from one social group to another.

(Excerpted from Jacob Mey. 2001. *Pragmatics: An Introduction.* pp. 136-137; 143, and George Yule. 1996. *Pragmatics.* pp. 71-72.)

Text B Turn-taking and Adjacency Pair

Sacks, Schegloff and Jefferson (1974) pioneered conversation analysis, an approach to analysis derived from sociology and known as ethnomethodology. It argues that conversation has its own dynamic structure and rules, and looks at the methods used by speakers to structure conversation efficiently. This means they look, for example, at the way people take turns, what turn types there are, such as adjacency pairs and at discourse markers which indicate openings, closures and links between and across utterances.

Ethnomethodologists observe that a conversation is a string of at least *two turns*, i.e. it is characterized by **turn-taking**: one participant, A, talks, stops; another, B starts, talks, stops; and so we obtain an A-B-A-B-A-B distribution of talk across two participants. These sequences of turns are called *adjacency pairs*. This occurs when one speaker's utterance makes a particular kind of response likely. Adjacency pairs are pairs of utterances that usually occur together.

Adjacency pairs have the following features: they are two utterances long; the utterances are produced successively by different speakers; the utterances are ordered — the first must belong to the class of *first pair parts*, the second to the class of *second pair parts*; the utterances are related and thus not any second part can follow any first part, but only an appropriate one; the first pair part often selects next speaker and always selects next action — it thus sets up a *transition relevance*, an expectation which the next speaker fulfils, in other words the first part of a pair predicts the occurrence of the second; 'Given a question, regularly enough an answer will follow'.

The most often used adjacency pair of the conversation is question–answer. A question, for example, in our culture is followed by an answer and is, therefore, a convenient way to introduce a new topic and to ensure a response.

The adjacency pair question–answer helps, therefore, in the structuring of a conversation. How much the question throws open the topic, however, can be dependent on the nature of the question. One of the most interesting types of question that can be used is a 'tag' question. How a tag question operates depends on the intonation used and the context it appears in. A tag question can show tentativeness and can reflect a desire for reassurance, as in '*This is a good match, isn't it?*' It can also be a very assertive device in prompting a response and in directing what the response should be, for example, '*You're not leaving, are you?*'

In the same way, it is difficult to avoid answering repeated questions and as the urgency of the question increases, the length of the question decreases. In other words, short, sharp questions are forceful in provoking a response.

As an accepted part of conversational structure, adjacency pairs have strong in-built expectations. Questions are answered, statements acknowledged, complaints are replied to and greetings are exchanged. If the rules are ignored and these patterns are broken, this immediately creates a response.

Sometimes the adjacency pairs are harder to spot because they can be separated by intervening utterances, which together make up what is called an **insertion sequence**.

A: Shall I wear the blue shoes?
B: You've got the black ones.
A: They're not comfortable.
B: Yeah, they're the best then, wear the blue ones.

The topic of the insertion sequence is related to that of the main sequence in which it occurs and the question from the main sequence is returned to and answered after the insertion.

Adjacency pairs can also be extended into **adjacency triplets**. Identified by Sinclair and Coulthard (1975), in their analysis of classroom conversations, and more commonly known as **exchanges**, they consist of three moves known as initiation, response and follow-up or feedback.

The following is a conversation that takes place in a chemistry lesson in the classroom of a college. SDR is a male teacher in his early fifties; FP is his pupil, a female 17-year-old student. Read the following transcription of a classroom conversation and think about the following questions:

1. What is the purpose behind the teacher's opening remarks?
2. Identify and explain the exchange in this conversation.
3. Explain the function of the adjacency pair at the end of the conversation.
4. How does the teacher pass on the turn and introduce the topics?
5. What is the reason for the repetition present in this conversation?

SDR:	that's good (.) that's excellent (.) so you can answer the questions (1) Fiona (.) if you heat up the reaction (.) what happens? (.) to the reaction
FP:	it goes quicker
SDR:	it goes quicker (.) so the key to any reaction at all is that it goes quicker (.) because all the molecules will be flying around faster (.) so it speeds up a reaction (.) but it speeds up a given (1) increase in temperature speeds of different reactions to different extents (1) Fiona (.) exothermic reactions (.) what is an exothermic reaction? (1)
FP:	one that gives out heat

The teacher's first three remarks, 'that's good', 'that's excellent' and 'so you can answer the questions', are concerned with the previous utterances made by the students. The evaluation offered here by the teacher is extremely positive and supportive in a way that could appear patronising in a normal situation.

The exchange that follows is initiated by the teacher's question, 'if you heat up any reaction what happens? (.) to the reaction (1)'. FP responds with the answer 'it goes quicker'. Then the teacher, as feedback, not only repeats the student's exact words but also reformulates the answer and summarises for the students what he hopes the exchange has taught them, 'so the key to any reaction at all is that it goes quicker'.

The adjacency pair at the end is asking the students to give a definition. This is a known-answer question in the sense that the teacher already knows what he wants to hear and Fiona's answer comes quickly and fluently in a way that implies the definition has been learnt almost by heart.

The teacher clearly dictates the turn by naming Fiona twice and the topics are introduced by two questions, 'if you heat up any reaction what happens?' and 'what is an exothermic reaction?' Interestingly, the final topic has already been signposted to the audience with the phrase, 'exothermic reactions'. Operating as a sub-heading would in a written text, the repetition of this phrase in the next sentence reflects the high amount of repetition already contained in the conversation.

The repetition shows the teacher's constant awareness of his larger audience and his purpose — to make sure all his students learn, not just the student he appears to be having a conversation with. Throughout the conversation, therefore, he is at pains by repetition to confirm the class's understanding.

(Excerpted from Francesca Pridham. 2001. *The Language of Conversation.* pp. 23-30.)

After You Read

Knowledge Focus

1. Decide whether the following statements are true or false based on Text A and Text B.

1) Greetings are the exchange of formalities.

2) In Sinclair and Coulthard's (1975) analysis, classroom exchanges consist of three moves known as question, response and feedback.

3) Conversation analysis is an approach to analysis derived from sociology and known as ethnomethodology.

4) Ethnomethodologists observe that a conversation is a string of at least four turns.

5) Adjacency pairs are pairs of utterances that usually occur together.

2. Discuss the following questions with your partner.

1) What is conversation?

2) Would you give examples to illustrate conversational structure?

3) What is an insertion sequence? Please identify insertion sequences in the following request-acceptance pair.

A: I wanted to order some more paint.

B: Yes, how many tubes would you like, sir?

A: Um, what's the price with tax?

B: Er, I'll just work that out for you.

A: Thanks.

B: Three nineteen a tube, sir.

A: I'll have five, then.

B: Here you go.

4) What are adjacency triplets? Can you show each other an example of classroom conversation?

Language Focus

1. Fill in the blanks with words or expressions in Text A and Text B.

1) True conversation, of course, never is the mere exchange of _____.

2) In the studies of conversation, we also focus on the topical organization of conversation

and how the topics are managed, either by _____ steering, or by covert manipulation.

3) A further point to be considered is the function of conversation in creating an 'ambience'; this is often the function of the kind of conversation called '_____ _____' or 'chit-chat'.

4) Any possible change-of-turn point in a conversation is called a _____ Relevance Place, or TRP.

5) In other words, short, sharp questions are forceful in _____ a response.

6) _____ _____ indicate openings, closures and links between and across utterances.

7) Adjacency pairs have the following features: they are two utterances long; the utterances are produced _____ by different speakers; the utterances are ordered.

8) Adjacency pairs have strong in-built expectations. Questions are answered, statements acknowledged, complaints are replied to and greetings are _____.

9) Sometimes the adjacency pairs are harder to spot because they can be separated by _____ utterances, which together make up what is called an insertion sequence.

10) Identified by Sinclair and Coulthard (1975), classroom conversations consist of three _____ known as initiation, response and follow-up or feedback.

2. Translate the following passage into English.

目前，语用学中会话交流的研究以多种不同的方式入手，反映出该领域的日趋多样化。其方法既将会话分析中会话结构和组织本身作为一种社会秩序又研究会话交流中出现的多种语用现象，包括程式化语言、语篇/语用标记语、指称和指示、预设、隐含、言语和语用行为、幽默、（不）礼貌以及身份和权力问题，等等。
(Allan, 2012: 251)

3. Translate the following passage into Chinese.

The latter study of pragmatic phenomena in conversational interaction draws from a wide range of approaches, including conversations reconstructed through the introspective methods of philosophical pragmatics, the study of naturally occurring conversations through ethnography of speaking, interactional sociolinguistics, philology, (critical) discourse analysis, interactional pragmatics and more recently corpora, and the study of conversation elicited through devices such as discourse completion tests or role plays.

(Allan, 2012: 251)

Comprehensive Work

1. Analyse the following conversation and try to identify the different types of sequences.

(*A is asking B to buy a ticket for him.*)

A: 买张北京的。
B: 白天还是晚上？
A: 晚上几点的？
B: 特快还是直达的？
A: 那个特快 60 (pause) 多少钱？
B: 二百多。
A: 几点？
B: 九点多要不就十点多。
A: 那就晚上（的）特快吧。
B: OK。

2. Work in group of three or four. Record and transcribe a television talk show conversation (English or Chinese), then observe how the conversation works. Write your findings regarding: a) how people open the conversation; b) how they take turns and at what point they take turns; c) how they change topics; d) how they end the conversation. Note that you should also observe the pauses, overlaps, delays, if any, and analyze their functions.

3. Record from movies and transcribe at least one English and one Chinese telephone conversation. Then in groups of two or three, discuss the differences between them in terms of opening and closing, adjacency pair, insertion sequence and back channel, etc.

Further Readings

Text C Pre-sequences

People do not have unlimited options in conversation, but typically follow general language patterns. Certain utterances are usually (in some instances, even always) felt to be 'precursors' to something else (another utterance, or perhaps a sequence of utterances). The classical examples are the so-called 'attention getters', such as:

Hey

You know something?

Excuse me

And so on, to which the usual answer would be:

Yes

What?

or something in the same vein.

After this initial exchange has been concluded, the real business can be dealt with. Utterances which serve as 'precursors' to others are often called *pre-sequences*. They can be considered as purely formal tools of conversation management, but usually, they are more than that, and occupy a position which is midway between the formal and the content aspect of conversation. Pre-sequences may include pre-announcements (such as 'Whaddyaknow', 'Guess what'), pre-invitations (e.g., 'Are you doing anything to-night?'), pre-threats ('Watch it') and numerous others (cf. Levinson, 1983: 346ff).

Some of the most frequent pre-sequences are the type sometimes called 'inquirers'. These usually precede a request of some kind; their function is to make sure that the request about to be made is indeed, for the point of the requestee, within the limits of the possible. For example, before purchasing an item in the shop or requesting information about something, help with a task, or any favor at all, we inquire about the available possibilities of obtaining that item, information, help or favor.

For instance, a well-known pre-sequence in shopping would be:

I wonder if you have X?

Do you by any chance have X?

Does your shop carry X?

(where X is some item that I might want to purchase).

When the shop clerk answers in the negative, the sequence usually comes to an end then and there (unless some information is requested or offered as to where else to buy the desired item). However, if the answer is affirmative, the 'pre-sequence' usually (though not necessarily) changes its 'activity type' (Levinson, 1979) form being a pre-sequence of an informatory kind to being a prelude to an act of buying. This act can, under the circumstances, be almost unavoidable, depending on the item (and, of course, the social conditions of the purchase). Thus, it may be all right for an American restaurant guest to inquire:

Waiter, do you have any oysters on the half shell tonight?

and subsequently, after the waiter has checked and come back with an affirmative response, decide not to have oysters after all, but lobster. In France, however, a request such as:

Are there any Coquilles St Jacques?

normally binds the guest to consume a portion if the waiter is able to confirm that there are indeed scallops on the menu.

Some of the clearest kinds of pre-sequence are **pre-invitations**, like the following:

1) →   A: Whatcha doin'?
           B: Nothin'
           A: Wanna drink?

2)   R: Hi John
           C: How ya doin =
  →   = say what'r you doing?
           R: Well we're going out. Why?
           C: Oh, I was just gonna say come out and come over here an' talk this evening, but if you're going out you can't very well do that

Further kinds of pre-sequence are **pre-requests** like the following:

3) →   C: Do you have hot chocolate?
           S: mmhmm
  →   C: Can I have hot chocolate with whipped cream?
           S: Sure (leaves to get)

4) → C: Do you have the blackberry jam?
S: Yes
→ C: Okay. Can I have half a pint then?
S: Sure (turns to get)

Other classes of pre-sequence of special interest are **pre-announcements** like the following:

5) → D: I forgot to tell you the two best things that happen to me today.
R: Oh super = what were they?
D: I got a B + on my math test …and I got an athletic award.
6) → D: Hey you'll never guess what your dad is lookih-is lookin' at.
R: What're you looking at?
D: A red range.

Let us now attempt to characterize such sequences. One way of thinking about them (and perhaps pre-sequences in general) is that they are made up of two superimposed adjacency pairs: a pre-pair (e.g. A: *Have you heard the news*? B: *No*.) and a second pair (e.g. B: *Tell me*, A: *John won the lottery*) — superimposed in that the second of the first pair and the first of the second pair occur in the same turn or position — namely position 2. Hence we often find in the turn occupying position 2 dual components of the kind in the second turn in 5), where *Oh super* looks backward to the prior turn, and *what were they* is a first part requiring the announcement as a second. We thus have the following structure for pre-announcements:

Position 1: pre-sequence first part, general checking on newsworthiness of potential announcement in position 3

Position 2: pre-sequence second, generally validating newsworthiness, and first part of second pair, namely a request to tell

Position 3: second part to second pair – the announcement delivered

Position 4: new receipt

(Adapted from Jacob Mey. 2001. *Pragmatics: An Introduction*. pp144-145, and S. C. Levinson. 1983. *Pragmatics*. pp346-350.)

Questions for Discussion

1. What is pre-sequence?
2. How many kinds of pre-sequence are there in Text C? Can you give other examples besides the ones in the text?

3. What kind of pre-sequence is the following example?

(The example is taken from Levinson (1983: 348).)

R: Erm (2.8) what are you doing today?

C: Er well I'm supervising at quarter past

(1.6)

R: Er yuh why (don't) er (1.5) would you like to come by after that?

C: I can't I'm afraid no

Text D Preference and Dispreference

A problem that arises with the notion of an adjacency pair concerns the range of potential seconds to a first part. Unless for any given first part there is a small or at least delimited set of seconds, the concept will cease, it seems, to describe the tight organization in conversation that is its principal attraction. But in fact there are, for example, a great many responses to questions other than answers which nevertheless count as acceptable seconds — (rather than, say, beginnings of insertion sequences prior to answers) — including protestations of ignorance, 're-routes' (like *Better ask John*), refusals to provide an answer, and challenges to the presuppositions or sincerity of the question. So while responses to, for example, questions may be restricted, they certainly do not constitute a small set, and this does seem to undermine the structural significance of the concept of an adjacency pair.

However the importance of the notion is revived by the concept of **preference organization**. The central insight here is that not all the potential second parts to a first part of an adjacency pair are of equal standing: there is a ranking operating over the alternatives such that there is at least one **preferred** and one **dispreferred** category of response. It must be pointed out immediately that the notion of preference here introduced is not a psychological one, in the sense that it does not refer to speakers' or hearers' individual preferences. Rather it is a structural notion that corresponds closely to the linguistic concept of **markedness**. In essence, preferred seconds are **unmarked** — they occur as structurally simpler turns; in contrast dispreferred seconds are marked by various kinds of structural complexity. Thus dispreferred seconds are typically delivered: (a) after some significant delay; (b) with some preface marking their dispreferred status, often the particle well; (c) with some account of why the preferred second cannot be performed. For the present a contrastive pair of examples will suffice to illustrate the notion:

1. Child: Could you .hh could you put on the light for my .hh room
   Father: Yep
2. (*In a telephone conversation*)
   A: Um I wondered if there's any chance of seeing you tomorrow sometime (0.5) morning or before the seminar
   (1.0)
   B: Ah um (.) I doubt it
   A: Uhm huh
   B: The reason is I'm seeing Elizabeth

In 1, a granting of a request is done without significant delay and with a minimal granting component Yep. In contrast in 2, a rejection of a request for an appointment is done after a one-second delay, and then, after further delay components (*ah um*, the micro-pause (.)), by a non-minimal turn (compare *I doubt it with No*), followed by an account or reason for the difficulty. In fact, rejections of requests are normally done in this marked way. Thus we can say grantings are preferred seconds (or **preferreds** for short) to requests, rejections are dispreferred seconds (or **dispreferreds**). This is a general pattern: in contrast to the simple and immediate nature of preferreds, dispreferreds are delayed and contain additional complex components; and certain kinds of seconds like request rejections, refusals of offers, disagreements after evaluative assessments, etc., are systematically marked as dispreferreds.

By ordering seconds as preferreds and dispreferreds, the organization allows the notion of an adjacency pair to continue to describe a set of strict expectations despite the existence of many alternative seconds to most kinds of first parts, with the exception that in greetings, returning greetings are more or less the only kind of second.

(Excerpted from S. C. Levinson. 1983. *Pragmatics*. pp.306-308.)

Questions for Discussion

1. Would you illustrate preferreds in conversation?
2. Would you illustrate dispreferreds in conversation?
3. What does the term 'Markedness' mean? Give examples in light of preference in conversation.
4. Do you agree to the argument that 'preference as a phenomenon of conversational organization probably is universal, its individual manifestations in different languages may display a great deal of variation'?

Text E The Place of Conversation Among the Speech-exchange Systems

The use of a turn-taking system to preserve one party talking at a time while speaker change recurs, for interactions in which talk is organizationally involved, is not at all unique to conversation. It is massively present for ceremonies, debates, meetings, press conferences, seminars, therapy sessions, interviews, trials, etc. All these differ from conversation (and from each other) on a range of other turn-taking parameters, and in the organization by which they achieve the set of parameter values whose presence they organize.

Such a sort of comparative investigation of the speech-exchange systems available to members of a single society, conceived of in terms of differential turn-taking systems, has barely been looked into by us. However, certain striking arrangements may be noted, if only to suggest the possible interest of this area.

It seems, as noted, correct to say that generally the allocational techniques for conversation provide for one turn-allocation at a time. But alternatives to such a mode of operation are readily found. Thus, in debates, the ordering of all turns is pre-allocated, by formula, with reference to 'pro' and 'con' positions. In contrast to both debates and conversation, meetings with chair-persons partially pre-allocate turns, and provide for the allocation of unallocated turns via the use of the pre-allocated turns. Thus, chair-persons have rights to talk first, and to talk after each other speaker, and they can use each such turn to allocate next-speakership.

The foregoing suffices to suggest a structural possibility: that turn-taking systems, or at least the class of them whose members each preserve 'one party talks at a time,' are, with respect to their allocational arrangements, linearly arrayed. The linear array is one in which polar type (exemplified by conversation) involves 'one-turn-at-a-time' allocation, i.e., the use of local allocational means; the other pole (exemplified by debate) involves pre-allocation of all turns; and medial types (exemplified by meetings) involve various mixes of pre-allocational and local-allocational means.

That the types can be so arrayed permits them to be compared, directly, in relevant functional terms. Thus one pole (local allocation of turns) permits maximization of the size of the set of potential speakers to each next turn, but is not designed organizationally to permit the methodological achievement of an equalization of turns among potential speakers; whereas the other pole (pre-allocation of all turns) is designed to permit the equalization of turns (or can be — it can be designed for other ends), which it does by specifying next speaker, thereby minimizing the size of the set of potential next speakers. If the range of turn-taking systems is arrayed on a continuum, ranging from full pre-allocation of turns to single allocation at a time, then any system may be found to maximize, to minimize, or not to be organizationally relevant to a range of functions such as equalization of turns among participants, maximization of potential next speakers, etc. The functions for which any system is design-relevant may then be explored; and the various systems may be compared with respect to their consequences on any given function of interest. On the two functions we have mentioned, equalization of turns and maximization of the set of next-speaker candidates, local allocation and full pre-allocation are polar-types – as indeed they might turn out to be for any function where turn-allocation is systematically relevant.

Given the linear array, the polar position of conversation, and the functions of which that position permits maximization, a characterization of the organization of turn-taking in conversation takes on more than merely ethnographic interest. Occupying such a functionally interesting structural position, conversation is at least a representative of the means by which one polar possibility is organizationally achieved.

(Excerpted from H. Sacks, E. A. Schegloff & G. Jefferson. 1974. *A Simplest Systematics for the Organization of Turn-Taking for Conversation*. pp. 729-730.)

Suggested Reading

Cutting, J. 2002. *Pragmatics and Discourse: A Resource Book for Students* [M]. London and New York: Routledge. pp. 23-33.

Levinson, S. C. 1983. *Pragmatics* [M]. Cambridge: Cambridge University Press. pp.284-370.

Mey, J. L. 2001. *Pragmatics: An Introduction* (2nd ed.) [M]. Malden, MA: Blackwell. pp. 136-153.

Schegloff, Emanuel. A. 2007. *Sequence Organization in Interaction: A Primer in Conversation Analysis* (Volume 1) [M]. Cambridge: Cambridge University Press. pp. 28-44.

Unit 8

Politeness

> Ceremonies are different in every country, but true politeness is everywhere the same.
> — Oliver Goldsmith
>
> Politeness is the art of choosing among your thoughts.
> — Madame de Stael

Objectives

- To understand what politeness is
- To learn how politeness is perceived in social studies
- To comprehend the principles of politeness in communication
- To learn the technical terms and expressions about the theories of politeness
- To improve critical thinking and intercultural communicative competence and comprehensive language skills
- To improve pragmatic competence, academic ability and relevant language skills

Before You Read

1. Can you name some ways which are used to show politeness?

2. Politeness is best expressed as the practical application of good manners or etiquette. It is culturally-bound, and therefore what is considered polite in one culture can sometimes be quite rude or simply eccentric in another cultural context. To what extent do you agree or disagree? Can you illustrate your points?

3. The following is a notice at a hotel. Read it carefully and decide on the writer's purpose and the strategies intended to achieve this purpose.

Dear Guest,

　　The items in this room have been provided for your convenience and remain the property of the Room Attendant in charge. Should you be interested to collect any of the guestroom items as souvenirs of your stay at the Petaling Jaya Hilton, you may purchase them from our Executive Business Centre at the Main Lobby.

Thank you.

Text A　Brown and Levinson's Linguistic Politeness Model

Goffman's Influence

　　Goffman is a sociologist whose ideas have helped directly and indirectly shape much of the linguistic facework and im/politeness research, including that of Brown and Levinson.

Goffman's (1967: 5) definition of face as 'the positive social value a person effectively claims for him- or herself is well known, as is his claim that:

> Face is an image of self delineated in terms of approved social attributes ... as when a person makes a good showing for his [or her] profession or religion by making a good showing for him [or her]self.

A less discussed characteristic of Goffman's concept of face is its dynamism: Goffman believed face to be: (i) on loan from society; (ii) liable to be withdrawn if an individual conducts him/herself in a way that is unworthy of it; and, hence, (iii) realized solely in social interaction (ibid.: 10). Fraser (1990: 22) has interpreted this to mean that:

> ...each society has a particular set of social norms consisting of more or less explicit rules that prescribe a certain behaviour, a state of affairs, or a way of thinking in context. *A positive evaluation (politeness) arises when an action is in congruence with the norm, a negative evaluation (impoliteness = rudeness) when an action is to the contrary.*

For Fraser, then, conversation relies upon our being polite — or operating within the terms of a 'conversational contract' (CC), albeit a CC which can always be renegotiated during actual interaction. Hence, politeness is viewed as an *unmarked norm*, and as the means of ensuring 'socially acceptable' behaviour. Brown and Levinson (1978/1987) and Leech (1983) also associate politeness with normal cooperative behaviour, and they've produced models by which we might categorize such linguistic politeness.

Brown and Levinson's Model

Brown and Levinson's (1978/1987) study of politeness documents the practices of Tamil speakers (from southern India), Tzeltal speakers (from Mexico) and English speakers (from America and Britain). Even so, the linguistic politeness model they propose is more rationalistic than it is empirical. This is because of their 'playful' adoption of 'Model Persons' (MPs) who recognize that:

> ...since people can be expected to defend their face if threatened, and in defending their own to threaten others' faces, it is in general in every participant's best interest to maintain each other's face.

(ibid.: 61)

The challenge MPs face is that they cannot completely eradicate face-threatening acts (FTAs) from their utterances. What MPs do, instead, is choose between a number of politeness superstrategies (see Figure 1), which Brown and Levinson situate on a cline of lesser-greater risk. The choice of the strategy is determined, then, by the MPs' assessment of: (i) the social distance between S (MP) and H; (ii) their relative power; and (iii) the size of the imposition in the cultural context.

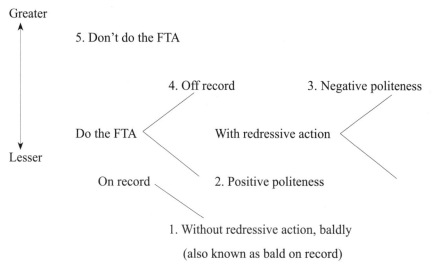

Figure 1   FTA strategies (adapted from Brown and Levinson, 1987: 60)

Let's consider each superstrategy in turn. The 'without redressive action, baldly' (or bald-on-record) superstrategy is used in contexts where maximally efficient utterances are acceptable because the risk to face (self and other) is considered to be minimal. We're most likely to hear bald-on-record utterances in emergency situations (cf. shouting Fire! As a means of getting others to quickly vacate a burning building) and in situations where the status/power differential between interlocutors is obvious (cf. *Get this to accounting asap*, said by a high-ranking boss to his subordinate).

If the risk to face is not considered to be minimal, MPs can use redressive language to help mitigate any face-threatening potential. The two on-record superstrategies used for this purpose — 'positive politeness' and 'negative politeness' — draw explicitly from two 'wants' which Brown and Levinson believe to be universal: the want to be approved of (also known as positive face) and the want to be unimpeded in one's actions (also known as negative face).

MPs make use of positive politeness when they explicitly want to signal that they are attending to their addressees' positive face. They might treat H 'as a member of an in-group' or 'friend', for example, and/or as someone 'whose wants and personality traits are known and liked'. Additional positive politeness strategies include: noticing H; exaggerating approval of /interest in H; seeking agreement; avoiding disagreement; presupposing/asserting common ground; joking, etc. Similarly, MPs make use of negative politeness when they explicitly signal their addressees' 'want' to be free to act without imposition in some way. If MPs need to make a request, for example, they are likely to redress the potential face threat 'with apologies for interfering or transgressing, with linguistic and non-linguistic deference, with hedges on the illocutionary force of the act' and/or 'other softening mechanisms that give' H 'a face-saving line of escape' and/or the sense that his/her 'response is not coerced' (ibid.: 70). Of course, how much of this mitigation MPs engage in will depend upon the social, familial and /or power relationship between them and their interlocutors as well as the size of the 'imposition'. Hence MPs will likely engage in less negative politeness work when asking a close friend to borrow a pen than they would if they asked the same friend to lend them their car for the afternoon!

The 'off-record' superstrategy comes into play when MPs deem an FTA to be such that an on-record superstrategy is inappropriate (because of being too face-threatening). This superstrategy is particularly useful when MPs want their utterances to have 'more than one ... attributable intention' according to Brown and Levinson. Consider their example, 'Damn, I'm out of cash. I forgot to go to the bank today', which can be interpreted as a statement of fact or as an indirect request for a (small) cash loan. Yet, the indirectness of the request is such that an MP can deny they ever intended to make a request.

To summarize, the above superstrategies equate to an 'estimation of face risk' scale with the on-record superstrategies being used in situations deemed to be of middle risk (in the case of positive politeness and negative politeness) and minimal/non-existent risk (in the case of bald-on-record). The off-record superstrategy, in contrast, is used when the risk to face is deemed to be quite high. The final superstrategy hightlighted in Figure 1 — 5. Don't do FTA — comes into play when MPs judge the threat to face to be too great and thus inadvisable in situations where face maintenance (self and other) is a priority.

(Adapted from Archer et al. 2012. *Pragmatics: An Advanced Resource Book for Students*. pp. 84-87.)

Text B Leech's Politeness Model

Leech (1983) advocates a conversational-maxim view to politeness, whereby a Politeness Principle (PP) complements Grice's (1975) Cooperative Principle (CP). The

PP is based on the premise that interlocutors seek to *minimize the expression of impolite beliefs and maximize the expression of polite beliefs*. Interlocutors draw on a number of politeness maxims to do so: these maxims are relabelled 'constraints' in Leech's 2007 work. The maxim (or constraints) seek to avoid discord first (see A) and seek concord second (see B) (see Figure 2)

As the repetition of 'expression of beliefs which imply...' in Figure 2 suggests, Leech's focus is how interlocutors avoid discord and foster concord *only in so far as these are evident in communication*. For Leech, then, politeness is an aspect of goal-oriented behaviour which is essentially pragmatic. Indeed, the basic question, for Leech, is What did S mean [to convey] by saying X?.

Interlocutors choose the most appropriate politeness strategy using three (inter-related) pragmatic scales, according to Leech: (1) the cost-benefit scale; (2) the optionality scale; and (3) the indirectness scale. Let's consider an utterance which involves the generosity maxim: *Have a chocolate*! with, first, the cost-benefit scale in mind. Although imperative in form, it is likely to be heard as benefitting H (unless he/she)'s on a diet or is lactose intolerant. *Could I have one of your chocolates*? in contrast, would likely be heard as being 'costly' to H, because he/she would have to supply the chocolate in this case. This is when the optionality

scale and indirectness scale become operationalized, according to Leech; for *Could I have one of your chocolates*? constitutes an indirect strategy, and its purpose is to give the addressee a choice as to whether to comply. Compare the imperative, *Give me one of your chocolates*! which doesn't allow H a choice. Leech suggests that (the scales of) indirectness and optionality often

A	Avoid discord by, for example, minimizing (expression of beliefs which imply) …					
	...cost to other	...benefit to self	...dispraise of other	...praise of self	...disagreement between self and other	...antipathy between self and other
That is	TACT	GENOROSITY	APPROBATION	MODESTY	AGREEMENT	SYMPATHY
B	Seek concord by, for example, maximizing (expression of beliefs which imply) …					
	... benefit to other	... cost to self	... praise of other	... dispraise of self	... agreement between self and other	... sympathy between self and other
That is	TACT	GENOROSITY	APPROBATION	MODESTY	AGREEMENT	SYMPATHY

Figure 2 Maxims subsumed by Leech's Politeness Principle

work together in this way when it comes to politeness:

> [i]ndirect illocutions tend to be more polite [...] because they increase the degree of optionality, and [...] because the more indirect an illocution is, the more diminished and tentative its force tends to be.
>
> (Leech, 1983: 108)

Whilst there might be an argument for linking indirectness with politeness in present-day English, we need to shy away from a one-to-one mapping. For a direct utterance can be the appropriate form — given the right context. Conversely, indirectness can be used for impolite or face-damaging purposes. Leech (ibid.: 171) provides the example of 'Haven't you something to declare?' spoken by an official at a border checkpoint, which could be argued to be 'progressively more impolite [and] more threatening than the ordinary yes-no question', because it seems to presuppose an affirmative response (as opposed to seeking one).

Leech's interest in impoliteness has grown in his later work (e.g. Leech 2007). Indeed, he suggests that his politeness maxims/constraints might be used to gauge instances when interlocutors appear to transgress the PP for some strategic gain. Bousfield (2008: 51) explains how this might work via an analogy to Grice's CP:

> [...] we may be able to say that Leech's PP maxims, or constraints, can be violated (covertly broken), flouted (overtly broken), infringed, suspended, or opted out of ... intentional linguistic impoliteness [would] occur at the level where one (or more) of Leech's PP maxims is flouted ... [in order] to generate an impolite implicature. Accidental offences ... would ... occur at the 'infringement' level. Emergency or other urgent situations would entail the suspension of the PP (cf. *bald-on-record* ...), and opting out of the PP would encompass those situations where people choose to *stay silent* when politeness might otherwise have been expected ... or where ... stated politeness may be considered to be offensive to the recipient (cf. *don't do the FTA* ...).
>
> (Adapted from Archer et al. 2012. *Pragmatics: An Advanced Resource Book for Students*. pp. 88-90.)

After You Read

Knowledge Focus

1. **Decide whether the following statements are true or false based on Text A and Text B.**

   1) For Fraser, politeness is viewed as a marked norm, and as the means of ensuring 'socially acceptable' behaviour.

   2) According the author, the linguistic politeness model Brown and Levinson propose is more rationalistic than it is empirical.

   3) The choice of the politeness strategy is determined, then, by the MP'S assessment of: (i) the social distance between S (MP) and H; (ii) their absolute power; and (iii) the size of the imposition in the cultural context.

   4) Interlocutors choose the most appropriate politeness strategy using three (inter-related) pragmatic scales, according to Leech: (1) the cost-benefit scale; (2) the effort-effect scale; and (3) the indirectness scale.

   5) The PP is based on the premise that interlocutors seek to minimize the expression of impolite beliefs and maximize the expression of politeness beliefs.

2. **Discuss the following questions with your partner.**

   1) How is positive/negative face related to politeness?
   2) When is the 'off-record' superstrategy adopted in social interaction?
   3) In what situations can the 'bald-on-record' superstrategy be found?
   4) How is Leech's Politeness Principle related to Grice's Cooperative Principle?
   5) Do people in different cultures observe the same maxims of the PP in performing the same speech acts?

Language Focus

1. **Fill in the blanks with words or expressions in Text A and Text B.**

   1) According to Goffman, the definition of face is 'the positive social value a person effectively _____ for him or herself.

   2) We're most likely to hear _____ utterances in emergency situations and in situations where the status/power differential between interlocutors is obvious.

   3) Positive politeness and negative politeness draw explicitly from two 'wants': the want

to be approved of (also known as positive face) and the want to be _____ in one's actions (also known as negative face).

4) The 'off-record' superstrategy comes into play when MPs deem an FTA to be such that an on-record superstrategy is _____.

5) The final superstrategy 'Don't do FTA' comes into play when MPs judge the threat to face to be too great and thus inadvisable in situations where face maintenance (self and other) is a _____.

6) Interlocutors draw on a number of politeness maxims to do so: these maxims are relabelled '_____' in Leech's 2007 work.

7) For Leech, politeness is an aspect of _____ behaviour which is essentially pragmatic.

8) A direct utterance can be the appropriate form - given the right context. _____, indirectness can be used for impolite or face-damaging purposes.

9) Leech suggests that his politeness maxims/constraints might be used to _____ instances when interlocutors appear to transgress the PP for some strategic gain.

10) Leech's PP maxims, or constraints, can be violated, flouted, _____, suspended, or opted out of ... intentional linguistic impoliteness would occur at the level where one or more of Leech's PP maxims is flouted ... [in order] to generate an impolite implicature.

2. Translate the following passage into English.

Brown 和 Levinson 对于面子威胁行为的过分突显受到批判。他们对于礼貌现象的理解完全以如何解决面子威胁为中心；他们也因其西方个人主义偏见而受到质疑。这种偏见与集体主义相冲突。他们主张所有说话人无论具有什么样的文化背景，都有相同的"面子需求"，因此，过分简化了重要差异性。(Archer *et al*, 2012: 87)

3. Translate the following passage into Chinese.

There is everyday politeness, of course, which does indeed prevent people from hurling bald threats and insults at each other. But what makes a direct request impolite? In a linguistic sense — in the sense developed as Politeness Theory (Brown and Levinson, 1978) — politeness involves the recognition and linguistic acknowledgement of much subtler threats to the self-image that a person presents publicly. The lay notion of 'saving face' corresponds to a more well-developed notion of face within this theory. A person's face is an aspect of their self-image, particular as they relate to other people. Each person has a positive face, which is their desire for interaction and solidarity with others, and a negative face, which is their desire to be autonomous, to be respected, and, in effect, to be left alone. When you phrase your utterance in such a way as to emphasize the solidarity between you an your interlocutor, you are appealing to their positive face; when you phrase the utterance in such a way as to allow them space and the freedom to decline solidarity or interaction, you are appealing to their negative face.

(Birner, 2013: 200-201)

Comprehensive Work

1. Use Leech's (1983) politeness model to explain impoliteness/ face damage in political interviews.

2. Study a particular speech act (e.g. compliment, invitation, refusal, etc.) by watching Chinese and English movies or TV series, and analyze how people in these two cultures perform the speech act and respond to it in light of Leech's Politeness Principle.

Further Readings

Text C Perspectives on Politeness

The primary purpose of this paper is to provide a critical overview of how scholars approach an account of politeness. I have attempted in the following to identify and explicate what I have found to be four major perspectives on the treatment of politeness: the social-norm view; the conversational-maxim view; the face-saving view; and the conversational-contract view. For each I provide a characterization of politeness embraced if not articulated by those writing from the perspective, and show how this notion gets played out in their account. I conclude with a brief set of comments of where one might expect future research to venture.

1. The social-norm view

The social-norm view of politeness reflects the historical understanding of politeness generally embraced by the public within the English-speaking world. Briefly stated, it assumes that each society has a particular set of social norms consisting of more or less explicit rules that prescribe a certain behavior, a state of affairs, or a way of thinking in a context. A positive evaluation (politeness) arises when an action is in congruence with the norm, a negative evaluation (impoliteness = rudeness) when action is to the contrary.

The social-norm approach has few adherents among current researches. There are, however, three somewhat separate approaches to an account of politeness within the recent linguistic literature.

2. The conversational-maxim view

The conversational-maxim perspective relies principally on the work of Grice (1967, published 1975) in his now-classic paper 'Logic and conversation'. In an attempt to clarify how it is that speakers can mean more than they 'say', Grice argued that conversationalists are rational individuals who are, all other things being equal, primarily interested in the efficient conveying of messages. To this end, he proposed his general Cooperative Principle (CP). The CP provides that you should say what you have to say, when you have to say it, and the way you have to say it.

Grice associates with the CP a set of more specific maxims and sub-maxims, which he presumes that speakers follow. Observance of the CP and maxims is deemed to be reasonable (rational). While one or more of the maxims may not be fulfilled by a speaker at a point in a conversation, Grice assumes that the CP is always observed and that any real or apparent violations of the maxims signal conversational implicatures: non-explicit messages intended by the speaker to be inferred by the hearer.

Grice notes that the relative importance of the maxims differs as does the significance of their violation, and suggests that there might be a need for others not mentioned in his article:

'There are, of course, all sorts of other maxims (aesthetic, social, or moral in character) such as 'Be polite' that are also normally observed by participants in talk exchanges, and these may also generate nonconventional (i.e. conversational) implicatures. The conversational maxims, however, and the conversational implicatures connected with them, are specially connected (I hope) with the particular purposes that talk (and so, talk exchange) is adapted to serve and is primarily employed to serve.' (1975: 47)

Lakoff (1973) was among the first to adopt Grice's construct of Conversational Principles in an effort to account for politeness. Unlike Grice, however, Lakoff explicitly extends the notion of grammatical rule and its associated notion of well-formedness to pragmatics. Extending this to the domain of politeness, she considers the form of sentences i.e., specific constructions — to be polite or not. In her later works she is more explicit, referring to politeness as 'a device used in order to reduce friction in personal interaction' (Lakoff, 1979: 64).

Lakoff (1973) suggests two rules of Pragmatic Competence:

(1) Be Clear (essentially Grice's maxims)
(2) Be Polite

She takes these to be in opposition to each other, and notes that they are at times reinforcing, at other times in conflict. In addition she posits sub-maxims (sub-rules), adapted as follows:

Rule 1: Don't Impose
    (used when Formal/Impersonal Politeness is required)
Rule 2: Give Options
    (used when Informal Politeness is required)
Rule 3: Make A Feel Good
    (used when Intimate Politeness is required)

Each of these is oriented to make the hearer 'feel good'.

These three rules are applicable more or less depending on the type of politeness situation as understood by the speaker. For example, if a speaker assesses the situations as requiring Intimate Politeness, window shutting might be requested by uttering 'Shut the window', while Informal Politeness might be met with 'Please shut the window'. The reader is never told how the speaker or hearer is to assess what level of politeness is required.

The position of Leech (1983) is a grand elaboration of the Conversational Maxim approach to politeness. Like Lakoff, Leech adopts the framework initially set out by Grice: there exists a set of maxims and sub-maxims that guide and constrain the conversation of rational people. He opts to treat politeness within the domain of a rhetorical pragmatics, his account of goal- directed linguistic behavior (For detailed discussions, refer to Text B).

3. The face-saving view

Certainly the best known of the recent approaches to an account of politeness is that in Brown and Levinson (1978, 1987), all references to the later edition, hereafter B&L. For B&L, a strong motivation for not talking strictly according to conversational maxims is to ensure politeness.

In contrast to Leech, they maintain that Grice's CP has a very different status in their theory from any so-called politeness principles. More specifically, the CP specifies a socially neutral framework within which ordinary communication is seen to occur, the operating assumption being 'no deviation from rational efficiency without a reason' (1987: 5). It is, however, considerations of politeness which do provide principled reasons for such deviation.

The operation of their model can be summarized into the following steps (1987: 90-91, adapted):

(i) Unless the speaker intends to perform an FTA with maximum efficiency, the speaker must determine that he/she wishes to fulfil the hearer face wants to some degree as a rational means to secure the hearer's cooperation, either for purposes of face maintenance or some joint activity, or both.

(ii) The speaker must then determine the face-threat of the particular FTA (the Wx) and determine to what extent to minimize the face-loss of the TA, considering factors such as need for clarity and the need to not overemphasize the degree of potential face-loss.

(iii) The speaker must then choose a strategy that provides the degree of face-saving consistent with (ii), above. Retention of the hearer's cooperation dictates that the strategy chosen meet the hearer's expectation of what is required at that point.

(iv) The speaker must then choose a linguistic means that will satisfy the strategic end. Since each strategy embraces a range of degrees of politeness, the speaker will be required to consider the specific linguistic forms used and their overall effect when used in conjunction with one another.

4. The conversational-contract view

The fourth and final approach to politeness is that presented by Fraser (1975), Fraser and Nolen (1981), and elaborated on here. While also adopting Grice's notion of a Cooperative Principle in its general sense (as quoted above), and while recognizing the importance of Goffman's notion of face, this approach differs in certain important ways from that of B&L.

We can begin with the recognition that upon entering into a given conversation, each party brings an understanding of some initial set of rights and obligations that will determine, at least for the preliminary stages, what the participants can expect from the other(s). During the course of time, or because of a change in the context, there is always the possibility for a renegotiation of the conversational contract: the two parties may readjust just what rights and what obligations they hold towards each other.

The dimensions on which interactive participants establish rights and obligations vary greatly. Some terms of a conversational contract may be imposed through convention; they are of a general nature and apply to all ordinary conversations. Speakers, for example, are expected to take turns (subject to the specific constraints of that sub-culture), they are expected to use a mutually intelligible language, to speak sufficiently loudly for the other to hear clearly, and to speak seriously. These are seldom negotiable.

Related are terms and conditions imposed by the social institutions applicable to the interaction. Speakers are expected to speak only in whispers, if at all, during a Protestant church service, everyone is expected to address the U.S. Chief Executive as 'Mr. President', and a witness in court is expected to speak only when questioned. Such requirements are also seldom, if ever, renegotiated.

And finally, other terms may be determined by previous encounters or the particulars of the situation. These are determined for each interaction, and most are renegotiable in light of the participants' perception and/or acknowledgments of factors such as the status, the power, and the role of each speaker, and the nature of the circumstances. These latter factors play a crucial role in determining what messages may be expected: both in terms of force and content.

A child, for example, is not ordinarily entitled to authorize a parent to do something; two close friends do not issue orders to each other; an employee is not free to criticize an employer; a felon does not christen a ship (except, perhaps, in Boston). And, while a podiatrist is entitled to ask questions, there are restrictions on the content: questions about your history and the reasons for the visit are expected; questions about your intimate moments are not.

In short, we enter into a conversation and continue within a conversation with the (usually tacit) understanding of our current conversational contract (CC) at every turn. Within this framework, being polite constitutes operating within the then-current terms and conditions of the CC.

Politeness, on this view, is not a sometime thing. Rational participants are aware that they are to act within the negotiated constraints and generally do so. When they do not, however, they are then perceived as being impolite or rude. Politeness is a state that one expects to exist in every conversation; participants note not that someone is being polite — this is the norm — but rather that the speaker is violating the CC. Being polite does not involve making the hearer 'feel good', à la Lakoff or Leech, nor with making the hearer not 'feel bad', à la B&L. It simply involves getting on with the task at hand in light of the terms and conditions of the CC.

The intention to be polite is not signaled, it is not implicated by some deviation(s) from the most 'efficient' bald-on record way of using the language. Being polite is taken to be a hallmark of abiding by the CP — being cooperative involves abiding by the CC. Sentences are not *ipso facto* polite, nor are languages more or less polite. It is only speakers who are polite, and then only if their utterances reflect an adherence to the obligations they carry in that particular conversation.

From this perspective much of what B & L take as politeness phenomena might be better treated as intended deference: 'that component of activity which functions as a symbolic means by which appreciation is regularly conveyed' (Goffman, 1971: 56). On this view, deference is a component of an activity, and is not associated with an activity, per se.

However, certain utterances can, in virtue of their meaning, encode speaker intention to convey deference. The use of 'Sir' as a title of respect and the use of 'please' are two such examples. The sentence 'Would you mind helping me today' used to indirectly convey a request, is certainly more deferential than 'Help me today'. The former conveys to hearers, if only symbolically, that they have a choice in deciding whether or not to comply, hence that they are more highly 'appreciated' in the estimation of the speaker.

Green captures this notion of deference when she writes of euphemisms that:

> 'as with many politeness techniques, the speaker is really only going through the motion of offering options, of showing respect [deference — BF] for the addressee's feelings. The offer may be a facade, the option nonviable, and the respect a sham. It is the fact that an effort was made to go through the motions at all that makes the act an act of politeness.' (1989: 147)

5. Conclusion

The foregoing has been an attempt to briefly present four perspectives on how to account for politeness: the social-norm; the conversational-maxim; the face-saving; and the conversational-contract. I think some clear conclusions follow.

First, there is little agreement among researchers in the field about what, exactly, constitutes politeness and the domain of related research. At times researchers seem more interested in defining the term 'politeness' than with understanding an interactive concept that appears to be relevant in all cultures. The distinction between linguistic and non-linguistic politeness is not drawn, if it indeed exists. The notion of politeness as universal is often proposed but seldom validated, even in B&L's work. And how the notion of politeness (assuming for the sake of argument it can be clarified) differs from that of deference, tact, civility, and the like requires serious consideration.

Second, assuming acceptable answers to the above issues, what form might an account of politeness take? It seems clear at the outset that a viable theory of politeness cannot rest upon a set of rules based on social, normative behavior. What we view as polite or impolite behavior in normal interaction is subject to immediate and unique contextually-negotiated factors and, as such, cannot be codified in any interesting way. The normative perspective must be rejected.

Third, a viable theory of politeness must be sufficiently precise to be assessed. It is one thing to adopt Grice's intuitively appealing Cooperative Principle. It is quite another to posit a host of maxims involving tact, modesty, agreement, appropriation, generosity, and the like, which are claimed to be guidelines for polite interaction, but without either definition and/or suggestions by which one could, on a given instance, determine the relative proportions of influence from these maxims. The conversational maxim perspective must be rejected as non-viable, for the same reasons that researchers have rejected Grice's program for conversational implicature (cf. Sperber and Wilson, 1987).

Fourth, while there are certain differences between the face-saving and conversational-contract perspectives (e.g., whether politeness is the result of deviation from a maximally efficient effort or is inherent in a maximally efficient effort; whether politeness is implicated (B&L) or anticipated (CC); whether the use of 'politeness strategies' is motivated by speaker concern for hearer face-loss or by concern to abide by the CP), they share the same orientation: choice of linguistic form is determined, in part, by the speaker's appreciation of a responsibility towards the hearer in the interaction. As such, they deserve to be pursued.

Finally, inasmuch as the B&L approach is the more fully articulated version, it seems clearly the one to be systematically challenged. For example, can what counts as 'face' be defined within a culture? Is their $Wx = D(S,H) + P(H,S) + Rx$ a viable summary of risk or, as it appears, much too simplistic? Is there sound empirical evidence that their claims about the use of politeness strategies correlate with naturally occurring conversations? To what extent is there persuasive evidence that their levels (degrees) of politeness are viewed consistently by native speakers of a language? To what extent is what they take as indirectness in performance a function of speaker intention of politeness? To what extent is their view of communication of a zero-sum game — the greater politeness, the less efficient the information transfer — an accurate assessment of speaker perceptions?

These raise but a few of the important questions to be asked in a pursuit of an understanding of just what politeness is, how it is used, and what factors influence a speaker's choice to be heard as polite. Optimists take the position that we can expect to arrive at a serious theory of politeness, where concepts of face and principles for interpretation are carefully articulated and well understood. Pessimists, on the other hand, take the position that while we all know polite behavior when we see it, we will never be able to speak definitively about it. Stay tuned.

(Adapted from Bruce Fraser. 1990. Perspectives on Politeness, *Journal of Pragmatics* 14, pp. 219-236.)

Questions for Discussion

1. Would you elaborate the social-norm view of politeness?
2. Would you summarize the conversational-maxim view?
3. How is Brown and Levinson's view different from Leech's in politeness?
4. In what ways does Fraser's views in politeness differentiate from Brown and Levinson's?

Text D Towards an Anatomy of Impoliteness

1. Introduction

Over the last twenty years politeness theories have concentrated on how we employ communicative strategies to maintain or promote social harmony:

> [The role of the Politeness Principle is] 'to maintain the social equilibrium and the friendly relations which enable us to assume that our interlocutors are being cooperative in the first place.' (Leech, 1983: 82)

> '... politeness, like formal diplomatic protocol (for which it must surely be the model), presupposes that potential for aggression as it seeks to disarm it, and makes possible communication between potentially aggressive parties.' (Brown and Levinson, 1987: 1)

> 'Politeness can be defined as a means of minimizing confrontation in discourse — both the possibility of confrontation occurring at all, and the possibility that a confrontation will be perceived as threatening.' (Lakoff, 1989: 102)

In this paper I shall investigate *impoliteness*, the use of strategies that are designed to have the opposite effect — that of social disruption. These strategies are oriented towards attacking face, an emotionally sensitive concept of the self (Goffman, 1967; Brown and Levinson, 1987).

The idea that the scope of a politeness theory might be extended to include antagonistic or confrontational communication is not new. Craig *et al.* (1986) and Tracy (1990) argue that an adequate account of the dynamics of interpersonal communication should consider hostile as well as cooperative communication. In analysing American courtroom discourse, both Lakoff (1989) and Penman (1990) extended their models of politeness to include features of confrontational discourse. However, none of these studies focus comprehensively on impoliteness in an attempt to improve our understanding of its operation and its theoretical basis.

In this paper I shall start by considering inherent impoliteness and mock impoliteness; I will then move on to discuss the contextual factors that are associated with impoliteness and to propose a list of impoliteness strategies. Here, as I will demonstrate, Leech's claim that conflictive communication tends to be 'rather marginal to human linguistic behaviour in normal circumstances' (1983: 105) does not apply.

2. Inherent impoliteness

Leech (1983) makes a distinction between 'Relative Politeness' and 'Absolute Politeness'. Relative politeness refers to the politeness of an act relative to a particular context, whereas absolute politeness refers to the politeness associated with acts independent of context. Within absolute politeness, Leech argues, 'some illocutions (e.g. orders) are inherently impolite, and others (e.g. offers) are inherently polite' (Leech, 1983: 83). Similarly, Brown and Levinson (1987), working within a face-oriented model of politeness, write that 'it is intuitively the case that certain kinds of acts intrinsically threaten face' (1987: 65); in other words, they argue that certain acts (e.g. orders, threats, criticisms) run counter to one's positive face, the want to be approved of, and/or one's negative face, the want to be unimpeded.

If one considers acts in the abstract, one might broadly concur with the idea that some acts are inherently polite, whilst others are inherently impolite. However, one must bear in mind that any assessment of politeness outside the theorist's vacuum will take context into account. Fraser and Nolan (1981) make this point:

'... no sentence is inherently polite or impolite. We often take certain expressions to be impolite, but it is not the expressions themselves but the conditions under which they are used that determines the judgment of politeness.' (1981: 96)

It is not difficult to think of examples where a supposedly impolite act will be judged as polite in a particular context (or as falling somewhere between the two extremes on a continuum ranging from politeness to impoliteness). An order could be conceived as polite in a context where it is thought to be of benefit to the target (for example, 'Go on, eat up' as an order for a dinner guest to tuck in to some delicacy).

However, in some instances the conjunction of act and context does give rise to impoliteness that may be said to be inherent, since it cannot be completely mitigated by any surface realisation of politeness. For instance, recently I was one of three passengers in a car driven by a somewhat nervous driver who had left the windscreen wipers on even though it was not raining. I wished to tell the driver to turn them off, but any form of request would have the unfortunate effect of drawing attention to the fact that the wipers had rather foolishly been left on, and thus damage the positive face of the driver. I was faced with a clash of goals: I wished to be polite, but no amount of politeness work could eradicate the impoliteness of the act I wished to perform. I reached an impasse and said nothing. A fellow passenger tried 'Is it raining?'. This did achieve its goal of getting the driver to turn off the wipers, but for all its superficially polite indirectness, it still embarrassed the driver in pointing out an apparent deficit in driving ability.

The notion of inherent impoliteness irrespective of contexts only holds for a minority of acts. For example, acts which draw attention to the fact that the target is engaged in some anti-social activity (e.g. picking nose or ears, farting) seem to be inherently impolite. It is difficult to think of politeness work or a change of context that can easily remove the impoliteness from an utterance such as 'Do you think you could possibly not pick your nose'? The reason why these acts may be described as inherently impolite is as follows. According to Brown and Levinson (1987: 1), politeness comes about through one's orientation towards what Goffman called the 'virtual offense' (Goffman, 1971: 138ff.). In other words, by demonstrating concern for the face-threatening potential of an act, one shows that one has the other's interests at heart. An inherently impolite act does not involve *virtual* or *potential* offence; it is in its very performance offensive and thus not amenable to politeness work. In the example, 'Do you think you could possibly not pick your nose?', the face-threatening potential in the request to desist from a particular line of activity can be mitigated by politeness work, but the face damage incurred in drawing attention to an anti-social habit cannot. This explanation for inherently impolite acts also applies to the inherent impoliteness arising from the conjunction of act and context, as in the windscreen wipers example. In both cases the fiction of the potential face threat is not available for politeness work. Instead, by drawing attention to an undesirable aspect of the addressee, the utterance inflicts unavoidable damage to his or her positive face.

3. Mock impoliteness

Mock impoliteness, or banter, is impoliteness that remains on the surface, since it is understood that it is not intended to cause offence. For example, I once turned up late for a party, and upon explaining to the host that I had mistaken 17:00 hours for 7 o'clock, I was greeted with a smile and the words 'You silly bugger'. I knew that the impoliteness was superficial, it was not really meant, and that I had been accepted into the party. Leech (1983) attempts to capture this kind of phenomenon within his Banter Principle:

> 'In order to show solidarity with h, say something which is (i) obviously untrue, and (ii) obviously impolite to h' [and this will give rise to an interpretation such that] 'what s says is impolite to h and is clearly untrue. Therefore what s really means is polite to h and true.' (1983: 144)

Leech argues that banter reflects and fosters social intimacy (i.e. relative equality in terms of authority and closeness in terms of social distance): the more intimate a relationship, the less necessary and important politeness is. In other words, lack of politeness is associated with intimacy, and so being superficially impolite can promote intimacy. Clearly, this only works in contexts in which the impoliteness is understood to be untrue. Leech, however, neglects to specify what these contexts might be.

If lack of politeness is associated with intimacy (an idea which is reflected in Brown and Levinson's model), surface impoliteness is, paradoxically, even more likely to be interpreted as banter in non-intimate contexts, where it is more clearly at odds with expectations. This can be illustrated with the advertising slogan, 'Eat beef — You bastards', used by an Australian meat retailer. One may suppose that the prototypical customer is both socially distant from the retailer and more powerful than the retailer (in so far as the customer has the power to determine the success or otherwise of the retailer's goals). Clearly, the retailer is not in a position to employ a derogatory term of address, and has nothing to gain from doing so: it is obviously banter. Some support for this argument can be found in Slugoski and Tumbull's (1988) investigation of the interpretation of ironic compliments and insults. Though the power variable was not included in their model, they did examine the effect of social distance. Subjects tended to interpret an insult as polite (i.e. as banter) in conditions of high social distance. More importantly, their study revealed the even stronger influence of affect (liking or disliking) operating as an independent variable. The more people like each other, the more concern they are likely to have for each other's face. Thus insults are more likely to be interpreted as banter when directed at targets liked by the speaker.

Banter, of course, also exists in a more ritualised form as a kind of language game. In America this is known variously as 'sounding', 'playing the dozens' or 'signifying', and takes place particularly amongst black adolescents. Labov's (1972) work has been influential in revealing the complexity of the insults used and the well-organised nature of this speech event. Typically, these insults are sexual, directed at a third person related to the target, and couched in rhyming couplets. For example:

Iron is iron, and steel don't rust,
But your momma got a pussy like a Greyhound Bus.
(Labov, 1972: 302)

The key to 'sounding' is that the insult is understood to be untrue, an interpretation that comes about on the basis of shared knowledge within the group. The effect is to reinforce in-group solidarity. There is a competitive element to 'sounding'; the winner is the one who has the widest range of ritual insults to hand and can use them most appropriately. Real time improvisation in the creation of ritual insults tends not to occur. A result of the formulaic nature of the insults is that it is easier to recognize that one is engaged in 'sounding' rather than personal insult. Labov also points out that 'weak' insults, ones that are not outrageously bizarre and so obviously untrue, are more dangerous in that they are more likely to be interpreted as personal insults.

Ritualised banter has been studied most extensively in America, but occurs in other cultures as well. Thompson (1935) found 'organised' swearing amongst the aborigines of Northern Queensland, and Montagu (1973) observed that a similar form of swearing is found amongst the Eskimos. Hughes (1991) points out that 'sounding' is similar to 'flytin'. This was a kind of competitive ritual insult that was common in Old Norse. With the Scandinavian settlement of England it made its way into English literature, but gradually died out. Vestiges of 'flyting' can be found in Shakespeare's plays (e.g. *Romeo and Juliet* II.iv, *The Taming of the Shrew* II.i). In all these cases ritualized banter seems to act as a societal safety-valve. It is a place where we can be impolite with impunity, since 'in ritual we are freed from personal responsibility for the acts we are engaged in' (Labov, 1972: 352-353).

4. When are we impolite?

There are circumstances when the vulnerability of face is unequal and so motivation to cooperate is reduced. A powerful participant has more freedom to be impolite, because he or she can (a) reduce the ability of the less powerful participant to retaliate with impoliteness (e.g. through the denial of speaking rights), and (b) threaten more severe retaliation should the less powerful participant be impolite. The fact that impoliteness is more likely to occur in situations where there is an imbalance of power is reflected in its relatively frequent appearance in courtroom discourse (Lakoff, 1989; Penman, 1990). As Penman points out, the witness has 'limited capacity to negotiate positive and negative face wants', whereas the barrister has 'almost unlimited capacity to threaten and aggravate the witness's face' (1990: 34).

In some circumstances it is not in a participant's interests to maintain the other's face. Participants may have a conflict of interests. For example, in zero-sum games, such as legal cases or sports contests, only one participant can win and in doing so causes the other participant to lose. Sometimes, it may be the case that a long-term goal can be best achieved by a short-term impoliteness strategy. For example, one might shame somebody into doing something that will be of long-term benefit to him or her. It may also be that a participant has some particular interest in attacking the other's face. For example, an assumption behind the American adversarial legal system is that direct confrontation will elicit the truth (Lakoff, 1989). In particular, Lakoff (1989) found systematic impoliteness in the case of defendants who havebeen found guilty of first-degree murder in a Californian court. Here the jury, having decided on the defendant's guilt, has the additional job of recommending the death sentence or life imprisonment without parole. The prosecution needs to demonstrate to the jury that the defendant is inhuman and loathsome. As a result, the prosecution uses impoliteness in the hope that the defendant will be provoked and lose control.

The factors influencing the occurrence of impoliteness in equal relationships are complex. If lack of politeness correlates with intimacy, can we assume that genuine impoliteness, as opposed to mock impoliteness, will be more likely to occur in an extremely intimate relationship? There is some evidence for this. Birchler *et al.* (1975) discovered that even in happy marriages spouses were typically more hostile towards each other than strangers. In a familiar relationship one has more scope for impoliteness: one may know which aspects of face are particularly sensitive to attack, and one may be able to better predict and/or cope with retaliation that may ensue. However, it seems absurd to argue that the more intimate one becomes with someone the more impoliteness one employs.

Part of the problem is that intimacy is a vague notion that covers a number of independent variables; it is not just familiarity. If one follows Brown and Gilman (1960) and takes intimacy to mean that intimate participants have more in common, then impoliteness may well be self-defeating. Close friends in this sense are more likely to have close identity of face wants (Brown and Levinson, 1987: 64). Thus the scope for impoliteness is reduced, since in normal circumstances one presumably wishes to avoid self face damage. Sometimes intimacy is also taken to mean affect (e.g. Baxter, 1984). It seems highly plausible that impoliteness correlates with negative affect. Slugoski and Turnbull's study (1988) provides evidence to the effect that people expect less concern for face when the relationship is one of dislike. It is worth noting that a particular characteristic of impoliteness behaviour in equal relationships is its tendency to escalate. Equal relationships - by definition - lack a default mechanism by which one participant achieves the upper hand. An insult can easily lead to a counter-insult and so on. Moreover, Harris et al.'s study (1986) of verbal aggression revealed that it is commonly assumed that the best way to save face in the light of verbal attack is to counter-attack. In fact, subjects assumed that the only way to terminate verbal aggression between male friends was through outside intervention. Not surprisingly, verbal aggression sometimes escalates into physical violence.

Of course, these are not the only circumstances in which impoliteness may occur. Infante and Wigley (1986), for example, conceptualise verbal aggression as a personality trait. In other words, some people are predisposed towards confrontation.

5. Impoliteness strategies

Impoliteness is very much the parasite of politeness. Each of the politeness superstrategies proposed by Brown and Levinson (1987) has its opposite impoliteness superstrategy. They are opposite in terms of orientation to face. Instead of enhancing or supporting face, impoliteness superstrategies are a means of attacking face.

(1) *Bald on record impoliteness* — the FTA is performed in a direct, clear, unambiguous and concise way in circumstances where face is not irrelevant or minimised. It is important to distinguish this strategy from Brown and Levinson's Bald on record. For Brown and Levinson, Bald on record is a politeness strategy in fairly specific circumstances. For example, when face concerns are suspended in an emergency, when the threat to the hearer's face is very small (e.g. 'Come in' or 'Do sit down'), or when the speaker is much more powerful than the hearer (e.g. 'Stop complaining' said by a parent to a child). In all these cases little face is at stake, and, more importantly, it is not the intention of the speaker to

attack the face of the hearer.

(2) *Positive impoliteness* — the use of strategies designed to damage the addressee's positive face wants.

(3) *Negative impoliteness* — the use of strategies designed to damage the addressee's negative face wants.

(4) *Sarcasm or mock politeness* — the FTA is performed with the use of politeness strategies that are obviously insincere, and thus remain surface realisations. My understanding of sarcasm is close to Leech's (1983) conception of irony. He states the Irony Principle (IP) as follows:

> 'If you must cause offence, at least do so in a way which doesn't overtly conflict with the PP [Politeness Principle], but allows the hearer to arrive at the offensive point of your remark indirectly, by way of an implicature.' (1983: 82)

This definition is not far removed from Brown and Levinson's notion of Off record politeness. However, Leech (1983) later expands:

> 'Apparently, then, the IP is dys-functional: if the PP promotes a bias towards comity rather than conflict in social relations, the IP, by enabling us to bypass politeness, promotes the 'antisocial' use of language. We are ironic at someone's expense, scoring off others by politeness that is obviously insincere, as a substitute for impoliteness.' (1983: 142)

This is, of course, the opposite of the social harmony that is supposed to be promoted through Brown and Levinson's Off record politeness. I prefer the use of the term sarcasm to Leech's irony, since irony can be used for enjoyment and comedy. Sarcasm (mock politeness for social disharmony) is clearly the opposite of banter (mock impoliteness for social harmony).

(5) *Withhold politeness* — the absence of politeness work where it would be expected. Brown and Levinson touch on the face-damaging implications of withholding politeness work:

> '... politeness has to be communicated, and the absence of communicated politeness may, ceteris paribus, be taken as the absence of a polite attitude.' (1987: 5)

For example, failing to thank somebody for a present may be taken as deliberate impoliteness.

Brown and Levinson's formula for assessing the weightiness of an FTA still applies for impoliteness. The greater the imposition of the act, the more powerful and distant the other is, the more face-damaging the act is likely to be. But how impoliteness superstrategies relate to the degree of face attack of an act and how they promote to the overall impoliteness of an utterance is an area for future research to investigate.

Much of Brown and Levinson's work is devoted to the linguistic realisations of output strategies for positive and negative politeness. Each output strategy is a means of satisfying the strategic ends of a superstrategy. Brown and Levinson provide open-ended lists of possible output strategies. Below I suggest a provisional list of some output strategies for positive and negative impoliteness. It must be stressed that this list is not exhaustive and that the strategies depend upon an appropriate context to be impolite.

Positive impoliteness output strategies:

Ignore, snub the other — fail to acknowledge the other's presence.

Exclude the other from an activity

Disassociate from the other — for example, deny association or common ground with the other; avoid sitting together.

Be disinterested, unconcerned, unsympathetic

Use inappropriate identity markers — for example, use title and surname when a close relationship pertains, or a nickname when a distant relationship pertains.

Use obscure or secretive language — for example, mystify the other with jargon, or use a code known to others in the group, but not the target.

Seek disagreement — select a sensitive topic.

Make the other feel uncomfortable — for example, do not avoid silence, joke, or use small talk.

Use taboo words — swear, or use abusive or profane language.

Call the other names — use derogatory nominations.

etc.

Negative impoliteness output strategies:

Frighten — instill a belief that action detrimental to the other will occur.

Condescend, scorn or ridicule — emphasize your relative power. Be contemptuous. Do not treat the other seriously. Belittle the other (e.g. use diminutives).

Invade the other's space — literally (e.g. position yourself closer to the other than the relationship permits) or metaphorically (e.g. ask for or speak about information which is too intimate given the relationship).

Explicitly associate the other with a negative aspect — personalize, use the pronouns 'I' and 'you'.

Put the other's indebtedness on record

etc.

There are other important means by which impoliteness can be transmitted. The structure of conversation itself is sensitive to violations. Brown and Levinson point out that

> '... turn-taking violations (interruptions, ignoring selection of other speakers, not responding to prior turn) are all FTAs in themselves, as are opening and closing procedures.' (1987: 233)

Moreover, we need to be aware of the fact that some areas of politeness are not well represented in Brown and Levinson's politeness model; otherwise those deficiencies could be carried over into an impoliteness framework. Their model is primarily geared to handling matters relating to linguistic form. A result of this, as they admit (1987: 11), is that impolite implicatures can slip through their framework. In contrast, Leech's politeness model is primarily concerned with linguistic content, and may be used to complement Brown and Levinson's model. Thus, reversing Leech's Politeness Principle (1983: 81), one general way of being impolite is to minimize the expression of polite beliefs and maximize the expression of impolite beliefs. Furthermore, Brown and Levinson have little to say about paralinguistic or non-verbal politeness. Avoiding eye-contact or shouting, for example, could be a means of conveying impoliteness.

6. Conclusion

In this paper I have brought together some ideas and observations about an area of discourse that has been much neglected. As Craig et al. (1986) argue, politeness theory needs to consider confrontational strategies, if it is to preserve analytical coherence. Furthermore, it is clear that in some circumstances impoliteness plays a key role, not a marginal one. This paper goes some way towards providing a framework that can capture this impoliteness. Many issues have been raised which could benefit from further research. For example: What factors lead to the interpretation that somebody is impolite? What factors influence the use of impoliteness in equal relationships? How do the impoliteness superstrategies relate to the degree of face attack of an act?

(Adapted from Jonathan Culpeper. 1996. Towards an anatomy of impoliteness. *Journal of Pragmatics* 25, pp. 349-367.)

Questions for Discussion

1. Would you exemplify what inherent impoliteness is?
2. Would you illustrate what mock impoliteness, or banter is?
3. Would you name some cases where interlocutors are genuinely impolite?
4. What impoliteness superstrategies are discussed in the paper?
5. How are these impoliteness superstrategies related to Brown and Levinson's politeness superstrategies?

Text E Geoffrey Neil Leech

Geoffrey Neil Leech (1936—2014) was educated at Tewkesbury Grammar School, Gloucestershire, and at University College London (UCL), where he was awarded a BA (1959) and PhD (1968). He began his teaching career at UCL, where he was influenced by Randolph Quirk and Michael Halliday as senior colleagues. He spent 1964-1965 as a Harkness Fellow at the Massachusetts Institute of Technology, Cambridge MA. In 1969 Leech moved to Lancaster University, UK, where he was Professor of English Linguistics from 1974 to 2001. In 2002 he became Emeritus Professor in the Department of Linguistics and English Language, Lancaster University. He was a Fellow of the British Academy, an Honorary Fellow of UCL and of Lancaster University, a Member of the Academia Europaea and the Norwegian Academy of Science and Letters, and an honorary doctor of three universities. He was not only the founder of the UCREL research centre for corpus linguistics at Lancaster University but also the first Professor and founding Head of the Department of Linguistics and English Language.

He was a specialist in English language and linguistics. He was the author, co-author or editor of over 30 books and over 120 published papers. His main academic interests were English grammar, corpus linguistics, stylistics, pragmatics and semantics. His contributions to linguistics — not only in pragmatics, but also in English grammar, corpus linguistics and stylistics — were immense.

Research

Leech's most important research contributions are the following:

- **English grammar**

Leech contributed to three team projects resulting in large-scale descriptive reference grammars of English, all published as lengthy single-volume works: *A Grammar of Contemporary English* (with Randolph Quirk, Sidney Greenbaum and Jan Svartvik, 1972); *A Comprehensive Grammar of the English Language* (with Randolph Quirk, Sidney Greenbaum and Jan Svartvik, 1985); and the *Longman Grammar of Spoken and Written English* (*LGSWE*) (with Douglas Biber, Stig Johansson, Susan Conrad and Edward Finegan, 1999). These grammars have been broadly regarded as providing an authoritative 'standard' account of English grammar, although the rather traditional framework employed has also been criticized — e.g. by Huddleston and Pullum (2002) in their *Cambridge Grammar of the English Language*.

- **Corpus linguistics**

Inspired by the corpus-building work of Randolph Quirk at UCL, soon after his arrival at Lancaster, Leech pioneered computer corpus development. He initiated the first electronic corpus of British English, completed in 1978 as the [Lancaster-Oslo-Bergen Corpus | Lancaster-Oslo/Bergen] (LOB) Corpus. Later, in the 1990s, he took a leading role in the compilation of the British National Corpus (BNC). The Lancaster research group that he co-founded (UCREL) also developed programs for the annotation of corpora: especially corpus taggers and parsers. The term treebank, now generally applied to a parsed corpus, was coined by Leech in the 1980s. The LGSWE grammar (1999) was systematically based on corpus analysis. Leech's more recent corpus research has centred on grammatical change in recent and contemporary English.

- **Stylistics**

Leech has written extensively on the stylistics of literary texts. The two stylistic works for which he is best known are *A Linguistic Guide to English Poetry* (1969) and *Style in Fiction* (1981; 2nd edn. 2007), co-authored with Mick Short. The latter book won the PALA25 Silver Jubilee Prize for 'the most influential book in stylistics since 1980'. The approach Leech has taken to literary style relies heavily on the concept of foregrounding, a term derived from P. L. Garvin's translation of the Czech term *aktualisace*, referring to the psychological prominence (against the background of ordinary language) of artistic effects in literature. In Leech's account, foregrounding in poetry is based on deviation from linguistic norms, which may take the form of unexpected irregularity (as in Dylan Thomas's *A grief ago*) as well as unexpected regularity (or parallelism — as in *I kissed thee ere I killed thee* from *Othello*). Further, Leech has distinguished three levels of deviation:

- *primary deviation:* deviation against the background of general linguistic norms;
- *secondary deviation:* deviation against the norms of conventional poetic regularity, as in metrical variation and run-on lines in verse;
- *tertiary deviation:* deviation against norms established within a literary text.

• Semantics

Leech's interest in semantics was strong in the period up to 1980, when it gave way to his interest in pragmatics. His PhD thesis at London University was on the semantics of place, time and modality in English, and was subsequently published under the title *Towards a Semantic Description of English* (1969). At a more popular level, he published *Semantics* (1974, 1981), in which the seven types of meaning discussed in Chapter 2 have been widely cited.

• Pragmatics

In the 1970s and 1980s Leech took a part in the development of pragmatics as a newly emerging subdiscipline of linguistics deeply influenced by the ordinary-language philosophers J. L. Austin, J. R. Searle and H. P. Grice. In his main book on the subject, *Principles of Pragmatics* (1983), he argued for a general account of pragmatics based on regulative principles following the model of Grice's (1975) Cooperative Principle (CP), with its constitutive maxims of Quantity, Quality, Relation and Manner. The part of the book that has had most influence is that dealing with the Principle of Politeness, seen as a principle having constituent maxims like Grice's CP. The politeness maxims Leech distinguished are: the Tact Maxim, Generosity Maxim, Approbation Maxim, Modesty Maxim, Agreement Maxim and Sympathy Maxim. This Gricean treatment of politeness has been much criticized: for example, it has been criticized for being 'expansionist' (adding new maxims to the Gricean model) rather than 'reductionist' (reducing Grice's four maxims to a smaller number, as in Relevance theory, where the Maxim of Relation, or principle of relevance, is the only one that survives). Leech is also criticized for allowing the addition of new maxims to be unconstrained (in defiance of Occam's Razor), and for his postulation of an 'absolute politeness' which does not vary according to situation, whereas most politeness theorists maintain that politeness cannot be identified out of context. In his article 'Politeness: Is there an East-West divide?' (2007), Leech addresses these criticisms and presents a revision of his politeness model.

Selected publications

- G. N. Leech (1969), *A Linguistic Guide to English Poetry*, London: Longman, pp.xiv +

240.
- R. Quirk, S. Greenbaum, G. Leech and J. Svartvik (1972), *A Grammar of Contemporary English*, London: Longman, pp.xii + 1120.
- G. Leech (1974), *Semantics*, London: Penguin, pp.xii + 386 (2nd edition, entitled *Semantics: the Study of Meaning*, 1981).
- G. Leech and J. Svartvik (1975), *A Communicative Grammar of English*, London: Longman, pp.324 (2nd and 3rd editions: 1994, 2002).
- G. N. Leech and M. H. Short (1981), *Style in Fiction: A Linguistic Introduction to English Fictional Prose*, London: Longman, pp. xiv + 402 (2nd edition, 2007).
- G. Leech, (1983), *Principles of Pragmatics*, London: Longman, pp.xiv + 250.
- R. Quirk, S. Greenbaum, G. Leech and J. Svartvik (1985), *A Comprehensive Grammar of the English Language*, London: Longman pp. xii + 1779.
- R. Garside, G. Leech and G. Sampson (eds.) (1987), *The Computational Analysis of English: A Corpus-based Approach*, London: Longman, pp. viii + 196.
- R. Garside, G. Leech and A. McEnery (eds.) (1997), *Corpus Annotation: Linguistic Information from Computer Text Corpora*, London: Longman, pp.x + 281.
- D. Biber, S. Johansson, G. Leech, S. Conrad and E. Finegan (1999), *Longman Grammar of Spoken and Written English*, London: Longman, pp.xxviii+1204.
- D. Biber, S. Conrad and G. Leech (2002), *Longman Student Grammar of Spoken and Written English.* London: Longman, pp.viii+487.
- G. Leech (2008) *Language in Literature: Style and Foregrounding.* Harlow, England: Pearson Longman, pp. xii+222.
- G. Leech, M. Hundt, C. Mair and N. Smith (2009) *Change in Contemporary English: A Grammatical Study*. Cambridge: Cambridge University Press, pp. xxx+341.

(Adapted from http://en.wikipedia.org/wiki/Geoffrey_Leech, and http://cass.lancs.ac.uk/?p=1358, Date of access: February 7, 2015)

Suggested Reading

Gu, Yueguo. 1990. Politeness Phenomena in Modern Chinese. *Journal of Pragmatics* 14: 237-257.

Leech, G. 2005. Politeness: Is There an East-West Divide? *Journal of Foreign Languages* (《外国语》) 6: 1-29.

Mey, J. L. 2001. *Pragmatics: An Introduction* (2nd ed.) [M]. Malden, MA: Blackwell. pp. 79-81.

Pecci, J. S. 2000. *Pragmatics*. Beijing: Foreign Language Teaching and Research Press. pp. 60-70.

Thomas, J. 2010. *Meaning in Interaction: An Introduction to Pragmatics*. Beijing: Foreign Language Teaching and Research Press. pp. 78-84.

Yule, G. 1996. *Pragmatics*. Oxford: Oxford University Press. pp. 50-51; 59-69.

Unit 9
Macropragmatics

> Every word has its fragrance: there is a harmony and a disharmony of fragrances, and hence of words.
> — Friedrich Nietzsche
>
> Man acts as though he were the shaper and master of language, while in fact language remains the master of man.
> — Martin Heidegger

Objectives

- To understand what macropragmatics covers
- To comprehend the distinction between micropragmatics and macropragmatics
- To learn how to approach pragmatics from a social, cultural and cognitive perspective
- To learn the academic notions about macropragmatics
- To improve critical thinking and intercultural communicative competence and comprehensive language skills
- To improve pragmatic competence, academic ability and relevant language skills

Before You Read

1. Suppose you were an exchange student in Sweden. You go to the hairdresser's and notice a sign on the wall saying:

   No Tipping, Please.

   Yet underneath the sign there is a small plate with coins and bills. You will immediately notice the discrepancy between what the sign says and what in fact happens. What do you think you will do in such a situation? (Hint: Which has a stronger effect on your decision, the sign or the plate?)

2. In what case can Chomsky's classical *Colourless green ideas sleep furiously* be put to use?

3. When you are making a request, what factors affect your wording?

4. How do you interpret the following lines of a poem?

蛀穿一张白纸，仅动用
三千多天失眠的蚕
邮票的突发奇想
源于一场感冒
晚秋的风太凉
……
　　　　——《绝响》（舒婷）

Start to Read

Text A　Variability, Negotiability and Adaptability

Using language must consist of *the continuous making of linguistic choices*, consciously or unconsciously, for language-internal (i.e. structural) and/or language-external reasons. These choices can be situated at any level of linguistic form: phonetic/phonological, morphological, syntactic, lexical, semantic. They may range over variety-internal options, or they may involve regionally, socially or functionally distributed types of variation. A theory

of language use should, therefore, be able to make sense of this 'making of choices'.

It seems that at least three, hierarchically related key notions are needed to understand the process of 'making choices' as the base-line description of language use. They are variability, negotiability and adaptability. Let us try to define them briefly.

Variability is *the property of language which defines the range of possibilities from which choices can be made*. More than two decades ago, Hymes said that 'in the study of language as a mode of action, variation is a clue and a key' (1974: 75). This statement may most readily evoke what is traditionally called 'varieties of language', whether defined geographically, socially or functionally. But given our pragmatic perspective on language use or verbal action, the statement remains true after generalizing the notion of variability to the entire range of variable options (also those that are strictly speaking 'variety'-internal) that must be assumed to be accessible to language users for them to be able to 'make choices'. The sexually harassed employee would not have been upset about the manager's *His behaveour is no doubt objectionable* if she had not had access to a wider range of options for adequately describing 'his behaviour', some of which were more suitable not only to her own emotional response but also to her assessment of what corporate policy should be in relation to the protection of her integrity, and if she had not assumed that the manager had the same access. Any change in this constellation — note that we are *really* talking about variability – could have made the employee adapt her interpretive choices and her subsequent reaction. For instance, knowing that the manager did not have access to the same range of options because of a less developed proficiency in English, she might have been satisfied with the phrasing of the verdict. Similar satisfaction might have resulted from an awareness that corporate policy banned words such as *unacceptable* and *outrage* from the vocabulary of managers, thus putting real limits on available options. The notion of variability must be taken so seriously that the range of possible choices cannot be seen as anything static or stable. It is not fixed once and for all; rather, it is constantly changing. It would be a mistake, moreover, to place this element of 'change' exclusively on a wide diachronic dimension. At any given moment in the course of interaction, a choice may rule out alternatives or create new ones for the current purposes of the exchange — though these effects can always be renegotiated, which brings us to our second key notion.

Negotiability is *the property of language responsible for the fact that choices are not made mechanically or according to strict rules or fixed form-function relationships, but rather on the basis of highly flexible principles and strategies*. Thus there is no rule that tells you when to choose I'm reasonably satisfied over I am not dissatisfied, representing two distinct logical forms of expression for a comparable state of mind; but there is a (manipulable) principle saying that the form with the double negation, even if it rules out real negation, is further down the negative end of the positive-negative scale than the utterance that avoids negation altogether. There is a long tradition in linguistics to contrast different structures and to relate them to each other on a scale of grammaticality and/or acceptability, marking the clearly ungrammatical or unacceptable cases with an asterisk. Negotiability is so strong, however, that pragmatics does not lend itself to this asterisk approach. Although it makes perfect sense for pragmatics to look at the possible as well as at the actual to learn about the principles of language use, a search for the limits of what is possible, i.e. the impossible (which, if found, would turn the principles and strategies into real rules), is futile. Remember Russell's classical example of an impossible, or meaningless, utterance, *Quadrilaterality drinks procrastination*, which was soon made to refer to post-WWII four-power meetings which failed to produce desirable results at a desirable speed. Even Chomsky's equally classical *Colourless green ideas sleep furiously* could be put to use if need be. Or look at what Meredith Quartermain does in poetry:

> Air
>   horse lips
>   breath
> hair
> on flat-palmed apple
> (From *Terms of sale*, Buffalo: Meow Press, 1996)

For all practical intents and purposes, this is a real utterance in English. Even if it is the business of poets to break the rules of language or to expand its potential, that does not make their poetry any less part of the language they are using. Brushing this aside as too exceptional to be relevant would be to put on a blindfold and might prevent us from seeing important aspects of the more mundane functioning of language.

Negotiability also implies indeterminacy of various kinds. First of all, there is indeterminacy in the choice-making on the side of the language producer. Language users operate under the constraint of having to make choices no matter whether they correspond exactly to their needs or not.

Second, there is also indeterminacy of choice on the side of the interpreter. Whatever is said can be interpreted in many ways, one of the reasons being that choices do not necessarily exclude their alternatives from the world of interpretation.

Third, indeterminacy is also involved because choices, once made, whether on the production or on the interpretation side, can be permanently renegotiated.

If using language consists of the continuous making linguistic choices from a wide and unstable range of variable possibilities in a manner which is not rule-governed, but driven by highly flexible principles and strategies, as well as permanently negotiable, it is only natural to ask how it is still possible then for language to be used successfully for purposes of communication. This is where our third key notion, adaptability, comes in - not as an explanation, but as a property which we must assume language to have in order for us to be able to understand that a certain degree of success can be achieved in verbal communication. But before going into this more deeply it should be pointed out that there is no reason to eulogize the powers of language. The properties of language use to which we have drawn attention so far, carry in them a guarantee of communicative difficulties and failure. We should realize that communicative success, except in some purely practical areas (or spheres of human activity, to borrow Bakhtin's term), is always extremely relative and can never be taken for granted.

Adaptability, then *is the property of language which enables human beings to make negotiable linguistic choices from a variable range of possibilities in such a way as to approach points of satisfaction for communicative needs*. This definition calls for a few caveats immediately. First of all, reference to 'communicative needs' does not mean that the needs served by language use all have to be 'communicative' in the strict sense of the word. Though we take the position that just about all language use is in some sense communicative (even if only one person is involved), we do not want to make this into a point of faith on which everything that follows should depend; we do allow for ways of using language that at least come close to being purely expressive without any communicative intent or effect. Second, the phrase 'communicative needs' may sound as if it meant to refer to needs that are somehow 'general'. We should stress, therefore, that the 'needs' in question mostly arise in context and can therefore be quite specific. Third, not that 'satisfaction' in the above definition is only 'approached' — which may happen to varying degrees. That term, moreover, should not be interpreted as precluding the possibility - already clearly offered earlier — of serious communication failure nor the incidence of circumstances under which there is a need for non-communication or even miscommunication.

Finally, adaptability *should not be interpreted unidirectionally*. The term itself may be conducive to a simplified vision of language choices being made in accordance with pre-existent circumstances. That, too, is involved. But it is not where the story ends. The other side of the coin is that circumstances also get changed by, or adapted to, the choices that are made. Consider, for instance, systems of politeness which are shaped by and simultaneously shape social relationships. The choice of a system of solidarity politeness (*tu*, first name, etc.) as opposed to a system of deference politeness (*vous*, family name, title, etc.) is typically based on closeness between the interlocutors. But when the closeness is absent, speakers may nevertheless opt for solidarity politeness. By doing so, an appearance of closeness is created to such an extent that it may be impossible to retreat from it without over hostility. After having spoken to someone on a first-name basis before, a switch to more formal forms of address can only be made for special reasons and will therefore carry extra (implicit) meaning. Typically, either playfulness or antagonism would be involved. In the latter case, the choices might be regarded as very impolite indeed, in spite of the objectively higher degree of politeness that would usually be associated with the linguistic choices involved. This example is at the same time an extra illustration of the negotiability of linguistic choice-making, or the lack of fixed form-function relationships.

The three notions we have introduced in this section are fundamentally inseparable.

They do not represent topics of investigation, but merely interrelated properties of the overall object of investigation for linguistic pragmatics, the functionality or meaningful functioning of language. Their hierarchical ranking is but a conceptual tool to come to grips with the complexity of pragmatic phenomena, which will allow us to use the higher-order notion of 'adaptability' as the point of reference in further theory formation and empirical research, keeping in mind that it has no content without both variability and negotiability.

(Adapted from Jef Verschueren. 2000. *Understanding Pragmatics*. pp. 55-63.)

Text B Pragmatic Acts and Action Theory

When we look at pragmatic acts from two points of view: that of the agent, and that of the act. As far as the individual *agent* is concerned, there are his or her class, gender, age, education, previous life history and so on. These are the factors identified by the ethnomethodologists under the caption of 'MR' ('member resources'), namely, the resources that people dispose of as members of the community; with regard to communication, these resources are 'often referred to as background knowledge' (Fairclough, 1989: 141). Another way of characterizing such resources is as constraints and affordances, imposed on the individual in the form of necessary limitations on the degrees of freedom that he or she is allowed in society.

The other point of view is that of the act; here, we are particularly interested in the language that is used in performing a pragmatic act. The question has two aspects: from the individual's perspective, I can ask what language I can use to perform a specific act; from the perspective of the context, the question is what language can be used to create the conditions for me to perform a pragmatic act.

As to the former perspective, following Verschueren (1987, 1999), we may invoke the *adaptability* of language, by which the individual members of society rely on language as their principal tool to adapt to the ever-changing conditions surrounding them and, in doing so, 'generate meaning', as Verschueren calls it (1999: 147). As to the latter perspective, the traditional speech acts are among the tools that we have at our disposal to control our environment, respectively adapt to it in various ways. As Levinson aptly remarks, the function of a promise as a speech act is to put one context to work to change another: speech acts are functions from context to context (1983: 276).

More specifically, Verschueren (1999: 149), in dealing with adaptability and linguistic choices, distinguishes among three ways of choosing the appropriate ('well-adapted') linguistic means: one is to appeal to the actual circumstances legitimating a particular choice, as they appear in the presuppositions that I am able to recognize (e.g., uttering 'I'm sorry to hear about your dog' presupposes that something bad has happened to the other's dog); another is to create, or invent, the circumstances that make a particular choice appropriate, as it happens in the case of conversational implicatures (e.g., asking at a newsstand 'Do you have the *Herald Tribune*?' implies that I want to buy the newspaper); and finally, an utterance may be well adapted only to certain circumstances that have to be actualized before the act becomes possible, suitable, legally binding or otherwise effective. For a typical case, consider the administering of the sacraments in the church, where the speech act 'I baptize thee' becomes effective *ex opere operato*, that is, contingent upon the pragmatic 'act having been performed': the baptismal formula depends, for its effect, on the actual flowing of the water on the body of the person to be baptized.

In all these cases, the pragmatic acting can be considered as *adapting* oneself, linguistically and otherwise, to one's world. And rightly so: in the final analysis, all our acting is done in that world, and within the *affordances* it puts at our disposal.

A pragmatic view of speech acting serves to replace, or at least readjust, the earlier focus on the individual speech acts as our unique (or at least, chief) means of verbal control of, and adaptation to, the environment. In pragmatic acting it is impossible to pinpoint a particular, predetermined use of any canonical speech act. Thus, when people practice 'indirect denial' or 'co-opting', the speech acts used are not commensurate with the pragmatic acts performed.

For the same reason, pragmatic acts cannot be simply considered to be some particular subtype of the indirect speech acts. For example, in a dinner-table situation, there is a difference between an indirect request such as:

Can you pass me the salt?
(compare the direct request 'Pass the salt')

And 'hints' or 'prompts' such as:

I'd like some salt.
or:
Isn't this soup rather bland?

Both the latter utterances can be seen as efforts to have somebody pass the salt, yet neither of them 'counts as' a request; rather, they are pre-sequences to requests ('pre-requests', to be exact), that somehow obtain the desired result most of the time, even without having to be developed into full-blown requests: the salt is passed on.

While speech acts, when uttered in contexts, are pragmatic acts, pragmatic acts need not be speech acts (not even indirect ones). A theory of action explains this by appealing to the 'underlying goal orientation' among the participants in the discourse (Jacobs and Jackson, 1983: 291), and which manifests itself in their interactional goals. The interpretation of a particular utterance relies on these interactional goals, a less interesting subset of which are the purely communicational ones. Thus, the hinting and prompting utterances in the example above are interesting not as informative statements (A: 'I'd like some salt'; B: 'Thank you for sharing this with me'), but as pre-requests to a request which is usually not formulated, and maybe not even needed for the interaction to be successful.

The developmental aspects of language use seem to bear this out as well. Children learn to deal with pragmatic acts long before they discover the existence of 'real' speech acts. The proper framing of a pragmatic sequence is often sufficient to obtain the right result, as every educator knows. In this context, even 'doing nothing' can figure as a recognized (pragmatic) act; compare the familiar story of Joshua and his mom:

MOTHER (calling out the window to child in yard): Joshua, what are you doing?
JOSHUA: Nothing ...
MOTHER: Will you stop it immediately!

Joshua's pragmatic act in this interchange could be described as trying to get out ('opt out') of a conversational minefield. And since there is no speech act (let alone a speech act verb) 'to nothing' (even though the philosopher Martin Heidegger did invent a word for it: '*Das Nichts nichtet*', literally: 'The nothing nots'; which can happen only in German), the next best thing is to use words that say as little as possible, in fact 'nothing'. One is reminded of Christopher Robin going off 'to do nothing':

What I like best is doing nothing ... It's when people call out at you just as you're going off to do it, 'What are you going to do, Christopher Robin?' and you say, 'Oh, nothing', and then you go and do it. (A. A. Milne, *The House at Pooh Corner*, ch. 10)

Learning how to manage speech acts, including their 'correct' verbal uptake, occurs later in the child's life than learning to respond to them in the form of an appropriate action. The individual speech acts, such as literal responses to requests, are acquired later than are appropriate reactions to pragmatic acts. As Jacobs and Jackson conclude, 'children have to learn that a literal response is possible' (1983: 295).

(Excerpted from Jacob Mey. 2001. *Pragmatics: An Introduction.* pp. 214-7.)

After You Read

Knowledge Focus

1. Decide whether the following statements are true or false based on Text A and Text B.

1) According Verschueren, language users can make choices based on three properties of language: variability, defeasibility and adaptability.
2) Adaptability is the property of language responsible for the fact that choices are not made mechanically or according to strict rules or fixed form-function relationships, but rather on the basis of highly flexible principles and strategies.
3) Adaptability should be interpreted unidirectionally.
4) Ethnomethodologists assume that member resources are the resources that people

dispose of as members of the community.

5) Pragmatic acts may not be speech acts, not even indirect ones.

2. Discuss the following questions with your partner.

1) In what aspects are the central ideas in this unit different from the ones in previous units?

2) Would you elaborate and exemplify variability, negotiability and adaptability? Are they related in any way?

3) What does it mean by 'pragmatic act'?

4) Would you illustrate the relationship of a pragmatic act and a speech act?

5) What does the author use Heidegger's example 'Das Nichts nichtet' to show in the Text B?

Language Focus

1. Fill in the blanks with words or expressions in Text A and Text B.

1) Using language must consist of the continuous making of linguistic _____, consciously or unconsciously, for language-internal (i.e. structural) and/or language-external reasons.

2) These choices can be situated at any level of linguistic _____: phonetic/phonological, morphological, syntax, lexical, semantic.

3) Adaptability, _____ and variability are the three key notions to understand the process of 'making choices' as the base-line description of language use.

4) _____ is also involved because choices, once made, whether on the production or on the interpretation side, can be permanently renegotiated.

5) We can look at pragmatic acts from two points of view: that of the agent, and that of the _____.

6) _____ is the property of language which defines the range of possibilities from which choices can be made.

7) As far as the individual _____ is concerned, there is his or her class, gender, age, education, previous life history and so on.

8) A pragmatic view of speech acting serves to replace, or at least readjust, the earlier focus on the individual speech acts as our unique (or at least, chief) means of verbal control of, and adaptation to, the _____.

9) In all these cases, the pragmatic acting can be considered as _____ oneself, linguistically and otherwise, to one's world.

10) Speech acts, when uttered in contexts, are _____ acts.

2. Translate the following passage into English.

Verschueren 认为使用语言是一个不断选择语言的过程。语言使用者之所以能够在使用语言时做出种种恰当的选择，是因为语言具有变异性、商讨性和顺应性。语言的变异性是指语言具有一系列可供选择的可能性；商讨性是指所有的选择都不是机械地或严格按照形式 - 功能关系做出的，而是在高度灵活的原则和策略基础上完成的；顺应性是指语言能够让其使用者从可供选择的项目中做灵活的变通，从而满足交际的需要。根据顺应论，要从以下四个方面描述和解释语言的使用：即语境关系的顺应 (contextual correlates of adaptability)、语言结构的顺应 (structural objects of adaptability)、顺应的动态性 (dynamics of adaptability) 和顺应过程的意识程度 (salience of the adaptation processes)。

3. Translate the following passage into Chinese.

Recent pragmatic theories follow two main lines: the cognitive-philosophical line and the sociocultural-interactional line. In pragmatic interpretation the cognitive-philosophical line of research appears to put more emphasis on the proposition expressed (e.g. Horn, 2005; Levinson 2000) while the socio-cultural-interactional line (e.g. Verschueren, 1999; Mey, 2001) emphasizes the importance of allowing socio-cultural context into linguistic analysis. *Cognitive-philosophical pragmatics*, often called Anglo-American pragmatics (as represented by neo-Gricean pragmatics, Relevance theory, and speech-act theory), is based on the centrality of intentions in communication. According to this approach, communication is constituted by recipient design and intention recognition. In contrast, the *sociocultural-interactional* paradigm questions the centrality of intention, considers it 'problematic,' and underlines its equivocality. According to this view, communication is not always dependent on speaker intentions in the Gricean sense. In fact, one of the main differences between the cognitive-philosophical approach and the sociocultural-interactional approach is that the former considers intention an a priori mental state of speakers that underpins communication, while the latter regards intention as a post factum construct that is achieved jointly through the dynamic emergence of meaning in conversation. In this process socio-cultural factors play the leading role. Since the two approaches represent two different perspectives, it would be difficult to reject either of them *in toto*.

Comprehensive Work

1. The following are some signs prohibiting smoking in pubic. Work in groups and discuss in what ways they are different in the choice of wording (Note that in one case no word is used). Find similar cases in everyday use of language, and discuss your findings with your classmates, then make a presentation to the class.

2. Record or note down the address forms in daily life (in a supermarket, a fast food restaurant, or a hotel, etc.) or in an institutional environment (a hospital, a business, or a university, etc.). Analyse your findings.

3. Make a contrastive study of the ways of blaming that American adults address to young children. Collect data from American movies or TV series and find whether blaming varies with age or gender, or any other social factors. (Note in what ways the

expressions that the blaming parents use with their own children and those they use with others' children could be different.)

Further Readings

Text C Intercultural Pragmatics

1. Definition

Intercultural Pragmatics is a relatively new field of inquiry that concerns how the language system is put to use in social encounters between human beings who have different first languages, communicate in a common language, and, usually, represent different cultures (Kecskes, 2004, 2010). The communicative process in these encounters is synergistic in the sense that it is a merger in which pragmatic norms of each participant are represented to some extent. Intercultural pragmatics represents a sociocognitive perspective on communication in which individual prior experience and actual situational experience conditioned by socio-cultural factors are equally important in meaning construction and comprehension. Research in intercultural pragmatics has four main foci: (1) interaction between native speakers and non-native speakers of a language, (2) lingua franca communication in which none of the interlocutors has the same L1, (3) multilingual discourse, and (4) language use and development of individuals who speak more than one language. The study of intercultural pragmatics supports a less idealized, more down-to-earth approach to communication than current pragmatic theories usually do. Whilst not denying the decisive role of cooperation, context, and politeness in communication, intercultural pragmatics also gives equal importance to egocentrism, chaos, aggression, trial-and-error, and salience in the analysis of language production.

2. Theoretical framework

Intercultural pragmatics relies on interculturality and adopts a sociocognitive approach (SCA) to pragmatics that takes into account both the societal and individual factors, including cooperation and egocentrism, which, as claimed here, are not antagonistic phenomena in interaction (Kecskes, 2008, 2010a).

2.1 The sociocognitive approach (SCA)

Before describing the main tenets of SCA a clear distinction should be made between Kecskes' approach and van Dijk's understanding of the sociocognitive view in language use.

Van Dijk (2008: x) said that in his theory it is not the social situation that influences (or is influenced by) discourse, but the way the participants define the situation. He goes further and claims that 'contexts are not some kind of objective conditions or direct cause, but rather (inter)subjective constructs designed and ongoingly updated in interaction by participants as members of groups and communities' (*ibid.*). SCA adopts a more dialectical perspective by considering communication a dynamic process in which individuals are not only constrained by societal conditions but also shape them at the same time. Speakers and hearers are equal participants of the communicative process. They both produce and comprehend speech, relying on their most accessible and salient knowledge expressed in their private contexts in both production and comprehension. Consequently, only a holistic interpretation of utterance and discourse from the perspective of both the speaker and hearer can give us an adequate account of language communication. It is very important that we realize that there are social conditions and constraints (contexts) that have some objectivity from the perspective of individuals. Of course, there can always be slight differences in how individuals process those relatively objective societal factors based on their prior experience. But it would be a mistake to deny the presence of any objectivity in social contexts.

When language is used, its unique property is activated in two ways. When people speak or write, they craft what they need to express to fit the situation or context in which they are communicating. But, at the same time, the way people speak or write the words, expressions, and utterances they use create that very situation, context, socio-cultural frame in which the given communication occurs. Consequently, two things seem to happen simultaneously: people attempt to fit their language to a situation or context that their language, in turn, helped to create in the first place (e.g. Gee, 1999).

This dynamic behavior of human speech and reciprocal process between language and context basically eliminates the need to ask the ever-returning question: Which comes first – the situation the speakers are in (e.g. faculty meeting, car renting, dinner ordering, etc.) or the particular language that is used in the given situation (expressions and utterances representing ways of talking and interacting)? *Is this a 'car rental' because participants are acting and speaking that way, or are they acting and speaking that way because this is a 'car rental'?* Acting and speaking in a particular way constitutes social situations, socio-cultural frames, and these frames require the use of a particular language. 'Which comes first?' does not seem to be a relevant question synchronically. Social and cultural routines result in recurring activities and institutions (e.g. Schank, 1982; Schank and Abelson, 1977). However, these institutions and routinized activities have to be rebuilt continuously in the here and now.

The question is whether these cultural models, institutions, and frames exist outside language or not. The social constructivists insist that models and frames have to be rebuilt again and again so it is just our impression that they exist outside language. However, the sociocognitive approach argues that these cultural mental models have some kind of psychological reality in the individual mind, and when a concrete situation occurs the appropriate model is recalled, which supports the appropriate verbalization of triggered thoughts and activities. Of course, building and rebuilding our world occurs not merely through language but through the interaction of language with other real-life phenomena such as non-linguistic symbol systems, objects, tools, technologies, etc.

The sociocognitive perspective on communication and pragmatics (Kecskes, 2002, 2008, 2010; Kecskes and Zhang, 2009) unites the societal and individual features of communication, and considers communication a dynamic process in which individuals are both constrained by and shape societal conditions (see above). In this paradigm, communication is driven by the interplay of *cooperation* required by societal conditions and *egocentrism* that is rooted in prior experience of the individual. Consequently, egocentrism and cooperation are not mutually exclusive phenomena. They are both present in all stages of communication to a different extent because they represent the individual and societal traits of the dynamic process of communication.

On the one hand speakers and hearers are constrained by societal conditions but as individuals they all have their own goals, intention, desire, etc. that are freely expressed and recognized in the flow of interaction.

In the sociocognitive approach framed by the dynamic model of meaning (Kecskes, 2008; Kecskes and Zhang, 2009) communication is characterized by the interplay of two traits that are inseparable, mutually supportive, and interactive:

Individual trait:	*Social trait:*
attention	intention
private experience	actual situational experience
egocentrism	cooperation
salience	relevance

Communication is the result of interplay of intention and attention motivated by sociocultural background that is privatized by the individuals. The sociocultural background is composed of dynamic knowledge of interlocutors deriving from their prior experience encapsulated in the linguistic expressions they use, and current experience in which those expressions create and convey meaning.

This sociocognitive approach integrates the pragmatic view of cooperation and the cognitive view of egocentrism and emphasizes that both cooperation and egocentrism are manifested in all phases of communication to a varying extent. While cooperation is an intention-directed practice and measured by relevance, egocentrism is an attention-oriented trait and measured by salience. Intention and attention are identified as two measurable forces that affect communication in a systematic way. The measurement of intention and attention by means of relevance and salience is distinct from earlier explanations (e.g. Sperber and Wilson, 1986; Wilson and Sperber, 2004).

2.2 Interculturality

Interculturality is a crucial notion for intercultural pragmatics. We should define interculturality in communication and separate it from intraculturality. There have been several attempts to explain the difference between the two terms. According to Samovar and Porter (2001) 'intracultural communication' is 'the type of communication that takes place between members of the same dominant culture, but with slightly different values', as opposed to 'intercultural communication', which is the communication between two or more distinct cultures. This approach has led to a common mistake that several researchers have committed. They have considered interculturality as the main reason for miscommunication. In fact, some researchers' findings show the opposite. The use of semantically transparent language by non-native speakers results in fewer misunderstandings and communication breakdowns than expected. The insecurity experienced by lingua franca speakers make them establish a unique set of rules for interaction which may be referred to as an 'interculture,' according to Koole and Ten Thije (1994: 69), a 'culture constructed in cultural contact'.

Blum-Kulka *et al*. (2008: 164) defined interculturality as 'a contingent interactional accomplishment' from a discursive-constructivist perspective. They argued that a growing literature explores interculturality as a participant concern. Nishizaka (1995) pointed out that interculturality is a situationally emergent rather than a normatively fixed phenomenon. The sociocognitive approach (Kecskes, 2008; Kecskes, 2010a; Kecskes and Zhang, 2009) explained in the previous section goes one step further and defines interculturality as a phenomenon that is not only interactionally and socially constructed in the course of communication but also relies on relatively definable cultural models and norms that represent the speech communities to which the interlocutors belong. Consequently, interculturality has both relatively normative and emergent components. In order for us to understand the dynamism and ever-changing nature of intercultural encounters we need to approach interculturality dialectically. Cultural constructs and models change diachronically, while cultural representation and speech production by individuals changes synchronically. *Interculturality is a situationally emergent and co-constructed phenomenon that relies both on relatively definable cultural norms and models as well as situationally evolving features* (Kecskes, 2011). Intercultures are ad hoc creations. They are created in a communicative process in which cultural norms and models brought into the interaction from prior experience of interlocutors blend with features created ad hoc in the interaction in a synergetic way. The result is intercultural discourse, in which there is mutual transformation of knowledge and communicative behavior rather than transmission.

Interculturality has both a *prior side* and *an emergent side*, which occur and act simultaneously in the communicative process. Consequently, *intercultures* are not fixed phenomena but are created in the course of communication in which participants belong to different L1 speech communities, speak a common language, and represent different cultural norms and models that are defined by their respective L1 speech communities. The following conversation between a Brazilian girl and a Polish woman illustrates this point well.

Brazilian: And what do you do?

Pole: I work at the university as a cleaner.

B: As a janitor?

P: No, not yet. Janitor is after the cleaner.

B: You want to be a janitor?

P: Of course.

In this conversation interlocutors represent two different languages and cultures (Brazilian and Polish), and use English as a lingua franca. This is the prior knowledge that participants bring to the interaction. They create an interculture, which belongs to neither of them but emerges in the course of conversation. Within this interculture the two speakers have a smooth conversation about the job of the Polish woman. Neither of them is sure what the right term is for the job the Polish woman has. There are no misunderstandings in the interaction because each participant is careful to use semantically transparent language in order to be as clear as possible. The Polish woman sets up a 'hierarchy' that is non-existing in the target language culture ('cleaner → janitor'). However, this is an emergent element of the interculture the interlocutors have been constructing.

Intercultures come and go, so they are neither stable nor permanent. They just occur. They are both synergetic and blended. Interculturality is constituted on the spot by interlocutors who participate in the conversation. But isn't this a phenomenon that also occurs in intracultural communication? Why and how should we distinguish intercultural communication from intracultural communication? Basically the currently dominant approach to this issue is that there is no *principled* difference between intracultural and intercultural communication (e.g. Wittgenstein, 2001). This is true as far as the mechanism of the communicative process is concerned. However, there is a qualitative difference in the nature and content of an intracultural interaction and an intercultural interaction. Speakers in intracultural communication rely on prior knowledge and culture of a relatively definable speech community, which is privatized by individuals belonging to that speech community. No language boundaries are crossed, however subcultures are relied upon and representations are individualized. What is created on the spot enriches the given culture, contributes to it, and remains within the fuzzy but still recognizable confines of that language and culture.

In the case of intercultural communication, however, prior knowledge that is brought into and privatized in the communicative process belongs to different cultures and languages, and what participants create on the spot will disappear and not become an enrichment and/ or addition to any particular culture or language. Intercultures are ad hoc creations that may enhance the individual and the globalization process but can hardly be said to contribute to any particular culture. This is exactly what we see in example (1) above. Speakers created a hierarchy between 'cleaner' and 'janitor' just to create common ground and assure their own mutual private understanding of a given situation. However, this interculture usually disappears when they stop talking. Intercultures can also be recurring for a while in certain cases such as international negotiating teams, international classrooms, international tourist groups, etc. Kasper and Blum-Kulka (1993) talked about 'intercultural style', which means that speakers fully competent in two languages may create an intercultural style of speaking that is both related to and distinct from the styles prevalent in the two substrata, a style on which they rely regardless of the language being used. Kasper and Blum-Kulka (1993) claimed that the hypothesis is supported by many studies of cross-cultural communication, especially those focusing on interactional sociolinguistics (e.g. Gumperz, 1982; Tannen 1985) and research into the pragmatic behavior of immigrant populations across generations (e.g. Clyne *et al.*, 1991).

3. Crossing language boundaries

An example of intracultural communication would be if a dentist in the dominant culture, say, in the United States, spoke about dental issues with a plumber belonging to the same U.S. culture. Their negotiation may not be entirely smooth because the plumber might not be very knowledgeable about dental terms. If, however, the dentist speaks with another dentist about dental issues they would certainly understand each other's language use quite well, although still there might be individual differences. This is what prompts the argument that a U.S. dentist would understand an English-speaking French dentist better than she would understand an English native-speaker plumber. However, we must be very careful with judgments like this. One intercultural situation may differ from another intracultural situation to a great extent. I have argued elsewhere (Kecskes, 2010b: 9) that it is important to make a distinction between a *quantitative change* and a *qualitative change*, and between changes occurring within a culture or across cultures. If a person moves from Albany, New York to New Orleans, Louisiana, and makes adjustments to the new Louisiana subculture, he may start to say things like 'I might could do this.' This scenario, however, cannot be compared *qualitatively* to the case where a person moves from Albany, New York to Lille, France. In the first case we can speak about peripheral rather than core changes in the language use of the person. Louisiana culture and Upstate New York culture can be considered subcultures of American culture, and Louisiana dialect and the Upstate New York dialect are dialects of American English. However, the change is different when a person moves from Albany, New York to Lille, France. Upstate New York dialect compares to the Picard dialect of Lille differently than to the Louisiana dialect. In this case we speak about dialects of different languages (English and French) while in the first case we speak about dialects of the same language (English). *There is a qualitative difference between crossing language boundaries and crossing dialects* (but staying within the confines of the core of one particular language).

The same is true for cultures. The relationship between American and French cultures qualitatively differs from the relationship between Louisiana subculture and Upstate New York subculture. English–French bilingualism may create qualitatively different changes in the mind and behavior of a person than Louisiana–Upstate New York bidialectalism (Kecskes, 2010b). I would like to emphasize that this view does not represent a homogenous approach to language and culture. Languages and cultures are never homogenous. *What is temporarily and relatively homogenous–like is the linguistic faculty (language system) that changes diachronically while language use changes synchronically.*

There is another major difference between intracultural and intercultural communication. Intracultural communication is dominated by preferred ways of saying things and preferred ways of organizing thoughts within a particular speech community (Kecskes, 2008). This is not the case in intercultural communication because the development of 'preferred ways' requires time and conventionalization within a speech community. Human languages are very flexible. They can lexicalize whatever their speakers find important to lexicalize. There are preferred ways of lexicalizing certain actions, phenomena, and things. Americans 'shoot a film', 'dust the furniture', 'make love', 'do the dishes', etc. One language has a word for a phenomenon that is important in that culture, and the other does not. In Russian they have the word *spargal'ki* to denote tools for cheating in school. In Hungarian the same phenomenon is denoted by the word *puska*, which can be translated into English as *gun*. However, we have no word for this phenomenon (tools for cheating in school) in American English. (British English has 'cribs', 'crib notes').

Knowing what expressions to select, what is appropriate or inappropriate in different situations, may be an important sign of *group-inclusiveness,* and 'native-likeness' (which is a notion with negative connotations nowadays). In intercultural communication this group-inclusiveness is created on the spot by speakers with different linguistic and cultural backgrounds who can hardly rely on the advantageous use of formulaic and figurative elements of a common language. In an empirical study Kecskes (2008) demonstrated that in lingua franca communication the use of formulaic language by the participants was less than 10 percent. Lingua franca speakers relied on semantically transparent language to make sure that their interlocutor could follow what they said. They also do this because they may not have had enough encounters with the target language and culture to be able to conventionalize the 'preferred ways of saying things' and 'preferred ways of organizing thoughts'.

In sum, it is erroneous to think that intercultural communication differs from intracultural communication because the former is more complicated than the latter, and the former leads to more miscommunication than the other. As we saw above, the dissimilarity is qualitative rather than quantitative, because there is a qualitative difference between crossing language boundaries and crossing dialects.

(Excerpted from Istvan Kecskes. 2012. Sociopragmatics and cross-cultural and intercultural studies. In K. Allan and Kasia M. Jaszczolt (eds.). *The Cambridge Handbook of Pragmatics.* pp. 608-615.)

Questions for Discussion

1. What is Kesckes' definition of intercultural pragmatics?
2. What are the differences between Kesckes' approach and van Dijk's understanding of the sociocognitive view in language use?
3. What are the main tenets of SCA?
4. Would you make a distinction between intracultural and intercultural communication?

Text D Variational Pragmatics

Intercultural pragmatics is usually associated with pragmatic differences between different languages. This seems to be the default reading of the term. However, this reading tacitly ignores that there is no one-to-one relationship between languages and cultures. Speakers who share the same native language do not necessarily share the same culture. For instance, native speakers of English in Ireland and the United States use language in different ways (e.g., Schneider, 1999, 2008). Neither do Americans in the US all use English in the same way. On the other hand, cultures may be shared by speakers with different native languages. Thus, as language use in interaction is shaped by cultural values, pragmatic similarities may occur across languages, while pragmatic differences may occur across varieties of the same language.

Variational pragmatics is a subdiscipline of intercultural pragmatics. Other subdisciplines include contrastive pragmatics, cross-cultural pragmatics, ethnopragmatics, interlanguage pragmatics, and postcolonial pragmatics. Contrastive pragmatics is concerned with inter-lingual differences, i.e., with pragmatic variation between different languages. Cross-cultural pragmatics, on the other hand, compares the ways in which different languages are used in communication. It also deals with native speaker — non-native speaker interaction and with lingua franca communication. Ethnopragmatics is concerned with explaining speech practices in terms of a culture-internal perspective (e.g., in terms of values) rather than in terms of presumed pragmatic universals. Interlanguage pragmatics focuses on the specific nature of language use conventions in learner language, e.g., in the English as a foreign language spoken by native speakers of German, and also on the acquisition of these conventions by learners . The use of second (as opposed to foreign) languages in interaction is studied in postcolonial pragmatics. In other words, this branch examines the use of the language of the colonizers in postcolonial societies, predominantly in public discourse and interethnic communication. English in India and English in Nigeria would be cases in point. Finally, variational pragmatics investigates intra-lingual differences, i.e., pragmatic variation between and across L1 varieties of the same language. It is an area of research which has been much neglected to date.

Variational pragmatics can be conceptualized as the intersection of pragmatics with sociolinguistics, or, more specifically, with dialectology as the study of language variation. It is assumed that the social factors analyzed in sociolinguistics have a systematic impact not only on pronunciation, vocabulary and grammar, but also on language use in interaction. Our framework includes two components, one in which social factors are specified, and one in which levels of pragmatic analysis are distinguished.

1. Social factors

In our framework, we distinguish five social factors. These are region, social class, ethnicity, gender, and age (less stable — and less studied — factors such as education and religion may be considered in addition). The impact of region on language was first studied in traditional dialectology, particularly in dialect geography. This study of regional differences was abandoned in the 1960s with the advent of sociolinguistics. Sociolinguists were not initially interested in regional, but only in social differences, particularly differences between speakers in cities (hence 'urban dialectology'). First and foremost, they were interested in the impact of social class and also of ethnicity, later and increasingly in the impact of gender, and finally also of age. Today, modern dialectology, especially in the United States, aims at integrating these two areas, i.e., the study of regional and the study of social factors.

While regional variation is usually mentioned alongside, or in contrast to, social variation, we wish to argue that regional variation is, in fact, a particular type of social variation. As is well known from the discussion of the gender concept, linguists and social scientists are not primarily interested in sexual differences and biological facts, but rather in much more complex social constructs of gender identities, of which there are more than just two, and the social construction of such identities, e.g., through language use in interaction. Similarly, we are not interested in race and such superficial properties as color of skin, hair, or eyes, but in ethnic identities which are based on choices, notably behavioral choices including linguistic choices. An obvious example is that in hip-hop culture white male adolescents may adopt a black identity. Regarding region, we can, by analogy, say that we are not interested in geographical facts, but in regional affiliations and identities as they manifest themselves in language use.

Accordingly, these five factors are all social factors. It is assumed that each of these factors has an impact on language, resulting in variety-specific preferences and features which can be employed to construe and project speaker identities. More specifically, the five factors identified here can be referred to as macro-social (or macro-sociolinguistic) factors. By contrast, micro-social (or micro-sociolinguistic) factors include power, distance, and other situational factors. The crucial difference between these two types of factors is that macro-social factors concern individual speakers, whereas micro-social factors concern speaker constellations.

The primary aim of variational pragmatics consists in determining the influence of each of the five macro-social factors on language use in interaction. A second aim is to examine the interplay of these factors, e.g., the interplay of gender and age. Other aims include an analysis of the interaction between macro-social and micro-social factors. Further factors to be taken into account are, among others, discourse type and genre, register and community of practice, also speech and writing and levels of formality; in short such factors which concern intra-individual variation .

As mentioned before, these macro-social factors impact not only on pronunciation (phonetics and phonology), vocabulary (onomasiology and semasiology) and grammar (morphology and syntactic features) — those linguistic features normally studied in variational linguistics — but also on pragmatic features of language use in interaction.

2. Levels of pragmatic analysis

It is assumed that the macro-social factors region, social class, ethnicity, gender and age have a systematic influence on language use in interaction and cause pragmatic variation. As long as this area is neglected, our understanding of language, language variation, and language varieties is incomplete. Indeed, Leech (1983) sees pragmatics and grammar as complementary domains in the study of language. He maintains that the nature of language can only be understood if both of these domains are considered and also the interaction between them. In this context, Leech uses the term 'grammar' in a broad sense as a synonym for the language system involving not only syntax, but also phonology and semantics (further levels of the language system, such as morphology or lexicology, are not mentioned). In the complementary domain, i.e., in the domain of pragmatics (pragmatics being a synonym for language use), no equivalent levels of analysis are specified.

In the present framework, by contrast, five levels of pragmatic analysis are distinguished. These are termed the formal level, the actional level, the interactional level, the topic level, and the organizational level. The analysis on the formal level takes linguistic forms as its starting point, for instance, discourse markers such as well. The aim is to establish the communicative functions of such markers in interaction (form-to-function mapping). On the actional level, the analysis starts with an illocution, e.g., request or apology, and here the aim is to establish the formal realizations available to perform the respective speech act (function-to-form mapping). On the interactional level, the analysis goes beyond individual acts and focuses on dialogical units; for instance, adjacency pairs, speech act sequences, and the structure of complete speech events. The topic level is the level on which propositions and sequences of propositions and also topic selection and topic development are dealt with.

Finally, the organizational level involves the turn taking mechanisms of dialogical discourse and also such phenomena as simultaneous speech and silence.

3. Some theoretical and methodological issues

The discussion has shown that variational pragmatics does not dictate any particular theory or methodology. The levels of pragmatic analysis detailed in section 2 display the influence of several different traditions in pragmatics. Investigations on the formal level are characteristic of present-day approaches in corpus linguistics and systemic-functional discourse analysis. Analyses on the actional level are, as a rule, rooted in speech act theory and conducted in empirical speech act analysis. Politeness theory is also relevant to this level of analysis in particular, albeit not exclusively. The interactional level, on the other hand, is the focus of sociolinguistic discourse analysis, while the topic level is studied especially in psycholinguistic discourse analysis, as well as in text linguistics and genre analysis. Finally, phenomena on the organizational level are those typically examined in ethnomethodology, and more particularly in conversation analysis.

As the component of our framework which details the different levels of pragmatic analysis reflects so many different traditions, the present overall approach could be said to be eclectic. However, we prefer to call it integrative, as we firmly believe that none of the existing approaches provides a full picture of the complexities of language use in interaction, and that therefore the best results are achieved by combining many different approaches. Of course, individual studies may well single out a certain phenomenon on a particular level of the framework and analyze it by adopting a specific approach considered most suitable for the purpose as the study of complex entities necessitates analytic separations and a certain amount of controlled reductionism.

Thus, generally speaking, it is not essential which particular theory or methodology is adopted. What is, however, really crucial for variational pragmatics is that varieties of a language are contrasted. Strictly speaking, it is not possible to establish any variety-exclusive and variety-preferential features of any (regional, socioeconomic, ethnic, etc.) dialect, if this dialect is not explicitly compared to a dialect of the same kind of this same language. For instance, specific features of youth language cannot be determined by analyzing only youth language without contrasting the sample under study with samples from other age groups. The same applies to all other macro-social factors. Ethnomethodologists have acknowledged this fact in relation to national varieties of English. Harvey Sacks and his collaborators, for instance, worked exclusively with American English data in their analyses. Even though they were not actually interested in the varieties of English and pragmatic variation, they note that the features of conversations which they identified in American English were not necessarily specific to American English conversations, but rather may possibly also be found in other national varieties of English to a significantly greater or lesser extent. They note: "that all conversations are in 'American English' is no warrant for so characterizing them. (...) That the materials are all 'American English' does not entail that they are RELEVANTLY 'American English'" (Schegloff and Sacks, 1973: 291; original emphasis). Thus, in general terms, a methodological principle can be formulated which can be termed the 'contrastivity principle'.

CONTRASTIVITY PRINCIPLE

Linguistic features can be considered variety-specific only if the variety under study is contrasted with at least one other variety of the same kind and of the same language.

Following this principle, features of, e.g., working class language or the language of African Americans can only be established by comparison to, e.g., middle class language or the language of European Americans respectively. In this connection, it must be emphasized that middle class language and the language of European Americans are not superior varieties, despite the fact that they may carry more overt prestige in many contexts.

While this principle is relevant to variational linguistics in general, it is central to variational pragmatics. Studies in variational linguistics focusing on features of pronunciation, lexis or grammar (implicitly) refer to an abstract standard, for which codified rules (explicitly) exist. Studies in variational pragmatics, on the other hand, aim at establishing the language use conventions (in terms of, e.g., appropriateness and politeness) of social groups, for which often no (abstract/explicit) standard exists. Hence, it is crucial to contrast two or more varieties to be able to identify similarities and differences.

Another important methodological principle is that variational pragmatics is empirical. In other words, studies in variational pragmatics are not based on impressionistic and episodical evidence or so-called introspective (i.e., intuitive and fabricated) data, but on collections of material observed or elicited. In an extensive methodological paper, Jucker (2009) reminds us that the use of intuitive data, which he refers to as an 'arm-chair method', has its merits too, and that the history of pragmatics has seen cases in which influential theories were developed on this basis alone. This certainly applies to Austin's and Searle's speech act theory. It also applies, of course, to Chomsky's work in linguistics outside pragmatics. However, theories such as Searle's or Chomsky's focus on language as such (or 'langage', to use Saussure's term) or languages (essentially in the sense of 'langue') conceptualized as homogeneous entities in which variation is abstracted away. Variational pragmatics on the other hand, like variational linguistics in general, conceives language as 'orderly heterogeneity' (Weinreich et al., 1968) and is interested in linguistic performance (or, maybe more precisely, 'parole'). Researchers in this area therefore must work empirically.

Regarding the question of which types of data can or should be used in the analysis, variational pragmatics, unlike approaches permitting no other type than naturally occurring conversation, acknowledges that each and every data type and data collection method has its advantages as well as its shortcomings, and this includes naturally occurring discourse. It further acknowledges that the choice of method depends entirely on the aims and research questions of a project, and that a method suitable for one purpose may not be suitable for other purposes.

Hence, variational pragmatics can be done with a wide range of data types and methods. These include, as the contributions to this special issue illustrate, the use of large electronic corpora (such as the British National Corpus), elicited conversation, role plays and sociolinguistic interviews. Elsewhere, production questionnaires have been used, but also naturally occurring everyday conversation.

As the primary aim of variational pragmatics is to study and establish the influence of macro-social factors on language use, and also the interplay of these factors, the best strategy, at least in the initial stages, seems to be to opt for a method which allows a high degree of variable control. Experimental methods, such as questionnaires, interviews and role play, are well suited for this purpose, since the social variables involved can be systematically manipulated. Elicited conversation in particular warrants near-natural data, while variables can be controlled fairly easily, and thus contrasts with naturally occurring conversation with all its accidentialities. In general, we can say that the higher the possibility of controlling the relevant variables, the higher the comparability of data from different varieties of the same language and therefore the greater the opportunity of identifying pragmatic differences between these varieties. For this reason, comparability is another crucial methodological issue in variational pragmatics.

A further methodological problem is posed by the macro-social factors themselves. While we generally assume that region, gender, ethnicity, etc. are social factors underlying the construction of identities, it is rather a challenging task to actually investigate them as such. Gender, for instance, is not just a matter of terminology. To simply substitute the term 'gender' for 'sex' in linguistic studies is largely misleading. The influence of such complex social concepts as gender on pragmatic variation can only be investigated properly by studying 'the everyday language use of individual women and men in the local communities where the social construction of gender and other identities takes place' (Cheshire, 2002: 425). In other words, what is actually required for this purpose are meticulous ethnographic case studies, which can be very time consuming and do not necessarily provide comparable data. Therefore, to enhance comparability, it is recommended to actually focus on sex rather than gender, because sex is much more easily identifiable. As Cheshire notes (2002) 'speaker sex is intended to be a purposely broad, unrefined social variable that can be easily taken into account at the data-collection stage of research. If all researchers categorize speakers in the same, albeit simplistic way, we can ensure replicability and can draw useful comparisons between studies carried out in a range of communities' (424–425).

At least in the initial stages of variational pragmatics, this type of reductionism seems useful, if not inevitable. Needless to say, it applies not only to gender but, in fact, to all macro-social factors considered in this framework.

Studying all macro-social factors individually helps to determine the impact of each of these factors on language use in interaction. Since, however, every speaker's identity depends on more than one macro-social factor — every speaker belongs to a particular age group, social class, etc. — the interplay of these factors has to be taken into account as well. For instance, the question 'to what extent does age interact with other social variables such as class, gender, and ethnicity?' (Eckert, 1997: 152) addresses a matter of central concern to variational pragmatics.

It is hoped that this paper will provide readers with novel and interesting perspectives on variational pragmatics, the study of intra-lingual pragmatic variation relative to such macro-social factors as region, social class, ethnicity, gender, and age.

(Adapted from Anne Barron and Klaus P. Schneider. 2009. Variational pragmatics: Studying the impact of social factors on language use in interaction. *Intercultural Pragmatics* 6-4: 425–442.)

Questions for Discussion

1. What is variational pragmatics?
2. Would you name some other subdisciplines of intercultural pragmatics and explain them?
3. What are the macro-social and micro-social factors on language use in interaction?
4. Would you elaborate the five levels of pragmatic analysis in the framework?

Text E Some Thoughts on Pragmatics, Sociolinguistic Variation, and Intercultural Communication

I would like to touch on the role of the social aspects in pragmatics from another point of view, focusing on intercultural (contrastive, cross-cultural, and interlanguage) pragmatics. Over the past twenty years this field has made substantial contributions to the extension of linguistic models and the understanding of the relation between language and culture, as well as expanding the basis for second language studies and language curriculum materials. I would like to draw attention to some dimensions which, to my knowledge, have so far been on the margins of the field, focusing first on the speech act of introduction, the very beginning of interpersonal interaction, which I will show varies even within speakers of German. This example raises the issue of variation in intercultural pragmatics and to pluricentric languages, ones with 'several interacting centres, each of which provides at least some of (their) own (codified) norms' (Clyne, 1992: 1). Different national varieties are linked to specific norms of expression and cultural values. Central to the discussion is the issue of what pragmatic norms should be expected of second language learners. In discussion of English, the most pluricentric and international of all languages, the power of the pragmatics and discourse of the 'native speaker' of particular varieties is critiqued within the context of certain cultural parameters.

1. Introduction

Let me begin with some reminiscences of a visit to Germany last year. My first task on arriving at my living quarters was to collect my room key. I went to the office to introduce myself: 'Guten Tag, ich bin Michael Clyne aus Australien.' (Good day, I'm Michael Clyne from Australia.) 'Und ich bin Frau Helmer' (And I'm Ms. Helmer), replied the woman in the office. I don't believe that her choice of a non-reciprocal introduction routine was intended to put me down. But clearly her first name was none of my business. Now I knew that I should have introduced myself as 'Clyne' or 'Professor Clyne.' And being involved in a project on address terms across a number of European languages, I was particularly sensitive to differences in address. Nevertheless, as an Australian bilingual, my personality and the interactional norms of my cultural value system automatically led me into an introduction routine that was inappropriate in Germany. Some weeks later, my wife joined me and I introduced her to the cleaning woman, who had saved me several times from the terrors of a German washing machine. 'Darf ich Ihnen meine Frau Irene vorstellen?' (May I introduce my wife, Irene?) I asked in what was perfectly polite 'Australian German.' To which my cleaning woman responded, 'Ich bin Frau Hombach.' In spite of my heightened sensitivity to German norms for introductions, I had failed to switch from Australian to German expectations, which called for me to introduce her as 'Frau Doktor Donohoue-Clyne.'

A few weeks earlier, an Australian economist working at the same German university had told me about a German colleague of hers who was interested in applying game theory to language policy, whom she wanted me to meet. Next day, while I was with a German linguist, I happened to run into the Australian economist with two men, whom she introduced to me as Barry and Reinhard. It appeared that the latter was the game theorist she had mentioned to me. I wanted to introduce all three of them to my German linguist friend, but was aware of being caught in a moment of cross-pragmatic confusion. This time bowing to German convention and knowing only first names, I pretended to have forgotten them and left everyone to introduce themselves. This time the game theorist gave his name as 'Selten.' 'Oh,' said my German linguist friend in German, 'I remember you from when I was university president. You won the Nobel Prize for your work on game theory.' The Australian system of informality and egalitarianism had suppressed my new contact's status and deprived me of some vital information.

Introduction is very much part of linguistic action that affects the entire exchange and, as we have already seen, is subject to substantial intercultural differences. It relates closely to its 2nd person counterpart, address, which in many languages is more deeply embedded in the grammatical system of the language through pronouns and in some (especially pro-drop) languages through verb morphology. This means that the pragmatics drives grammatical decisions from the very start of an interaction. Choice of address pronominal (such as tu or vous in French) and/or nominal (such as first names/surnames/titles) generally denotes social distance and therefore plays a crucial role in human relations with the interlocutor and with many others. The transition from du to Sie relations has been described by one of the German informants in our project as 'perhaps the greatest step you ever take'. Introductions and address choice both indicate that verbal action carries with it a management of power relations and of sociolinguistic variation, and it is essential for the language user to be aware of this fact. Clearly, this would call for closer collaboration between the sub-disciplines of pragmatics and sociolinguistics.

2. Pragmatic variation in pluricentric languages

Most accounts of contrastive pragmatics studies abound with examples of individual variation. This is often captured in percentages of different individual responses to discourse completion tests. But they are rarely discussed in terms of sociolinguistic variation —

different sub-groupings within the sample with different conventions. Nor is there much discussion of the sociolinguistic rules underlying cultural variation. The scope of the speech act realizations encompassed under a language umbrella such as 'English,' 'German,' 'Spanish' or 'French' has usually remained outside critical consideration. Usually, the source country (though rarely the region) of the informants is indicated. The assumption is either that the pragmatic formulae will apply to the 'entire' language (usually the standard language) or that the variation within the language is not of importance. Any variation is implicitly attributed to the formality of the situation or to social distance factors, such as relative age and status. However, English is contrasted with German or Japanese or French or Spanish. English may be British, American, Australian or Canadian English; Spanish may be Castilian or Argentinian or another Latin American national variety; French may be French or Canadian French.

Very few studies so far have focused on pragmatic variation between different national varieties of a pluricentric language. There are a few brief sketches of the pragmatics of a number of languages in papers in Clyne (1992), but hardly any contrastive studies. Among the exceptions are Gumperz's many pragmaprosodic studies of communication breakdown between speakers of 'Indian' and 'Western' English. Other exceptions include Herbert (1989) on compliments in South African and American English, Muhr (1994) on speech act variation between German and Austrian speakers of German, Muhr's (1987) study of the use and non-use of modal particles by Germans and Austrians in German, and Barden, Grosskopf, and Auer (1996) and Birkner and Kern (2000), on the way eastern and western Germans manage interaction in job interviews, reflecting previous communicative practices in the two former German states. Creese (2001) compared existing non-contrastive data from British and American English as a preliminary to her pilot interviews to elicit British and American speakers' perceptions of variation in communication patterns of the two national varieties.

A study of communicative styles of couples of whom one was originally German, the other originally Austrian, most of whom had been living in Australia for many years (Clyne, Fernandez & Muhr, 2003), took as its point of departure Muhr's earlier studies of German and Austrian pragmatics in the source countries. It was intended to explore to what extent convergence had taken place over time between the pragmatics of the two German national varieties. The study focused on apologies and directives and on modal particles, in which issues of face and politeness reflecting differing cultural values would come to the fore. Most of the variation is in keeping with the contrasts between homeland national varieties (Muhr, 1987; 1994), with those of Austrian background preferring lower levels of directness and more negative politeness (Brown & Levinson, 1987) in comparison with those of German background. The latter prefer conventional responses indicating respectability while the Austrian-background informants are less conventional, preferring more creative responses, and also focus more on blame and guilt. This all indicates not only that national variation at the pragmatic level is not trivial; it shows that pragmatic routines are deeply ingrained through early socialization and even under conditions very conducive to convergence. It is difficult for speakers to change their norms of interaction. This takes us back to a more general discussion of how much we can expect second language learners to master the pragmatic norms of the target language, for pragmatics is rooted in cultural values which may affect people's personal identities. Of course, much depends on the objectives of the learner and the program. As Neustupny (1978) reminds us, 'foreignness' is still, to a large extent, marked as 'inadequate.' While many teachers consider balanced biculturalism the ideal, it is not frequently achievable except by very young learners. In addition, there is also a moral dimension to holding native-like pragmatics as the standard in all situations — urging someone to conform to your communicative behavior may be an act of cultural imperialism or suppression, or at least assimilation (Clyne, 1994: 208). It would seem that a more democratic standard to strive for would be a mutual understanding of and tolerance for the others' communicative behavior, and as much of an active command of pragmatic rules as is possible without threatening one's own face and identity. The near-absence of contrastive and interlanguage pragmatics research on (speakers of) the national varieties of a pluricentric language is related to the teaching of dominant national varieties of a language (for example, British and American English, French French, German German). This is changing, with Australia and New Zealand becoming very active in the TESOL scene in the Pacific and beyond and Latin Americans teaching their norms to second language learners in North America and elsewhere. Spearheaded by the research of Muhr (2000) and others, there is now an Austrian effort to offer an alternative international curriculum and certification for German, based on a pluricentric model, incorporating elements of pragmatics. Discussion among sociolinguists on the pluricentric model for German (for example, Clyne, 1984; Clyne, 1995) has eventually led to a pluricentric dictionary of German. Claes and Gerritsen (2002) have contrasted communication patterns in the Dutch of the Netherlands and Flanders (Belgium), which can be attributed to variation in basic cultural values. If pluricentricity is an issue for German, it certainly is far more for English, the most pluricentric and international of all languages, being a widespread lingua franca. Kachru (for example, 1997) has categorized the English-using nations in terms of a trichotomy — inner, outer, and expanding circles. While the 'circles' broadly correspond to L1 national varieties, 'New' (indigenous) Englishes, and 'English as a foreign language' varieties, dividing lines between the three categories are blurred by ethnic (including indigenous) Englishes in all the 'inner circle' nations. The relatively unexplored territory of pragmatic variation between national varieties requires much research.

Just as an example of distinctive Australian English pragmatics, let us consider the use of the word 'right.' It can occur in 'Are you right?' (Context: a customer waiting in a shop), an invitation to be served next. But the same utterance, in the context of someone walking around part of a shop which is 'out of bounds' for customers or non-employees, can be an indirect reproach (You shouldn't be here) or a request for justification (What are you doing here?) 'Are you right for getting home?' (Context: guests at a dinner or party are about to leave), on the other hand, is an offer of a lift in a car. Another distinctively Australian usage is 'Please bring a plate' with an invitation to a social gathering — which is a request to bring an item of food for one course. Such distinctive formulae occur in each of the national varieties and regularly lead to communication breakdown between people whose L1 is a different national variety as well as between those with a different language as L1.

The New Englishes draw on cultural values from Southeast Asia, the Pacific, West Africa, and the Indian sub-continent, to name just a few places. (*Examples of Singapore English speech acts may be found in Anna Wierzbicka's forthcoming book, English: Culture and Meaning.*) To understand a speech act in an originally non-native variety requires some basic information on and preferably experience of the appropriate cultural context (Eades, 2003; Holmes, 2003; Kramsch, 2003). But producing a speech act in someone else's cultural terms may go against the grain of a speaker. Pragmatic variation between national varieties of English raises a number of issues. First, the one that has been raised in the literature from time to time (Clyne, 1994: 209; Seidlhofer, 2000) — now that English is an international language, should English as a Foreign Language programs continue to assume that everyone is learning English to communicate with the English/British or Americans, or even Canadians, Australians or the Irish? The reality is that most learners of English need to be equipped to communicate with first, second, and foreign language users from a range of cultures. Seidlhofer's corpus in Vienna will facilitate the development of curriculum material for programs that prepare students for communication with all these categories of speakers. Second, English is an instrument of intercultural communication, and the study of culture-bound variation in communication styles in English will sensitize people to such styles and the cultural values that underpin them. This should be of importance not only to speakers of English as a second or foreign language but also to English native speakers, especially monolingual, monocultural ones, who may have had little opportunity to be confronted with different ways of behaving communicatively. For reasons I will explain in the following section, in the long term, I believe that it will not be possible for the inner circle to monopolize the norms of English. All English speakers will eventually need to learn the distinctive pragmatic features of the Englishes of the outer and extended (as well as inner) circles to be able to fully participate in international networks in the English language. It may be that over time some collaborative corpus planning will be needed for English as an international language.

3. Englishes and intercultural communication

Estimates of the number of L1 English speakers in the world vary a great deal, but we can assume that there are about 350 to 380 million. If we estimate that about a billion L2 speakers of English use the language regularly for intercultural communication, we see that L1 speakers are now very much in the minority among users of the English language today. Yet at present, the inner circle nations (the minority) are imposing their norms on the others (the majority). There is a need for an acceptance of pragmatic variation because it expresses an acceptance of people of other cultures. Linguists have an important role to play in investigating pragmatic variation and sensitizing the public to it. This field was pioneered by Gumperz and his colleagues (for example, Gumperz, Jupp & Roberts, 1981; Gumperz, 1982). They found that intercultural communication breakdown occurred for three main reasons (Gumperz, Jupp & Roberts, 1981: 5):

1) 'Different assumptions' about situation-appropriate behavior
2) 'Different ways of structuring information or an argument'
3) Different conventions for speaking (for example, prosody) and their interpretation.

Failure to recognize such variation in intercultural pragmatics can contribute to stereotypes about speakers of other varieties. It is these differences that put Black Americans and South Asian immigrants in the U.S. and Britain respectively at a disadvantage in a range of situations including job interviews and service encounters. East Germans were in a similar situation following German unification (Barden, Grosskopf & Auer, 1996; Birkner & Kern, 2000). The three issues highlighted by Gumperz et al. continue to provide the basis for a program of vital research in this field. Further scholarly work in intercultural communication showing that there are different ways of being polite, such as Hickey and Stewart (2005) on politeness in 22 countries and, within the CCSARP framework, different degrees of directness (Blum-Kulka, House & Kasper, 1989) can heighten cultural sensitivity. I will cite only a few areas.

A study of workplace communication in English as a lingua franca among immigrants from various backgrounds, mainly continental European, Southeast, and South Asian, in Melbourne (Clyne, 1994) demonstrated intercultural variation in the turn length, especially where the content is potentially face threatening, with Style A tending to cluster mitigating speech acts to counteract the effects of the main speech act, thereby lengthening turns, and Style C avoiding tension by expressing a face threatening speech act in a short turn. Style B tends to exhibit long turns with much repetition and parallel discourse. Style A is most prevalent among continental Europeans and Latin Americans, B among South Asians, and C among Southeast Asians, but some cultures in the region show only peripheral tendencies towards one of these styles or combine aspects of different styles. Turn maintenance and appropriation conventions also varies between European, South Asian, and Southeast Asian groups. Much of the variation in style is confirmed in Fitzgerald's (2003) Australian data. She differentiates six styles, which she identifies culturally: instrumental/exacting (Anglo, Northern, and Western European), spontaneous/argumentative (Eastern European), involved/expressive (Southern European/Latin American), elaborate/dramatic (Middle Eastern), bureaucratic (South Asian), succinct/subdued (Southeast Asian). Such assertions should not be regarded as stereotypes but as tendencies, to demonstrate that communication styles are not universal and to interpret how they are underpinned by cultural values and history.

The increasing internationalization of scholarship and the widespread use of English as an academic lingua franca have introduced new challenges to the linguistic study of intercultural communication. With most international journals appearing mostly or entirely in English, scholars from English-speaking backgrounds are able to exercise power over the acceptance of research. The credibility of academic scholarship rests at least partly on the acceptance by 'inner circle' English-speaking scholars of the academic discourse styles of people from other cultures, who have been socialized through a different education system into different priorities as to what is important in writing. This applies both to reviews of books and to the refereeing process for journal articles (for example, Clyne, 1987; Ammon, 2000), both of which are increasingly acting as gate-keepers for appointment, promotion, and for justifying the representation of certain disciplines in institutions. It is particularly problematic to evaluate on the basis of formal criteria the research of scholars from cultures with a strong content orientation, such as most continental European cultures. While texts by people from any culture will be more or less linear, that is, with the propositions following in a more or less linear order, English speakers' texts are generally more linear than those by German, Czech, Polish, and Finnish speakers (Clyne, 1987; Clyne, 1994; Duszak, 1997). These European cultures attach far greater importance to the content. In fact, in an empirical, synchronic or practical text, Central European cultures need to include what English speakers consider to be 'digressions,' that is, a theoretical, historical or ideological perspective, all of which Galtung (1985) consider to be integral features of German-based intellectual style. Chinese, Japanese, and Korean speakers tend to be less linear for historical reasons or (at least in the case of Japanese) cultural reasons of politeness, which requires implication rather than explicit linear presentation (see Kirkpatrick, 1992 for Chinese; Hinds, 1980 for Japanese; Eggington, 1987 for Korean).

Among other things, there is a canon of good English academic writing in the humanities and social sciences revealed in a survey of German and Australian linguists and sociologists (Clyne, Hoeks & Kreutz, 1988), which does not have currency among comparable German scholars, for instance. It includes a high degree of linearity and of symmetry between different propositions (that is, each section of the text is more or less equal in length), the early placement of definitions and of advance organizers. Similar issues have been discussed in relation to cultural variation in the conduct of meetings (Clyne, 1994: 125–136; Byrne & Fitzgerald, 1996).

4. Concluding remarks

The increased use of English as an international lingua franca carries with it a special social responsibility for the researcher in intercultural pragmatics. The study of intercultural communication aims at understanding the point of view of a person from another culture and responding accordingly. One important goal involves bridging the 'gap' between two or more sets of cultural understandings. Impartial, scholarly study reveals that every discourse community develops its own rules of community behavior, which becomes part of their individual and group identity. Failure to recognize this creates stereotypes, a belief in the normative status of one's own (group's) communicative behavior, and the negative evaluation of those behaving differently. This is particularly so within a pluricentric language and may limit access by and to those who communicate differently. Intercultural pragmatics and the adjoining field of intercultural discourse hold a key to the crucial understanding and respect. There is a great deal of research needed on a large range of spoken and written cross-cultural encounters. This brief paper has attempted to develop a rationale for including the sociolinguistic notion of national variation in intercultural pragmatics. Doing so is particularly important in the case of English because of the New Englishes and the significance of English as a lingua franca.

> (Adapted from Michael Clyne. 2006. Some thoughts on pragmatics, sociolinguistic variation, and intercultural communication. *Intercultural Pragmatics* 3-1: 95–105.)

Suggested Reading

Jaszczolt, K. M. 2004. *Semantics and Pragmatics: Meaning in Language and Discourse.* Beijing: Peking University Press. pp. 330-340.

Mey, J. L. 2001. *Pragmatics: An Introduction* (2nd ed.). Malden, MA: Blackwell. pp206-235; pp. 262-288.

Verschueren, J. 2000. *Understanding Pragmatics.* Beijing: Foreign Language Teaching and Research Press. pp. 227-237.

Unit 10
Pragmatics and Its Interfaces

> No idea is isolated, but is only what it is among all ideas.
> — Friedrich Von Schlegel
>
> It was an initiation into the love of learning, of learning how to learn ... as a matter of interdisciplinary cognition — that is, learning to know something by its relation to something else.
> — Leonard Bernstein

Objectives

- To understand the multidisciplinary nature of pragmatics
- To learn to describe the relationship of pragmatics to its academic neighbours
- To comprehend the importance of research beyond disciplines
- To learn the academic notions about pragmatics in relation to other relevant disciplines
- To improve critical thinking and intercultural communicative competence and comprehensive language skills
- To improve pragmatic competence, academic ability and relevant language skills

Before You Read

1. A man sees his neighbour's son running in his garden, and says to his neighbour:

   Man: *What is your son doing in my garden?*

   How many interpretations can you make of the man's utterance?

2. In naturally occurring conversations, people usually do not express complete propositions. Study the following utterances, and think what YOU would say in similar situations.

   1) (A mother assures her child who cut his finger.)

      You are not going to die, Peter.

      (Compare: *You are not going to die from this cut, Peter.*)

   2) *I haven't eaten.*

      (Compare: *I haven't been to the Mars.*)

   3) A: What time is it?

      B: *It's five.*

      (Compare: B: *It's 1 minute 30 seconds past five.*)

   4) (A boy comes to his mum.)

      Boy: *Everyone's got a bike.*

   5) *I'm too tired.*

3. Which is bigger, the 'Small Elephant' or the 'Big Ant'?

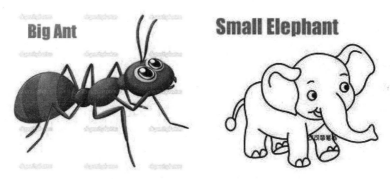

4. Based on what you have learned in previous chapters, think about the relationship between pragmatics and semantics.

5. Can you name a few neighbouring areas of enquiry which can usefully contribute to the study of pragmatics?

Start to Read

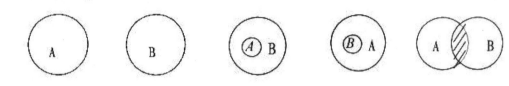

Text A The Semantics/Pragmatics Distinction

The semantics/pragmatics distinction is one of the most discussed topics in the philosophy of language today. Several collections have been devoted specifically to it (e.g. Turner, 1999; Bianchi, 2005; Szabo, 2006), and a number of important recently published works address issues that crucially hinge upon the relationship between semantics and pragmatics (e.g. Levinson, 2000; Perry, 2001; Carston, 2002; Borg, 2004; Recanati, 2004; Cappelen and Lepore, 2005; Predelli, 2005, and numerous journal articles).

The problem of the semantics/pragmatic distinction is, roughly, how to define 'semantics' and 'pragmatics' in a coherent and empirically plausible way. The source of the problem lies in the tensions among several initially plausible criteria that, at least at a first glance, may be used in drawing the line between semantics and pragmatics. The three main criteria may be roughly formulated as follows:

(i) ('lexical encoding'): Semantics deals with elements that are lexically encoded in the meaning of the words, pragmatics deals with elements that are not lexically encoded;

(ii) ('context-independence'): Semantics deals only with elements whose meaning does not depend on any contextual factors; elements that depend on the context belong to pragmatics;

(iii) ('truth-conditionality'): Semantics deals with elements that bear upon truth and truth conditions; pragmatics deals with elements that go beyond truth conditions, such as implicatures.

It takes little to realize that the criteria do not converge unproblematically towards a single distinction. Consider a sentence such as:

(1) I have had enough.

Whether or not this sentence, on a given occasion of use, is true, arguably depends not only upon the lexical (linguistic, conventional) meaning associated with this sentence, but on a number of other issues: who is the speaker, when was the sentence uttered, what is the thing of which enough has been had, and finally, what counts as enough. This generates a clash between criteria (ii) and (iii), since all these issues are determined by context, but are also relevant to the truth value of (1). Indexical elements, such as the pronoun 'I', are clearly context-dependent, but it is generally agreed that they are an object of study to *semantics*, rather than (just) to pragmatics. The case of the pronoun 'I' also suggests some clash between criteria (i) and (ii), since the context-dependence of 'I' is *lexicalized*: the lexical meaning of the first person pronoun is precisely that the pronoun is used to refer to the speaker (Kaplan, 1977). Presented with context-dependent elements that should count as semantic according to criteria (i) (lexical encoding) and (iii) (truth-conditionality), philosophers were led to distinguish between two notions of context, 'narrow' versus 'broad', where narrow context specifies the speaker, the place, the time, and perhaps the world (hence it is context in Kaplan's sense), while broad context includes that and 'all the rest' (see e.g. Bach, 2000). But that will help little in solving the problem. Fix the narrow context — suppose it is David Kaplan who says (1) on January 31, 2007, at noon. Determining the truth conditions of (1) still seems to depend upon further contextual factors. Whether he says (1) to his wife while she is serving him salad (meaning that he has had enough of the salad), or to a friend in course of a conversation about students' term papers (meaning that he has had enough of papers to grade) may give rise to different truth values. And even if we fix the subject matter — suppose it is the students' papers — whether he means to be saying that he has had enough for the rest of the day, or for the rest of the year, or for the rest of his career, are again contextual elements that neither belong to the narrow context nor are lexicalized (at least, not in any fruitful sense of 'lexical encoding'), and yet, appear to reach into the truth-conditional content of (1).

The studies of quite a few scholars attempt to shed new light on these problems. Robyn Carston argues that something very similar to criterion (i) is central to drawing the line between semantics and pragmatics. By the end of her paper, Carston also addresses the issue of what is needed to get pragmatic inference started. This issue is also discussed by Kepa Korta and John Perry. They show how their proposal, based on the 'reflexive-referential' theory of Perry (2001), avoids what they call 'the pragmatic circle': the idea that (broadly) contextual reasoning may be required for determining the semantic content (as the example of (1) suggests), and yet that, according to the standard Gricean picture, semantic content (or 'what is said') is one of the main inputs to pragmatic inference.

Christopher Gauker challenges the view, endorsed by many, that determining the reference of deictic elements, such as demonstrative pronouns, most often involves pragmatic reasoning about the speaker's beliefs or intentions, and outlines an alternative theory of demonstratives that does not appeal to pragmatics (understood in this sense). Brendan Gillon discusses linguistic evidence that suggests that only lexical (or grammatical) context-dependence may reach into semantics, and concludes that, in the case of quantifier domain restriction, the context-dependence is pragmatic rather than semantic. Finally, Napoleon Katsos offers new perspectives on the kind of considerations that may bear upon the delineation between semantics and pragmatics. Discussing the particular case of scalar implicatures, he demonstrates how the experimental paradigms used in psycholinguistics may shed light on such prima facie philosophical issues as that of the semantics/pragmatics distinction.

(Adapted from Isidora Stojanovic. 2008. The semantics/pragmatics distinction. *Synthese* 165: 317–319.)

Text B Pragmatics and Grammar

Previous approaches to the relation between grammar and pragmatics

The problem of the interaction between grammar and pragmatics can only be investigated within a particular theory, depending on how it conceives of the concepts of grammar and pragmatics. Since both terms are used with differing connotations and denotations in different theories, 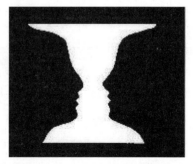 it is necessary to overview and compare very carefully their different definitions in order to grasp what similarities and differences the particular theories have in the treatment of the issue of the interaction between grammar and pragmatics according to their particular conceptions of grammar and pragmatics.

On the basis of their similarities and differences, approaches to the relation between grammar and pragmatics can be classified into four groups. In the first group of approaches, grammar and pragmatics are not separated from each other since language and language use are not distinguished from each other. The factors considered pragmatic by other theories are included in grammar and not treated separately. This treatment is followed by holistic cognitive grammars and functional grammars, as well as by construction grammars, according to which pragmatic information either is involved in the constructions, i.e. in the meaning-form pairs of the grammar, or it provides the necessary motivation for the existence of a construction (e.g. Goldberg, 1995, 2005). Similarly, in head-driven phrase structure grammar (HPSG) pragmatic information is included in the grammar (Pollard and Sag, 1994; Engdahl, 1999). In HPSG, the SYNTAX- SEMANTICS (SYNSEM) attribute contains the attribute CONTEXT (CONX) in addition to the attributes CATEGORY (CAT) and CONTENT (CONT). The attribute CONX involves information that bears on certain context-dependent aspects of semantic interpretation. Since pragmatic information is included, but not separately, in the grammars mentioned here, the question how grammar and pragmatics interact cannot be raised in the first group of approaches.

The second group contains frameworks which consider pragmatics a functional perspective on any aspect of language and not an additional component of a theory of language (e.g. Mey, 1993; Verschueren, 1999). Pragmatics, in this view, concerns all levels of language and examines linguistic phenomena at any level according to the motivation and effects of the linguistic choices communicators make. Pragmatics has a considerable social relevance in these frameworks. The relationship between grammar and pragmatics cannot really be examined in functional pragmatics either. The research in functional pragmatics does not concern the questions how an utterance meaning is constructed by a speaker according to her/his intentions and how a hearer interprets the utterance meaning intended by the speaker, but, instead, addresses the questions why an utterance is produced, why the particular linguistic form is selected by the communicator, and also what consequences the communicator's linguistic choices have. Pragmatics examines and describes linguistic phenomena at all levels of language from the point of view of the properties and the course of use. Although pragmatics is situated outside of grammar, there is no possibility to relate it to grammar.

In the third view, pragmatics is one of the components of grammar (e.g. Levinson, 1983). It intrudes into the lexicon, semantics and syntax (Levinson, 2000). For example, in the lexicon some kinds of contextual information should be taken into consideration to define the meanings of lexemes. In this case we involve pragmatic information in the lexicon of grammar. The semantic component of grammar also requires pragmatic information, e.g. to construct the meaning of the sentences with deictic and indexical phrases we should necessarily rely on the context. Levinson (2000) convincingly argues that syntax can also rely on pragmatics. The theory of generalized conversational implicatures helps syntax to account for anaphoric relations in a more adequate way. Newmeyer (2006) also considers pragmatics a component of grammar. In harmony with the generative framework he assumes grammar with a modular architecture, taking pragmatics into account as a module of grammar. Newmeyer presupposes different principles for each component of grammar, i.e. syntax, semantics and pragmatics. However, he emphasizes an intensive interaction between these modules. To summarize approaches in the third group, we can say that here pragmatics as a component of grammar and other components of grammar are in a close relationship.

And finally, the fourth group of theories considers pragmatics a component outside of grammar. There are two different approaches in this group. In addition to grammar, pragmatics is either a component of a theory of language (e.g. Kasher, 1986) or cognition (e.g. Sperber and Wilson, 2002). In the first case, pragmatics is mainly defined with regard to semantics, which is a component of grammar. There are theories which draw a strict dividing line between semantics and pragmatics considering semantics truth-conditional and pragmatics postsemantic, as well as non-truth-conditional (e.g. Gazdar, 1979), and theories which allow pragmatics to contact grammar through its semantic component (e.g. Leech, 1983). Grammar and pragmatics are distinguished in the research framework of generative linguistics as well, but the treatment of the relationship between them has changed in the history of the theory. The generative framework defines grammar and pragmatics on the basis of the distinction between grammatical competence and pragmatic competence, which are two separate modules of the human mind. According to Chomsky (1977) and Kasher (1986), grammatical competence is independent of pragmatic competence. Consequently, grammar is independent of pragmatics. However, pragmatics as a model of the faculty of language use cannot be considered independent of the grammar, its operation is based on grammar, i.e. the model of the knowledge of language. In the latest version of generative grammar, i.e. in the Minimalist Program, Chomsky (1995) emphasizes the interface character of the two interpretive components – phonetic and logical forms – in grammar. The logical form can be related to the conceptual-intentional system of the human mind. This potential relationship makes it possible to treat grammar and pragmatics as not independent, but to assume an interface between them (Engdahl, 1999).

The second approach which situates pragmatics outside of grammar considers pragmatics a component of cognition outside of the theory of language (Sperber and Wilson, 2002). Its task is to describe and explain how ostensive-inferential communication operates. Since ostensive-inferential communication does not refer only to verbal communication but also to the various types of non-verbal communication as well as to the kinds of communication without any code use, pragmatics as a theory of ostensive-inferential communication is not an exclusively linguistic discipline. Natural languages enter ostensive-inferential communication in order to make information transmission in communication more effective and reliable, i.e. one of the main functions of languages in ostensive-inferential communication is to fulfill communicators' informative intention. Language and linguistic communication are not independent in verbal communication, consequently, a contact can be supposed between grammar as a theory of language and pragmatics as a theory of communication.

On the basis of this brief overview and comparison, it is obvious that the question of interaction between grammar and pragmatics can really be dealt with in the fourth group of approaches. However, the third group of approaches, according to which pragmatics is included in grammar, is worth taking into consideration, because it assumes a close relationship between various components of grammar including pragmatics. And, further, according to the approaches in the first group, grammar also contains pragmatic information. To summarize: the majority of the theories mentioned in this section agree on the point that grammar cannot work adequately without pragmatics.

New definitions of grammar, pragmatics and the relationship between them

Developing the ideas of the third and fourth groups of approaches, we define grammar as the explicit model of the knowledge of language, i.e. grammatical competence which is a component of the theory of language, not independent of pragmatics, and we treat pragmatics as the model of the faculty of language use, i.e. pragmatic competence which is another component of the theory of language, not independent of grammar. Pragmatic competence is not restricted to one module of the human mind. It contains and organizes procedural and declarative knowledge concerning not only communicative but all possible forms of language use. Consequently, pragmatics as a model of pragmatic competence should describe and explain not only communicative language use, i.e. verbal communication, but other forms of language use, e.g. informative language use and manipulative language use, as well.

Thus, we basically consider the interaction between grammar and pragmatics a co-operation of two separate components of the theory of language in contexts of language use. Nevertheless, we also accept that detached from its contexts, some contextual information becomes not only context-independent, i.e. general pragmatic information, but also such encyclopedic information or information concerning the use of language can be fixed in semantic representations of lexical entries as integral parts.

It is worth noting that our definitions of grammar and pragmatics do not rely on the classic, strict modularity hypothesis proposed by Fodor (1983), according to which modules of the human mind are unique, independent, informationally encapsulated systems. In addition to neurolinguistic evidence, Sperber's (2000) extended modularity hypothesis has served as one of the starting points to formulate our definitions. The extended modularity hypothesis suggests that in addition to peripheral systems there is not only one central system in the human mind as Fodor (1983) proposes. Instead, peripheral systems are connected with more than one conceptual module. The conceptual modules themselves are not independent of each other, an intensive interaction can be supposed between them.

Our approach to grammar and pragmatics as well as to their interaction can be related, first, to Leech's (1983) idea that pragmatics is a component of the theory of language situated outside of grammar, second, to Chomsky's (1977, 1995) as well as Kasher's (1986) proposals according to which grammar and pragmatics are models of the grammatical and pragmatic competences, i.e. faculties of the human mind, respectively, and third, to Sperber's (2000) and Sperber and Wilson's (2002) extended modularity hypothesis, which allows an intensive interaction between grammar and pragmatics. A possibility of the interaction between grammar and pragmatics through the logical form is also provided in Chomsky's (1995) Minimalist Program. Fourth, in connection with the appearance of encyclopedic information or information concerning the use of language in the lexicon of grammar, we have to refer to Levinson's (2000) similar idea of the intrusion of pragmatics into the lexicon of grammar.

However, our views of grammar and pragmatics as well as of their relationship differ from Leech's (1983), because we do not restrict the interaction between grammar and pragmatics to the relationship between semantics and pragmatics. In this respect we agree with Levinson's (2000) and Newmeyer's (2006) suggestions that pragmatics can intrude into all components of grammar, including the lexicon, semantics and also syntax. At the same time, we do not consider pragmatics a component of grammar as Levinson and Newmeyer do. We define pragmatics as the model of pragmatic competence and grammar as the model of grammatical competence. Most recent neurolinguistic and neuropragmatic research (e.g. Paradis, 1998) supports the ideas of both the real existence of pragmatic competence and the separate location of grammatical and pragmatic abilities in the brain. While grammatical competence is located in the left hemisphere, pragmatic competence is located in the right one. In contrast with damage in the left hemisphere, lesions in the right hemisphere do not lead to grammatical (i.e. phonological, morphological, or syntactic) deficits, i.e. to a kind of aphasia, but they result in considerable systematic disfunctions in the course of production and interpretation of pragmatic phenomena such as indirect speech acts, conversational implicatures, metaphors, humor, and discourse coherence. However, grammatical and pragmatic abilities interact in language use. On the basis of these neurolinguistic and neuropragmatic results, if grammatical and pragmatic competences are conceived of as two separate but interacting abilities, it is reasonable not to take pragmatics as a component of grammar, but, instead a separate component of the theory of language in addition to grammar, while an intensive interaction must be assumed between them.

Our approach also differs from Chomsky's (1977) and Kasher's (1986), since it does not treat grammatical competence as independent of pragmatic competence, so it does not draw a strict, impenetrable boundary between grammar and pragmatics. Our proposal is different from Chomsky's (1995) solution in Minimalist Program as well, because we do not restrict the interaction between grammar and pragmatics to an interface between the logical form of grammar and conceptual-intentional system of mind. And finally, our approach also differs from Sperber's (2000) and Sperber and Wilson's (2002), because we regard pragmatics, i.e. a model of pragmatic competence, as a component of the theory of language which is responsible not only for verbal communication, but also for all forms of language use.

To summarize: in our approach both grammar and pragmatics are considered components of the theory of language, and an intensive interaction is assumed between them. We also deem an interaction between grammar and pragmatics possible in such a way that encyclopedic information or information concerning the use of language can be fixed in the lexical-semantic representation.

(Adapted from E. T. Nemeth and K. Bibok. 2010. Interaction between grammar and pragmatics: The case of implicit arguments, implicit predicates and co-composition in Hungarian. *Journal of Pragmatics* 42: 503–506.)

After You Read

Knowledge Focus

1. Decide whether the following statements are true or false based on Text A and Text B.

 1) Broad context specifies the speaker, the place, the time, and perhaps the world.

 2) Christopher Gauker claims that determining the reference of deictic elements, such as demonstrative pronouns, most often involves pragmatic reasoning about the speaker's beliefs or intentions.

3) Newmeyer presupposes different principles for each component of grammar, i.e. syntax, semantics and pragmatics. However, he emphasizes an intensive interaction between these modules.

4) Leech's (1983) considers pragmatics to be a component of the theory of language situated outside of grammar.

5) Pragmatic competence contains and organizes procedural and declarative knowledge concerning not only communicative but all possible forms of language use.

2. Discuss the following questions with your partner.

1) According the author of Text A, what is the source of the problem of the semantics/pragmatic distinction?

2) What is the 'pragmatic circle'?

3) What does Napoleon Katsos' study demonstrate?

4) What are the four approaches to the study of the relation between grammar and pragmatics discussed in Text B?

5) What do the majority of the four approaches above have in common?

6) In what aspects is Sperber & Wilson's positions on pragmatics and grammar different from Chomsky's based on Text B?

Language Focus

1. Fill in the blanks with words or expressions in Text A and Text B.

1) The problem of the semantics/pragmatic distinction is, roughly, how to define 'semantics' and 'pragmatics' in a coherent and _____ plausible way.

2) A number of important recently published works address issues that crucially _____ upon the relationship between semantics and pragmatics.

3) The three main criteria may be roughly _____ as lexical encoding, context-independence and truth-conditionality.

4) Whether or not a sentence, on a given occasion of use, is true, arguably depends not only upon the _____ (linguistic, conventional) meaning associated with this sentence, but on a number of other issues.

5) Napoleon Katsos discusses the particular case of scalar implicatures and demonstrates how the experimental _____ used in psycholinguistics may shed light on the semantics/pragmatics distinction.

6) Levinson's (2000) and Newmeyer's (2006) suggest that pragmatics can _____ into

all components of grammar, including the lexicon, semantics and also syntax.

7) Chomsky (1995) emphasizes the _____ character of the two interpretive components — phonetic and logical forms — in grammar.

8) Kasher (1986) takes pragmatics into account as a _____ of grammar.

9) Sperber's (2000) extended modularity hypothesis suggests that _____ systems are connected with more than one conceptual module.

10) In contrast with damage in the left hemisphere, lesions in the right hemisphere do not lead to grammatical (i.e. phonological, morphological, or syntactic) _____, i.e. to a kind of aphasia.

2. Translate the following Chinese into English.

语言和言语的区分问题主要集中于语义学和语用学的界面之争。关于语义学和语用学的关系，主要有两种不同的理论观点：简约论和互补论。简约论可以细分为语义简约论和语用简约论。前者主张语用学完全归属于语义学，而后者认为语用学完全涵括语义学。互补论将语义学和语用学视为语言学中不同且互补的子学科。

3. Translate the following English into Chinese.

Sometimes, it may be clear to the audience that an aspect of prosody is being accidentally revealed rather than intentionally conveyed. So a speaker's tone of voice may simply betray the fact that she is anxious or assured, cross or collected. In more sophisticated cases, a speaker may covertly manipulate her tone to suggest to an audience that she is accidentally betraying her feelings rather than wanting them to be recognized as part of her meaning in the full Gricean sense. As well as being used covertly, a communicator may also overtly show her feelings to an audience. She may do this by deliberately producing, and perhaps exaggerating, a natural sign or signal (e.g. an anger tone of voice); or she may do it by making no attempt to conceal a spontaneously produced natural sign or signal in circumstances where it is obvious to both communicator and audience that she could have taken steps on conceal them.

(Allan, 2012: 574-575)

Comprehensive Work

1. Study the different views on the relationship between pragmatics and semantics and present them in your group.

2. Read and summarize a journal article on the interface between pragmatics and any other disciplines.

Further Readings

Text C Pragmatics and Prosody

We all know that it is possible to say the same words in many different ways, and that our tone of voice can have as much effect on the listener as the words we choose. This is evident from our own experience and also through the medium of fiction, where writers often describe their characters' voices in a way that allows us to 'hear' something of their state of mind or attitude. We might find, for example, something like: *Yes, he said firmly, or No, she murmured sympathetically, or Go away, he snapped abruptly.* Each adverb, and sometimes the verb itself suggests a way of  speaking that conveys how the speaker feels, either about the addressee or about the message itself (Brown, 1977). This expression of emotional and attitudinal meaning has been claimed as the primary function of tone of voice, or 'prosody', but it also conveys other less elusive kinds of meaning, including focus of information, utterance type (question, statement), topic structure and the organization of turns in conversation. However, prosody does not have any propositional meaning, and this is the main reason why prosody is considered to belong primarily to the domain of pragmatics rather than semantics. (Archer *et al*, 2012: 96)

Prosody, speech acts and implicature

A pragmatic role of prosody is to signal speech acts, and it does this partly through the choice of final melody or 'nuclear tone' which is associated with the nuclear syllable — normally the last prominent syllable in the tone group. The exact number of contours available in English is controversial, but most agree that there are at least three: a rising contour; a falling contour; and a contour that falls and then rises (if necessary on a single syllable). These are referred to as *falls*, *rises* and *fall-rises*. The power of pitch contours to generate pragmatic meaning relies, as with prominence placement, on a default pattern typically associated with certain speech acts. Much work has therefore been carried out to establish what these 'default' contours are, from which speakers can then strategically deviate, which they frequently do.

Tonal contours with a high endpoint (rises, fall-rises) are generally assumed to indicate openness or non-finality, and generally occur at a non-final point in an utterance suggesting 'more to come'. Thus, if they occur at a final point in the utterance, it is unsurprising that they are typically associated with questions, so that the suggestion of 'more to come' refers to the answer that is being elicited. Falling contours, on the other hand, are associated with closedness or finality, and are therefore typical of statements. Wh-questions are an exception, since the default tone is a fall. In this respect they sound more like statements, and could perhaps be understood to have the underlying declarative meaning of *I want to know*.... When a rising tone is used with a wh-question, as in *What's your name*?, it could be in order to check the name against a list. The rise here usually begins in mid-range. If the rise is extended, beginning lower in the speaker's voice but ending high, it tends to be with children and can sound slightly patronizing if addressed to an adult.

If there is a discrepancy between the form of the utterance and the contour, it is generally the contour that determines how we interpret the force of the utterance. For example, if an utterance with declarative form (e.g. *you are hungry*) normally typical of a statement, is spoken with a rising tone, it is understood as a question and not as a statement of fact (i.e. you are hungry?).

A nuclear tone that lends itself particularly well to conveying some implied meanings is the fall-rise. As we said above, this contour typically indicates non-finality, meaning that more is coming, and therefore frequently occurs on sentence elements that are part of a larger structure. As in:

I went to \/town | and then ...
\/ Sometimes I w like to ...

However, the fall-rise can also occur on utterances that are pragmatically complete, such as statements. This creates a mismatch between the finality of the syntax and the non-finality of the intonation. According to Wells (2006: 27): '[b]y making a statement with the fall-rise, the speaker typically states one thing but implies something further. Something is left unsaid – perhaps some kind of reservation or implication.' Wells gives a number of examples, including the following (*ibid.*: 28):

A: What do you think of Hubert?
B: He's very met\/ticulous
A: /But?
B: Utterly boring

As Wells explains, the implicational fall-rise can be used simply to imply that the speaker has reservations. *Is she coming? I ∨think so*. The fall-rise here underlies the uncertainty or tentativeness of the reply, but the reason for the uncertainty is not specified. This lack of specificity is something exploited strategically: it enables us 'to imply things without actually saying them... to be tactful and politely indirect... (or) hypocritical and devious' (ibid.). In the following example (from ibid.):

What's she like as a colleague? Well she ∨works very hard. (Or: She works very ∨hard)

'... the unspoken implication might be but she has no imagination or but she's not a good teacher or but she doesn't get on with her colleagues or something else uncomplimentary' (ibid.: 29). By using the fall-rise it is possible to say something complimentary but imply (but not say) something critical.

Intonation and Social Rituals

Social rituals, such as thanking and apologizing do not have fixed intonation contours: these depend on the context in which they occur. In the case of *thank you* a falling tone conveys genuine gratitude, while a fall-rise or a rise is closer to an acknowledgement of receipt rather than an expression of gratitude. We can imagine then that if someone receives a gift and says /*thank you*, i.e. with a rising tone, effectively just acknowledging receipt, the giver may well be offended.

In the case of apologies, the intonation patterns depend very much on the seriousness of the offence for which the speaker is apologizing. A detailed study of apologies has been made by Aijmer (1996) including a description of the intonation contours typically occurring with *sorry* and other expressions of apology (*I apologize, pardon* and *excuse me*). The use of sorry was by far the most common, constituting over 80 per cent (ibid: 86) of the occurrences in the corpus data. Knowles (1986: 194) suggests that a serious apology normally has a final falling contour, as in *I'm (very)\sorry*, while if it is more casual, then a fall-rise is more usual (*∨sorry*). Aijmer's study finds that there are many more rising or falling-rising contours on 'sorry' than falling, which suggests that the majority of these apologies are in fact fairly routine, and that there are many fewer expressions of deep regret.

In other expressions with *sorry*, the expression is expanded to include reference to the offence as in *I'm \sorry I'm /late*, or *\Sorry about /that* or to include a vocative as in *\Sorry / Neil*. If the apology is intensified, the prosodic prominence is often transferred to the intensifier: *I'm \so/sorry* or *I'm \so \sorry* or *∧am sorry*.

At the least apologetic end of the scale, there is evidence that sorry in some contexts is routinized to such an extent that it has become a pragmatic marker. This occurs when there is a disturbance in the flow of conversation, for example if the speaker makes a slip of the tongue e.g. *It'll be Tues ... sorry* Wednesday, or wished something to be repeated:

A: Pete's arrived

B: /Sorry

A: I said Pete's arrived

Aijmer refers to these as 'talk offences' which require an apology. It is likely, however, that they are no longer perceived as true apologies. Such tokens of *sorry* are spoken quickly, sometimes so quickly that all that remains is something like [soi] or even [so]. This loss of phonetic material is typical of the process of grammaticalization, a process of semantic change whereby lexical items lose their propositional meaning over time and take on grammatical, discoursal or pragmatic meaning.

(Adapted from Archer et al. 2012. *Pragmatics:*
An Advanced Resource Book for Students. pp96, 100-101; 103-104.)

Questions for Discussion:

1. What is relationship between pragmatics and prosody in general?
2. Would you illustrate the pragmatic role of prosody in signaling speech acts?
3. Would you exemplify the intonation contours of thanking and apologizing in different context respectively?

Text D Literary Pragmatics: An Overview

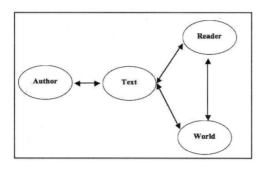

Language and literature can be integrated by their common feature of being communicative. Literature is for the users, and the use of language is what determines pragmatics, so the combination of literature and pragmatics clarifies the relationships between humans, their words, and their worlds. The first attempts are based on the concept of proposition, in an attempt to connect questions debated in the philosophy of language to research in the language of fiction. 'Recently, an increasing interest in the pragmatics of literary texts has been making itself felt across the disciplines of both literary science and linguistics' (Mey, 2001: 787). It is widely acknowledged that at the present stage stylistics should be based on the principles of interdisciplinarity, integrity and expansionism. Genuine interdisciplinarity is both possible and necessary for a meaningful and constructive modern-day poetics. Literary pragmatics thus can be seen as an interdisciplinary approach to the systematic studies of literature with pragmatic principles. The interrelation of pragmatics and style is a very close one. Pragmatic components are indispensable in stylistics. Literary pragmatics, as defined by Jacob Mey (1999), goes one step further and includes

> the kind of effects that authors, as text producers, set out to obtain, using the resources of language in their efforts to establish a 'working cooperation' with their audiences, the consumers of the texts. Such efforts rely on a precise understanding of the conditions of use of those resources, when directed at a particular audience among the consumers of the literary work.
>
> These pragmatic effects cannot rely on the linguistic elements involved alone. [...] What is required beyond those linguistic techniques is a thorough exploitation of all the contextual factors determining the use of those linguistic items. (Mey, 1999: 12)

According to Hickey, if stylistics studies the form of linguistic utterances, while pragmatics is interested in the formal analysis of the dependence of a text in respect of its situation or context or in 'that part of linguistic knowledge and behaviour which pertains to speaker-sentence-context relations' (1989: 10-11), it seems certain that only a stylistics which includes a pragmatic component can claim to be complete. In *Pragmatics of Language and Literature*, Teun A. van Dijk (1976) also makes the claim that what appears to be inadequacies in the models for the descriptions of either language or literature can be remedied by introducing pragmatic elements into them. The pragmatic factors greatly influence the functioning of stylistic means and govern the process of transmission, perception and interpretation of the conceptual information. Such pragmatic parameters as intentionality, focusing, the point of view, social and cultural context, the position of the addresser and the addressee should be taken into account while analysing the literary communication.

Literary pragmatics is a pragmatic analysis of literary works. Wales (1989: 238) defines literary pragmatics as a term that came into prominence in the 1980s. It follows developments in the field of linguistic pragmatics, in speech act theory, text linguistics and also in stylistics itself, concerned with literature as discourse in its interactional and social context, and with reader reception. Hence literary pragmatics looks at the linguistic features of texts which arise from the real interpersonal relationships between author, text and reader in real historical and sociocultural contexts. Consideration is made of features such as speech act, deixis, modality, mutual knowledge, presupposition, politeness and tellability, etc. Pragmatics can be illuminating discussions in literary works, and hence a new perspective into literary appreciation and criticism. For instance, it is of great help to understand a piece of work by focusing on its deictic expressions. Pragmatic notions such as speech act, cooperation, politeness, and relevance, can also shed light on the analysis of development of dialogues in novels, dramas, and poems.

Over the past four decades, an increasing number of pragmatic approaches to literature have appeared at home and abroad. A preliminary discussion of literary pragmatics is Michael Hancher's (1978) attempt to use Grice's implicature in interpreting literature. Hancher was from the Department of English, University of Minnesota, Minneapolis. At the Twentieth Annual Meeting of Midwest Modern Language Association held 2-4 November, 1978, in Minneapolis, Minnesota, he read his paper entitled 'Grice's 'implicature' and literary interpretation: background and preface'. Besides Hancher, the earliest scholars who combined pragmatics and literature were van Dijk (1976), Ohmann (1971, 1973), and Pratt (1977). Since Hancher, there appeared numerous discussions. Among the numerous good discussions of pragmatic analysis of literary works is Roger D. Sell's (1991) *Literary Pragmatics*. Jacob Mey (1999) has also written a book on literary pragmatics, and a special issue of the journal *Language and Literature* is edited by Adrian Pilkington. It is devoted to the Relevance Theory and literary studies. Pilkington believes that poetic effects can be used to explain 'literariness'. If that idea were developed sufficiently, relevance theory might be able to offer a theory of literature (Black, 2006: 150).

The interaction of stylistics and pragmatics is an interesting area for both disciplines. Literary pragmatics must concern itself with textual meanings beyond the linguistic structure of the literary text itself. Literary pragmatics must be able to encompass both methods of considering the relationships between the linguistic structures of the literary text, the 'users' of those texts, and the contexts in which the texts are produced and interpreted (Sell, 1991: 27). Any literary pragmatics must include a top-down perspective from the start:

the pragmaticist knows that he will be relating whatever aspects of the text he selects for discussion to the world in which the text functions communicatively (Sell, 1991: xv).

There have been productive studies of the pragmatics of literature by such people as Richard Ohmann and, notably, Mary Louise Pratt in her book, *Towards a Speech act Theory of Literary Discourse* (1977), studies which merge into work going under such names as text comprehension and reception aesthetics. All such work can be subsumed under the general heading of 'pragmatics' when it is given the scope it has in C. W. Morris's 1938 definition of pragmatics as encompassing the study of the relations between signs and their users. This is because 'users' includes hearers and readers as well as speakers and writers. The pragmatic study of literary activity focuses on the features that characterize this dialectic aspect of literary production: the text as an author-originated and -guided, but at the same time reader-oriented and -activated, process of wording. The reader is constrained by the limitations of the text; but also, the text provides the necessary degrees of freedom in which the reader can collaborate with the author to construct the proper textual universe, one that is consonant with the broader contextual conditions that mark the world and times in which the reader lives (Mey, 2001: 788).

Literary pragmatics addresses the relationship between language and those who use it, or between texts and their readers. The aim of literary pragmatics is to 'recontextualize'. The interaction of literary stylistics and pragmatics is an interesting area for both disciplines. The application of pragmatic approaches leads to a deeper and more far-reaching understanding of many aspects of literature.

Questions for Discussion:

1. What is literary pragmatics?
2. Why does pragmatics provide a new perspective into literary appreciation and criticism?
3. Would you briefly outline the development of literary pragmatics?

Text E Anticipatory Pragmatics

1. Introductory remarks

My role at this workshop has been described as 'advisor'. Now, an advisor clearly has one specific task in front of him or her: namely, to give advice. What kind of advice seems appropriate to offer at this point of the workshop when it is nearing its conclusion?

One can distinguish between 'pre-advice' and 'post-advice': advice either given

before the fact, and advice provided as feedback on what has happened. But there is a third kind of advice, which I would call 'pro-advice': advice about things to come, an advice that tells us how to handle current problems in the future but also anticipates future problems and how to deal with them, based on our historical experiences, in accordance with the Italian/US philosopher George Santayana's famous dictum: 'He who has not learnt from history will have to repeat it.' One could call this kind of advice 'feed-forward', as opposed to 'feedback', and it is this kind of advice I will present to you today.

But first a matter of terminology: why do I call my advice 'anticipatory'? Heeding Santayana's warning, let's have a short look at history.

2. Emancipatory and anticipatory

The term 'anticipatory pragmatics' is, in a way, an extension of the earlier coined term 'emancipatory linguistics' (see Mey, 1976, 1979, 1985, 1994, 2001). Now, the first question to ask is what is meant by 'emancipatory'? What or who do we emancipate ourselves from?

In classical times, the term was used to characterize the process by which slaves were freed from their bonds (called *mancipium*, the 'taking by the hand'), and, metonymically, the enslaved individuals themselves. The emancipation of the slaves in the US in the 19th century was replicated in the emancipation of the working classes in the Western world in general; also, the freeing from religious oppression was often called 'emancipation' (the struggle of the Dutch Catholics to obtain full citizenship rights in the Netherlands in mid-19th century provides an instance).

When it comes to emancipatory linguistics, the term was originally intended to signify the freeing of the language users from the societal oppression, among others as it was manifested in language. In the latter half of the 20th century, sociolinguists such as Basil Bernstein remarked on the fact that social origin often leads to societal inferiority in matters of education and use of language. The socially inferior were also underprivileged with regard to culture and the workings of democracy. An emancipatory linguistics was thought of as ideally serving the underprivileged, and as such was seen as part of the social struggle.

Recently, however, and thanks to the work of Sachiko Ide and her co-workers (see Hanks *et al.*, 2009), the notion has been broadened to comprise emancipation from all sorts of linguistic bondage, not just social; in particular, with regard to pragmatics, 'emancipatory' denotes the special status in linguistics of a discipline that does not obey the usual circumscription of linguistic work: conversely, and by the same token, pragmatics, according to many of the traditional practitioners of the art (the phonologists, the syntacticians, the semanticists, and others) does not really 'belong' there.

As a consequence, pragmatics is often seen as an 'intruder' (cf. the term 'pragmatic intrusion', as used by Levinson (2000) or Capone (2008) and many others): an illegitimate offspring, a kind of bastardized linguistics. For some even, the idea of pragmatics as a 'wastebasket' of linguistics (in particular semantics) seemed attractive enough to relegate the burgeoning discipline to the outer reaches of the linguistic realm. In addition, many pragmaticists were initially hide-bound in their philosophical and semantic traditions; at best, they considered pragmatics as rightfully belonging in either of those disciplines and did not see the need for an independent area of research.

3. Emancipation and anticipation

As we know, pragmatics is all about the use of language and the people who use language; emancipating them from the bondage of false beliefs and societal oppression is thus an appropriate task of an emancipatory pragmatics. But emancipation in and by itself is not enough: there is a life after emancipation, as the freed slaves of the American South got to experience, often to their disadvantage. Without knowing where to go, or whom to approach for a 'free' labor connection, many of them sunk into a misery that was often worse than the slavery they had been emancipated from. Similarly, emancipating pragmatics from its linguistic bondage must include some blueprint for the next series of steps. In other words, in order to be successful, emancipation presupposes *anticipation*. Pragmatics must not just liberate itself; it has a paramount role in the liberation of the users, and must follow up the emancipatory process in sustained supportive action.

Such a task is not just confined to the here and now; we must look ahead, and this is where the 'anticipatory' comes in. If pragmatics is about the use of language, an emancipatory pragmatics deals with how to use language in a non-oppressive, even liberating way. Looking ahead, then, we will see that our task is to proactively promote a language use that will prevent people from abusing the gift of language to their own egoistic ends. The task of an anticipatory pragmatics is then to foresee and prevent such abuses, and enable the users to counteract abusive language (in the widest sense of the word), even before it starts being accepted as a normal way of dealing with the world. ('Politically correct' language may, despite its sometimes 'holier-than-thou' connotations, represent a step in the right direction).

In the following I will give some examples.

4. Use and abuse in language

In every day usage, 'abusive language' is thought of as consisting of abusive and vituperative words and expressions, as when we call people names, or diminish their dignity as humans by comparing them to low-prestige animals (as the Iraqi journalist did when he threw his shoes at former President George W. Bush during a press conference in Baghdad and called him a 'dog'). The language of religious fanaticism (as in 'unclean unbelievers') belongs here, and in general all ideology-laden invective and depreciative discourse.

In a broader context, the terminology we create for controversial natural and social phenomena often is abusive in that it puts the user in a double bind: thus, we have to use a term like 'climate change' in order not to offend our audience (who may be shocked by hearing 'global warming' being defined as the real problem). Here, an anticipatory pragmatics should look for ways to express sensitive matters in such a way that we do not offend our listeners, yet maintain the integrity of our speech.

In this connection, one may think of the recent international debates on whether or not to interfere in other nations' internal affairs. Cases like the former Yugoslavia and the conflict in the Darfur region of Sudan come to mind. Here, the right to interfere (RTI) has been a matter of hot controversy; in contrast, fewer people will be offended (both nationally and internationally) when we proactively define our interference as a 'responsibility' to protect (RTP).

5. Fighting the common discourse

The term 'discourse' is often used to characterize not just (a) speech (as in French *discours*), but a total attitude of people vis-à-vis their life world, as it manifests itself in language and is handled and nurtured by language, specifically by the way we express our ideologies in language. Discourse in this sense creates and recreates the social fabric on which it is predicated; in a dialectically turning of the screw, it conditions us towards accepting the societal order that we happen to live under, as natural.

As an example of a proactive use of discourse in this sense, consider the fight that Abraham Lincoln had to wage against his contemporaries when he opposed the secessionists. Many of those who wanted to preserve the Union and opposed secession, were not at all convinced that slavery was at the root of the secessionist discourse; actually five of the 'loyal' Southern states of the Union were slave states, whose governments had little or no interest in abolishing slavery (examples: Kentucky and Maryland). Lincoln skillfully turned the problem on its head and persuaded these people that the discourse of slavery had to be replaced by a discourse of freedom, as the only way to preserve the Union. His anticipatory pragmatic view prevailed in the end, albeit at the cost of many lives and a deep scar in the minds of the American people and the collective consciousness of the US — a scar, which even today is not entirely healed.

Other discourses come to mind: the discourse of oppression, of sexual discrimination, of colonialism, and so on. Recently, we have witnessed a rising discourse of terrorism, by which acts of violence are glorified as heroic deeds; in the cities of the US and Europe a new attitude among mainly young immigrant populations sees the discourse of terrorism as an example on which to model their own fight for independence and a better livelihood (the inner cities of Britain serve as egregious examples).

In order to turn back the wave of violence that is rolling in over our society, we need to redefine the mentality that is expressed in this discourse; but also, proactively and emancipatorily, we need to replace the language used in the terrorist discourse. Why should a suicide bomber be called a martyr and not a mass murderer? Replacing the discourse of terror with a discourse of 'doing no harm' in the Gandhian tradition of *ahimsa* is a necessary step towards eliminating terrorism itself.

Similarly, in the current financial mess, we should proactively deflate the discourses glorifying the 'captains of industry', when they in reality are robber barons and committers of grand larceny, often in collusion with the politicians (not all of whom get caught.). Here, the proactive discourse that US President Obama is introducing points the way to a true emancipation of the tyranny, not only of the language of evil, but of the social evils that are at the bottom of the abusive language itself.

6. Conclusion: emancipation, anticipation, and control

One caveat is in order here, though. As Neal Norrick has remarked during the Third International Workshop on Emancipatory Pragmatics (Norrick, 2009), anticipating people's needs can be used to control those very people whose needs we intend to meet. The manipulative character of this kind of anticipation is clear: we may overstep the boundaries of other people's 'territories of information', or we may impinge on the private sphere of people whose sufferings we want to empathize with, as has been pointed out by John Heritage in his discussion of the boundaries of 'empathy' (2007). An emancipatory pragmatics with a proactive, anticipatory thrust should be aware of these dangers, and not fall back in the old groove of paternalistic colonialism, by which the poor natives were considered as unruly children, to be educated and formatted according to the principles and beliefs of the colonizers.

Here, emancipatory pragmaticists should be aware of the dangers, but still stride boldly ahead; for even less preferable actions are better in the end than no action at all, as we have seen demonstrated repeatedly in the crises that plagued the former Yugoslavia, and are still rampant in Central and East Africa. But our action should be embedded in theoretical insights, and this is where emancipatory pragmatics, in its proactive, anticipatory version comes in. If pragmatic linguistics has as its aim to unveil the abuses of language, then emancipatory pragmatics will have to anticipate such language and prevent it from being acknowledged as the 'correct' way of discoursing about our actual problems, be they of a political, social, and even ecological nature.

In this sense, my advice is for all pragmaticists to proactively engage in the counter-discourses of emancipation, by depriving all corruption, impunity, and terrorism of the protective cloak that language and its abusive users willfully and consistently have wrapped around themselves. In this sense, too, I feel that the venue of this talk, the Third International Workshop on Emancipatory Pragmatics, has had a vision to defend that is of importance not just to its participants, but on a wider, global scale of emancipatory pragmatic thinking and practice.

(Adapted from Jacob L. Mey. 2012. Anticipatory Pragmatics, *Journal of Pragmatics* 44: 705–708)

(Note: This is a speech given by Jacob L. Mey at *The Third International Workshop on Emancipatory Pragmatics* (2009) as an advisor.)

Suggested Reading

Green, G. M. 2006. Some Interactions of Pragmatics and Grammar. In Horn, L. R. & G. Ward (eds.) *The Handbook of Pragmatics*. Oxford: Blackwell. pp. 407-426.

Mey, J. L. 2001. *Pragmatics: An Introduction* (2nd ed.). Malden, MA: Blackwell. chp. 9.

Pecci, J. S. 2000. *Pragmatics*. Beijing: Foreign Language Teaching and Research Press. pp. 71-83.

Racanati, F. 2006. Pragmatics and Semantics. In Horn, L. R. & G. Ward (eds.) *The Handbook of Pragmatics*. Oxford: Blackwell. pp. 442-462.